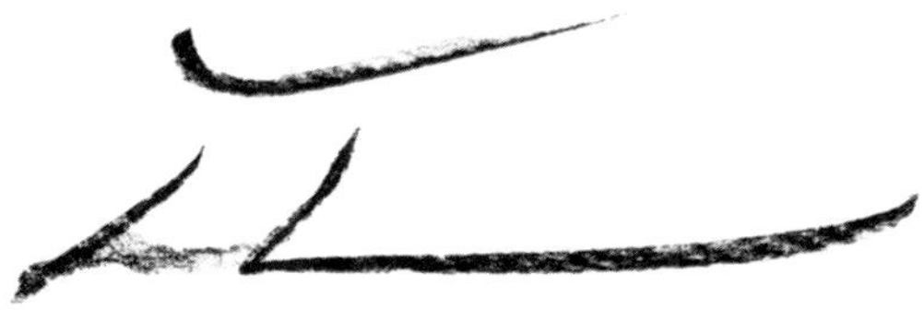

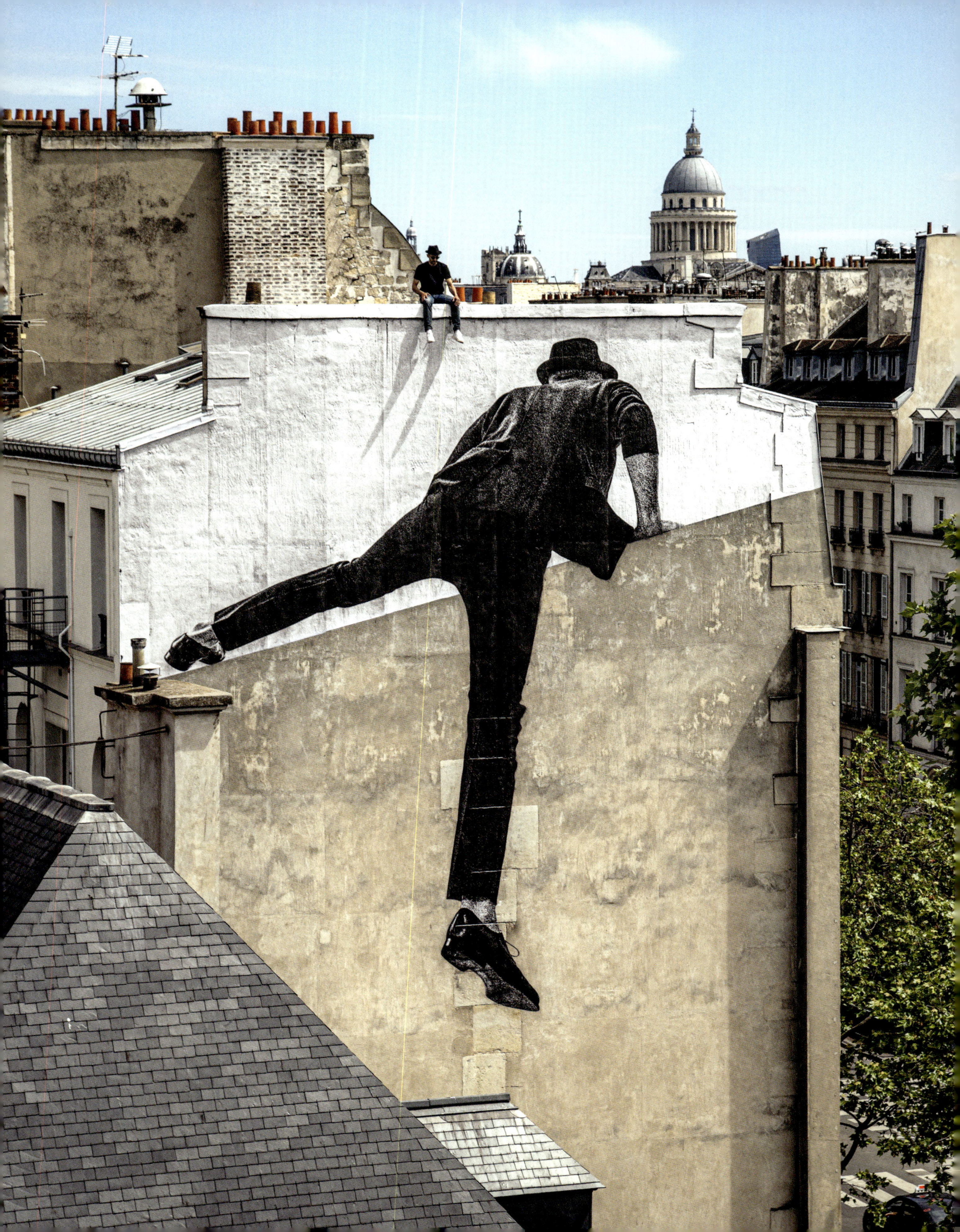

Janis Mink

JR

TASCHEN

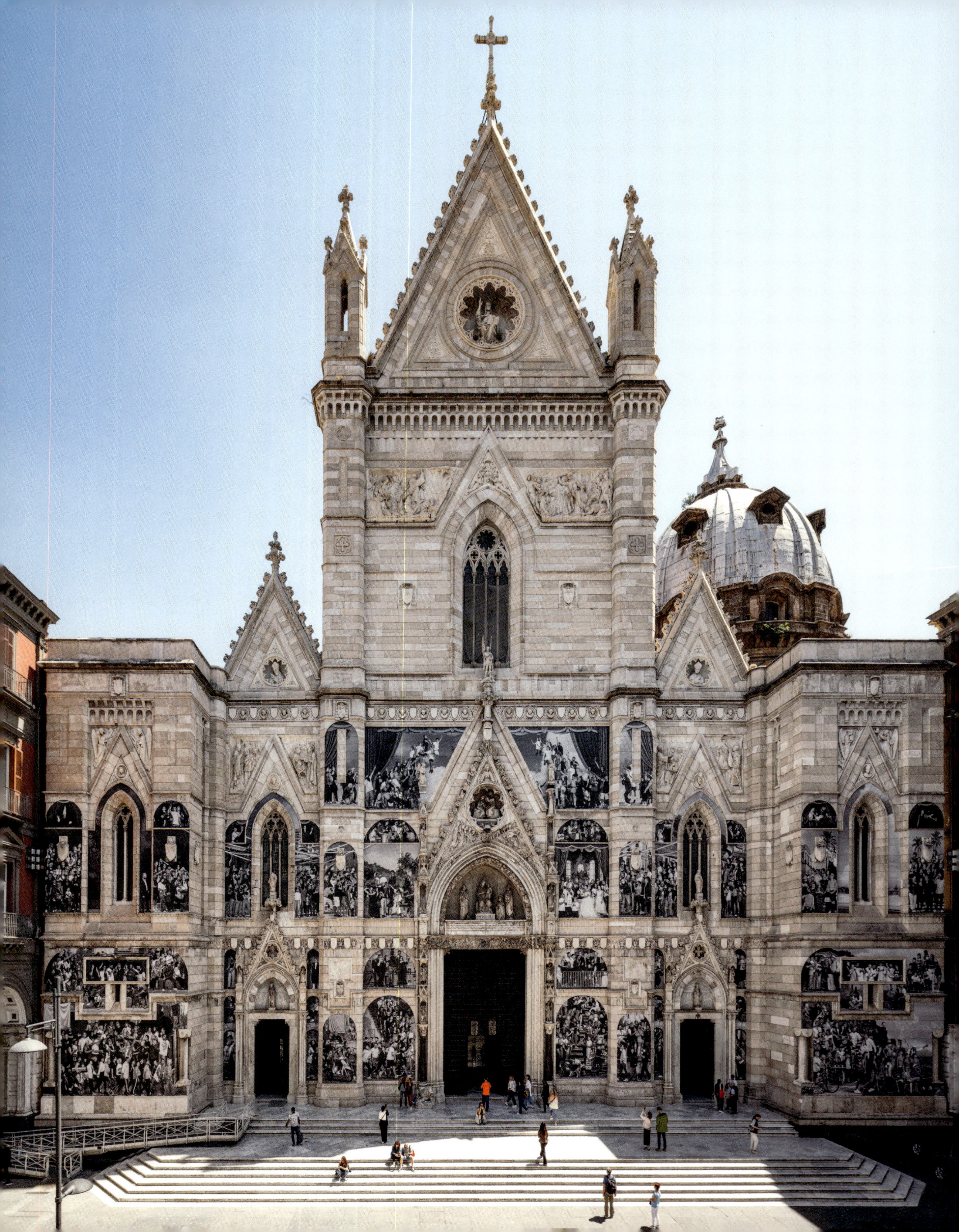

Contents

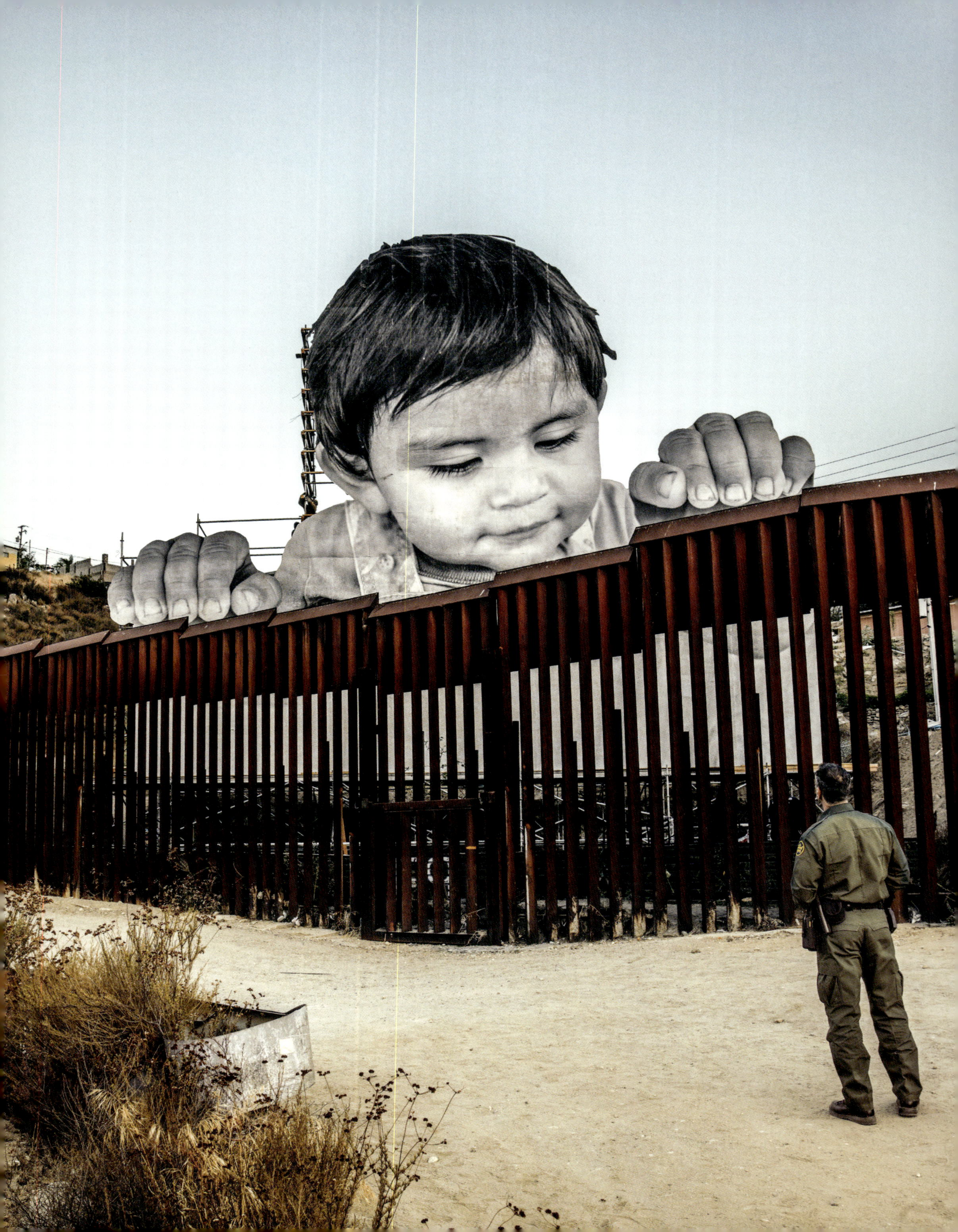

Introduction: A Question of Perspective

At first glance, the documentary photograph *Giants* (2017, p. 6), seems to show a small child looking over a high fence at a toy soldier. The scale and reality of the scene shifts when it becomes clear that the color photograph shows the man wearing green fatigues within a naturally colored desertscape, while the child reveals itself as a looming, flat, shaped, photograph—actually a 65-foot-high billboard. On patrol, the US border guard looks up at the Mexican toddler, as large as a dinosaur, who seemingly seeks to breach the fence. His posture, head position, and hand gestures convey a mix of consternation, interest, assessment, and even a hint of amusement. Need measures be taken to protect the demarcation line between countries?

The artist JR met the toddler, Kikito, at home with his family in 2017, near the eastern edge of the city of Tecate, Mexico, adjacent to the United States border. The artist had traveled there from France, drawn by news of a proposed permanent wall between the countries. Writing and pasting images onto outside walls was how he made his start as an artist.

Of neither Mexican nor US heritage, JR intuitively felt that the fortifying of this area with a wall made it ripe for exploration and intervention. As an artist, he moves toward places of conflict, not away from them. Tecate provided an environment of potential interaction where he could discover something, see what happened. Filmed by his usual collaborators, JR walked along the high fence separating one stretch of desert from another, musing that there was no solid wall yet. The footage JR's team took would later be incorporated into his documentary film *Paper & Glue* (2021).

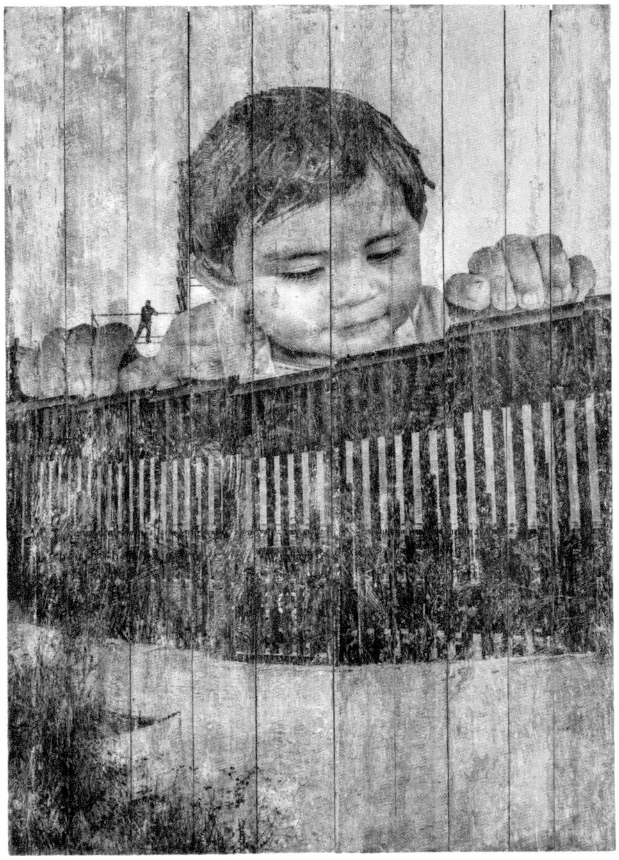

GIANTS, Kikito, September 6, 7:01 p.m., Tecate, Mexico – United States, 2017
Ink on wood, 249 x 180 x 7 cm
(98 x 71 x 2 ¾ in.)

Having heard so much rhetoric about the wall and after traveling so far, JR was surprised by how little was happening at the border, though he found more contacts on the Mexican side. There, one simple house interested the artist—the one closest to the fence. He considered using the house's roof somehow, and when he approached was surprised to find that the woman of the house recognized him by his signature hat and sunglasses—she followed his work on

OPPOSITE
Giants, Kikito, September 6, 2017, 7:02 P.M.
Tecate, Mexico – United States, detail

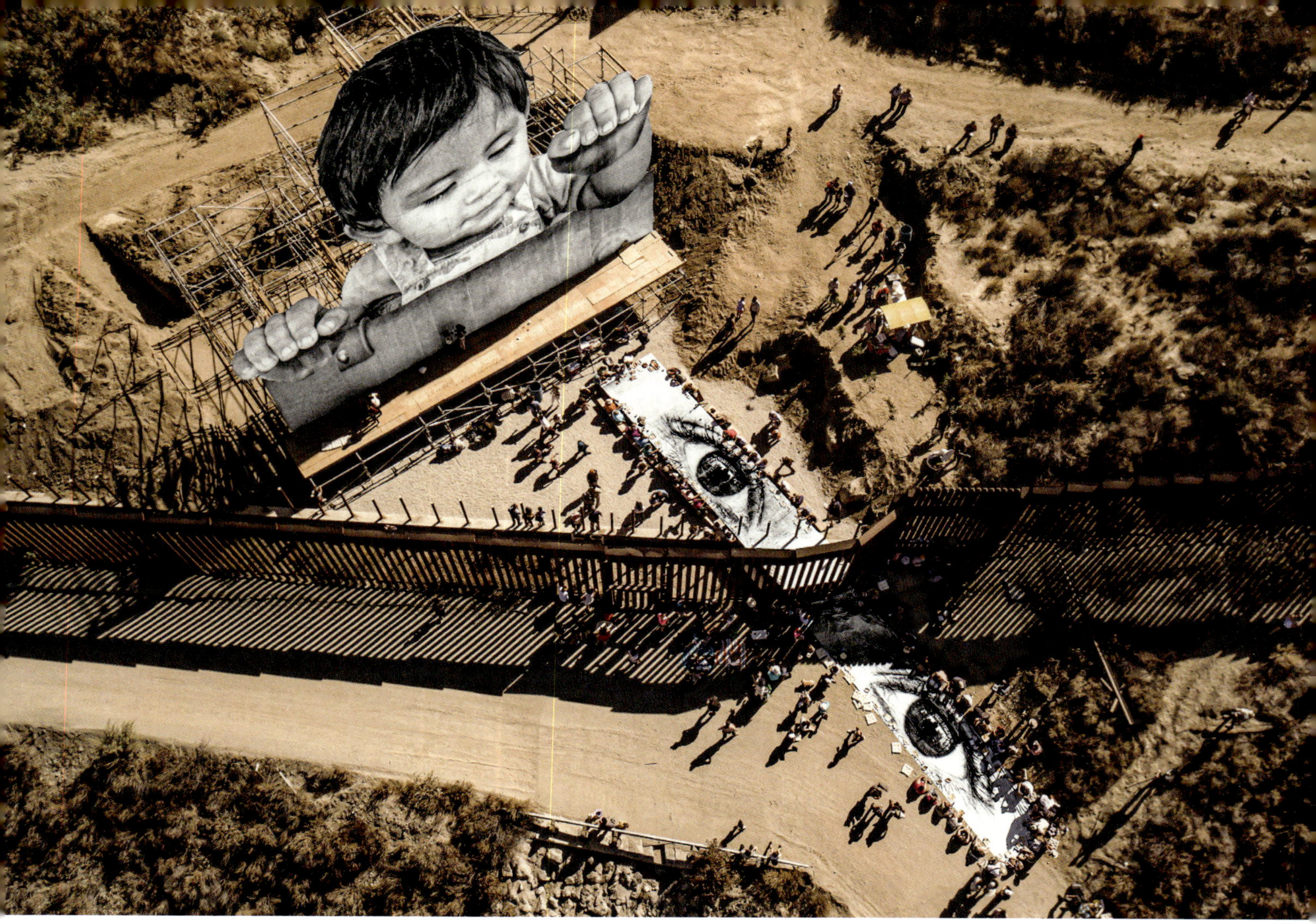

Migrants, 2017
Picnic across the border
General View, Tecate, Mexico – United States

Facebook. He talked to the family and asked if he could take some photographs. Kikito had pulled himself up in his playpen on the porch and traveled along the railing with his hands, as children who are just learning to walk often do, ranging about his protected space, smiling and looking out at … the fence. JR snapped his picture. The artist sensed that the peaceful, innocent toddler peering from his pen could become a humane image that made light of a separating wall. Kikito's charm could disarm.

No appointed or elected official allowed the installation of the large photograph. Although he was used to trespassing, this time JR tried to get permission to use the land along the Mexican side of the border fence. But no one seemed to know who owned the property. He rented a bulldozer and leveled some ground; no one stopped him. Nor were the artist and his crew hindered when rented scaffolding arrived and the team raised a tall structure that supported a plywood wall, onto which printed paper strips that assembled into Kikito's hands and face could be pasted. After the pasting, the child's silhouette was shaped by cutting away the plywood corners. The toddler rose above the border fence on the Mexican side, while the watchful US side of the fence provided the main viewpoint.

The installation hadn't been commissioned by anyone and was paid for solely by the artist himself. Made from ephemeral and rented materials, the installation remained in place for only about a month. Nonetheless, it became known through social media, and many people came and took selfies with Kikito in the background, making Tecate and Kikito's fame grow. JR celebrated the end of the installation run with a *finissage* picnic, to which he invited the public through social media and word of mouth. A band, divided in half, played together through the fence, with several members standing on each side. While an actual table could only be built on the Mexican side—the US border patrol did not want a table encroaching on the road—a spontaneous workaround was found by passing a tablecloth through the fence's openings and spreading it out on the ground. One US border guard, watching from afar, did not object to this use of the tablecloth. Food was shared through the fence.

The special long tablecloth bore another JR photograph: a close crop of a young woman's face, highlighting her eyes. JR had recently photographed her in San Francisco. A so-called Dreamer (a beneficiary of the 2001 DREAM Act, which stands for Development, Relief, and Education for Alien Minors), this young woman, Mayra, was brought to the United States as a child. Like many Dreamers, she grew up and attended school in the United States and identified as American but did not have permanent-resident status. By 2017, many Dreamers began to feel vulnerable about their ability to remain in the United States. After the tablecloth printed with Mayra's eyes was spread on the ground, JR launched a drone to photograph the picnic and the tablecloth as it crossed through the fence—he wanted that aerial shot. Mayra's eyes look up into the sky; the border runs right through the middle of her forehead, an eye in each country. Only photographs and film of Kikito's installation and the picnic document their occurrence. JR's action started with photography (and building, pasting, collaborating, and feasting) and ended with more photography.

Remarkably, Mayra attended the picnic in person, despite the possibility that border patrol could arrive at any moment. When the US border guard finally appeared to suggest that the picnic should wind down, JR adapted to the moment by offering a beverage to the guard, who took time to share tea with JR through the fence while he stood on the Mexican side. The guard also engaged in a friendly conversation with Mayra, who stood on the US side.

Thus, a neighborhood on the edge of a Mexican border town, local residents, US border guards, a French artist, his crew, and their social media followers interacted in the desert for a time, under the black-and-white eyes of an impish toddler. Together they enacted a poetic essay about overcoming barriers and borders. JR instigated the situation, allowed it to evolve, and guided it, assisted stalwartly by his team. He decided on the project's forms—a giant billboard and a printed tablecloth—and documented the whole process, including a bird's-eye view, so it could be remembered and seen by people who were not there. For the artist, however, the most important part of the multimodal project was intangible: the conversations along the Mexican–US border. Conversation, close to music in its sense of dynamic, rhythmic exchange, is itself an art form.

FOLLOWING SPREAD
Déplacé.e.s, 2023
Procession, Turin, Italy

Between 2022 and 2023, JR worked on the "Déplacé·e·s" series, in which he depicted refugee children worldwide. For each work, he used a 148-foot-long photo tarp printed with the image of a child forced to flee home, though the photo emphasizes the child's joy and love of life. The long tarps were each carried by hundreds of volunteers in individual local public processions that ended with picnics. Once all five of the "Déplacé·e" tarps were carried by more than a thousand volunteers and united in the Piazza San Carlo in Turin, the aerial photo made the children appear to be playing together.

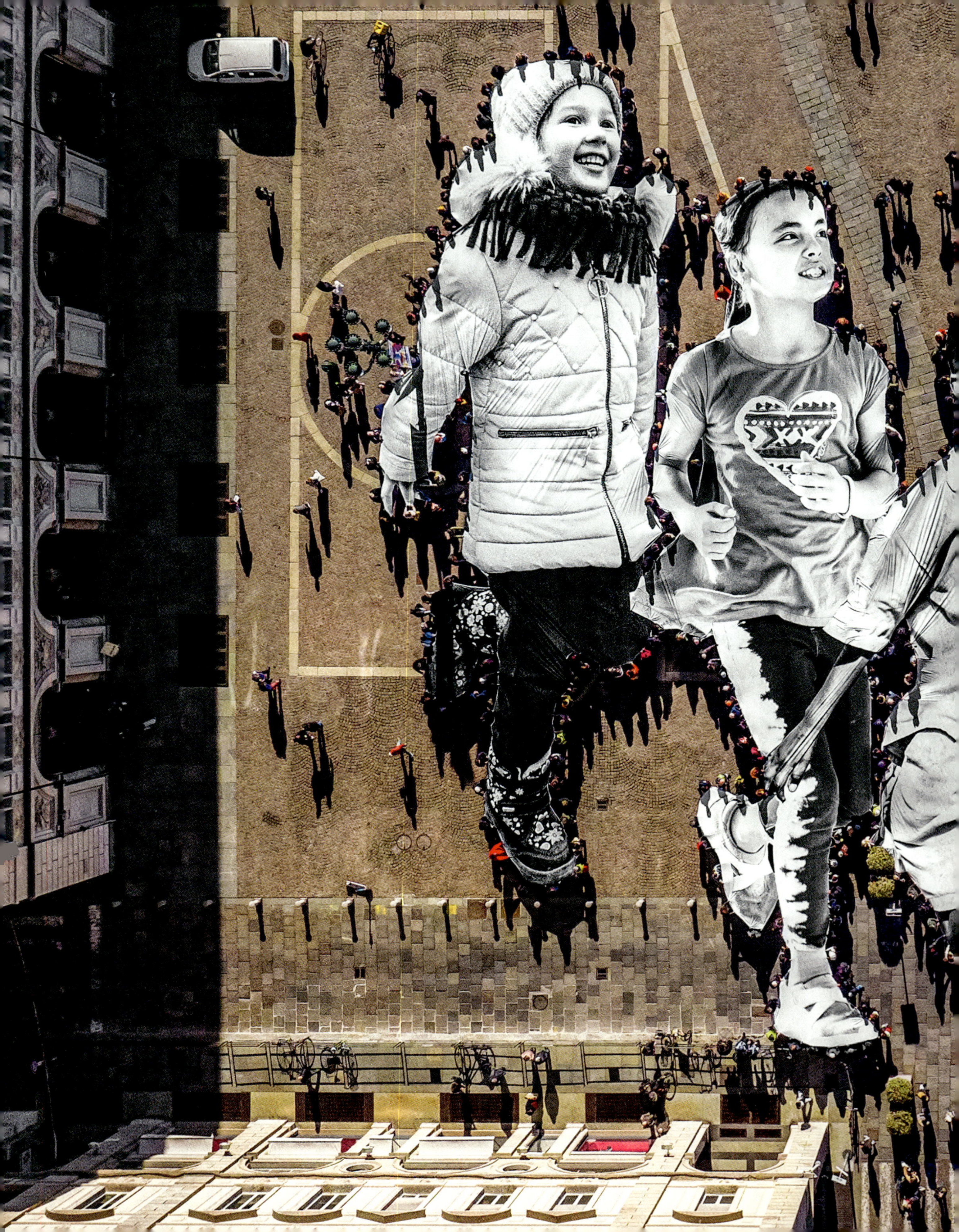

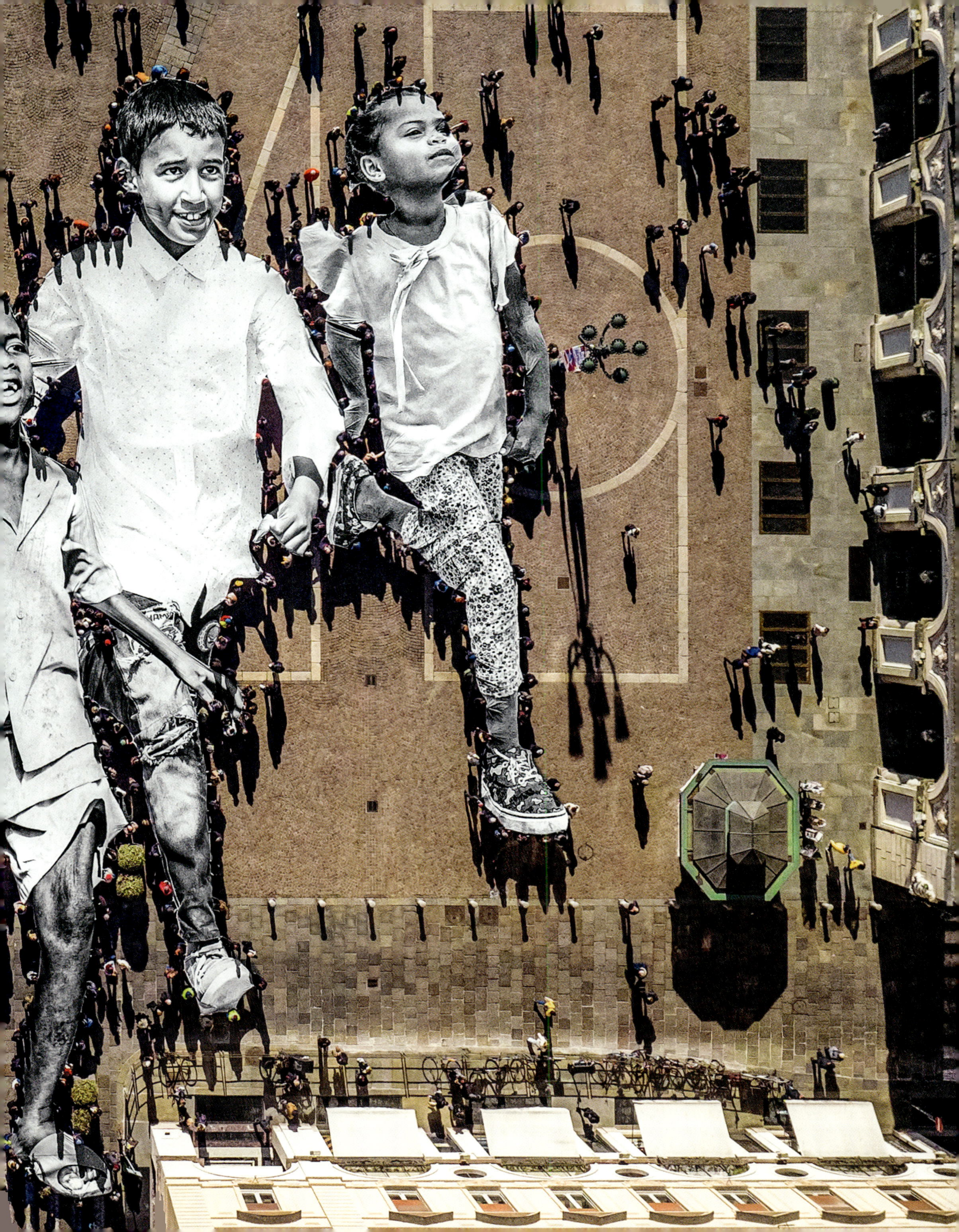

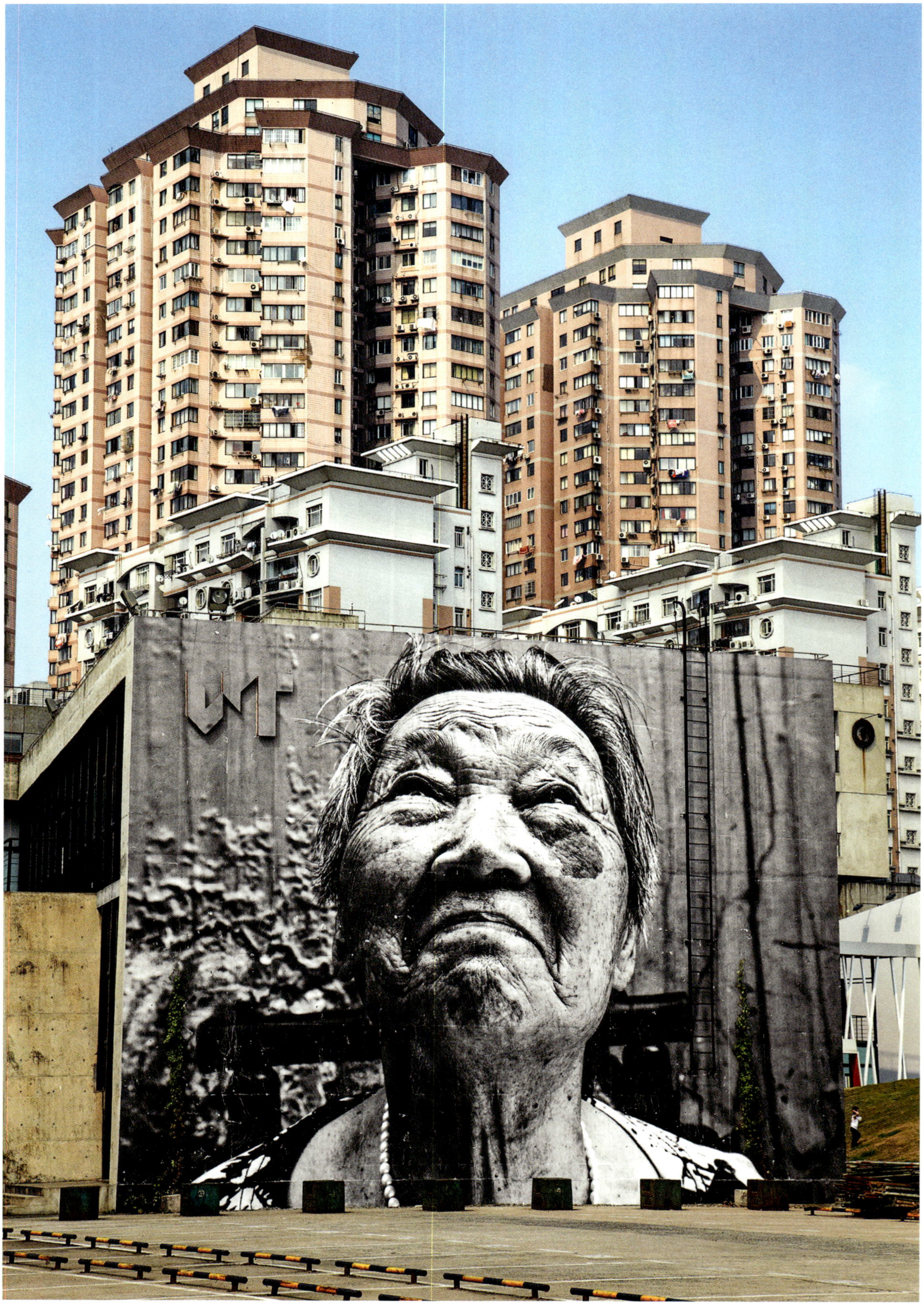

Tagger from the Streets: The Rooftops

JR was born on February 22, 1983, to immigrant parents, his father from Eastern Europe and his mother from Tunisia. Nothing about JR's schooling or home life indicated he would become an artist. One of three siblings, he grew up in a lower-middle-class suburb of Paris, where his family lived in a large housing complex shared by multigenerational families of diverse nationalities. At times an elderly neighbor looked out for him, or he for her. His grandmother came to live with the family. JR seems to have internalized an appreciation for the elderly and their histories, as shown by his later friendship and artist collaborations with the Nouvelle Vague filmmaker Agnès Varda (1928–2019, p. 92) and his series of actions held in several cities titled "The Wrinkles of the City" (2008–15)—"The Wrinkles of the City" started in Cartagena, Spain, and spread to several cities around the world where the "wrinkles" on elderly people and worn buildings could be matched. JR pasted portraits on walls in Cartagena (2008, p. 13), Shanghai (2010, p. 12), Los Angeles (2011), Havana (2012, in collaboration with Cuban American artist José Parlá), Berlin (2013), and Istanbul (2015).

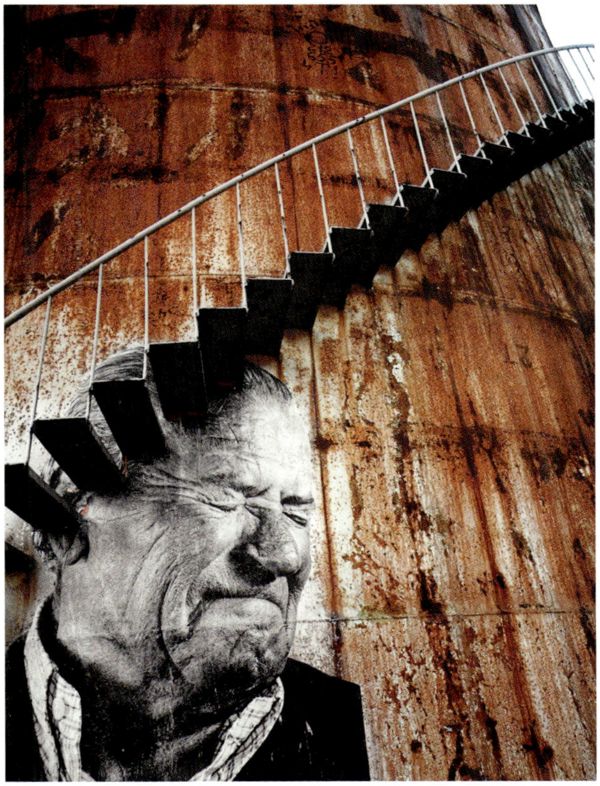

The Wrinkles of the City, 2008
Marino Saura Oton, Cartagena, Spain

As a child, he never felt poor. His parents slept in the living room, decorated with only a poster of Astérix and Obélix on a flying carpet. They knew when their children came and went. Because they trusted their children's decisions, JR had lots of freedom. As an energetic child who liked DJing and breakdancing, school bored him. He did, however, appreciate his good teachers, although he acknowledges he was not one of their best or even most memorable students. His teenage years coincided with the early years of the internet, and the public's growing acquaintance with it as it evolved. Visits to art museums were not significant to him, nor did he learn about art and artists as a child. He didn't like to draw. He instead made his mark by carving the initials of his first name into the top of his desk so they could not be washed off. It meant, "I'm here. I exist." "JR," abbreviated from his initials, became his preferred name.

He designed a unique symbol by using the horizontal line of the capital *J* as a roof for the *R* and giving the two letters the same stem (p. 15), thus forming a

OPPOSITE
The Wrinkles of the City, 2010
Action in Shanghai, Shi Li, Red Town, China

BELOW
Expo 2 Rue, 2001
Paris, France

OPPOSITE AND FOLLOWING SPREAD
JR and ROL.K, ***Expo 2 Rue***, 2002
Bastille, Paris, France

"People were calling us 'vandals' and then 'street artists,' and the 'artists'—and I think 'artist' is what I've always been, in a way, without knowing it. Now that I understand the meaning of it, I feel proud to be able to use that name."
JUXTAPOZ MAGAZINE (2018)

single, architectural mark reminiscent of a torii gate or an attempt at a kanji letter. He extended and curved the *R*'s leg to mirror the *J*'s hook so the symbol appears to run or take a flying leap into the air, like an athlete taking a hurdle, with arms and legs akimbo. He would later conjure his photography into ink-on-wood paintings that often depict refugee boys running and playing (p. 29).

Because risky locations confer prestige in graffiti culture, graffiti artists often take risks to tag "heaven spots"—dangerous, elevated sites like bridges or rooftops that often require a jump (pp. 14–17). Later, JR became the artist's tag when, ever adventuresome, he began to follow some neighbors about 10 or 15 years older than he who did graffiti. Not one to stay at home smoking a joint in front of a console, adolescent JR joined the older boys when they climbed onto rooftops to tag anything that rose above the city. The Paris rooftop still makes its presence felt today in a corner of the artist's loft in New York: a raised, inhabitable architectural sculpture by the artist Takao Shiraishi is covered with the distinctive zinc material cut from actual Paris rooftops.

JR and his friends also entered the labyrinths of the underground to tag trains and tiled *métro* tunnels. On those excursions, JR discovered the city's mechanical workings, entering unauthorized spaces and approaching Paris from odd, dangerous angles. The neighbor who took him along was a well-known tagger who had founded the ABC crew, which had a reputation for violence. The TPK and the UV were two other such Parisian groups. They could use force when necessary, sometimes going out in groups of 30 or so and even blocking a train while some members sprayed as the driver called for help. JR never felt as accomplished as they were, nor as tough. JR usually tagged his symbol neatly,

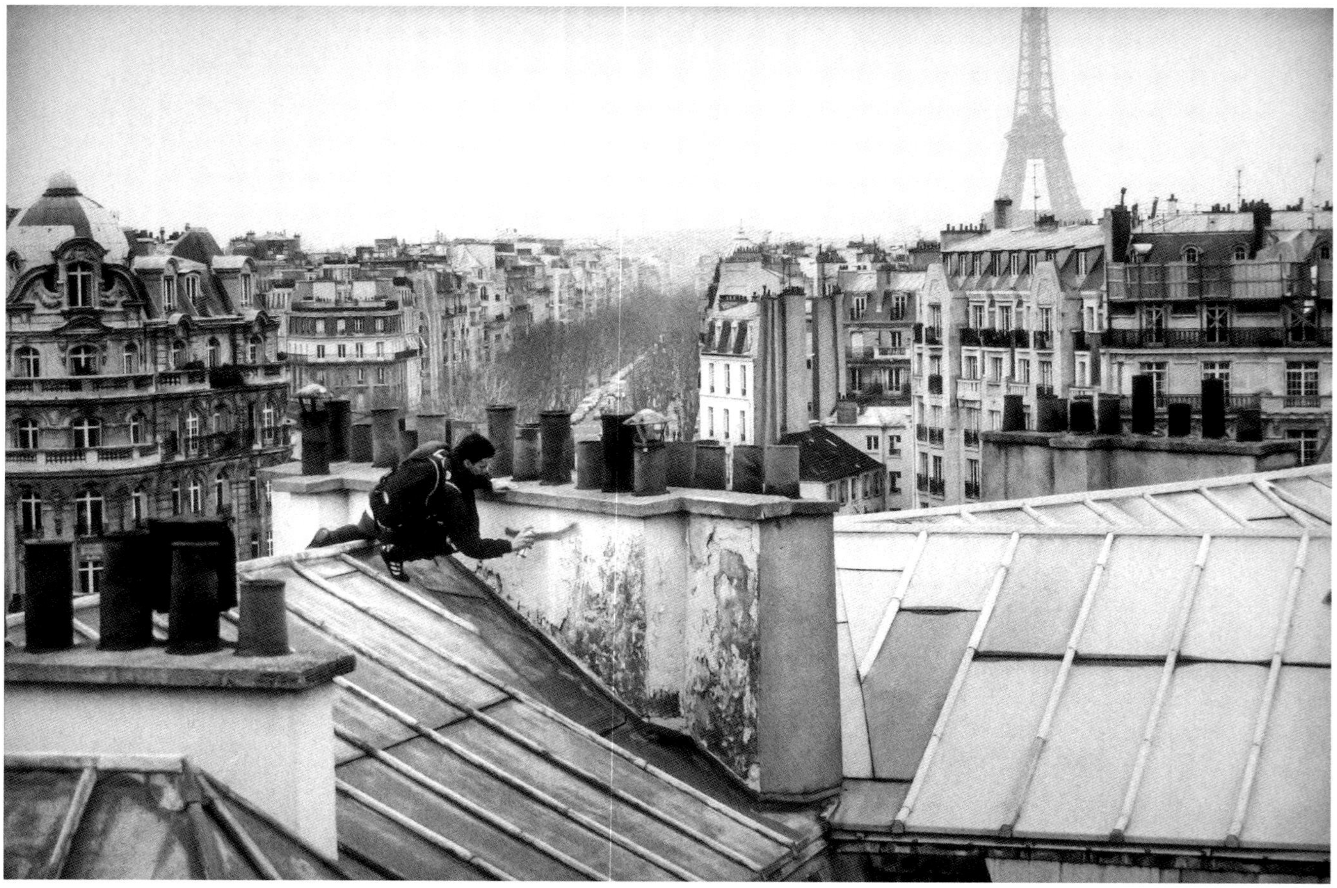

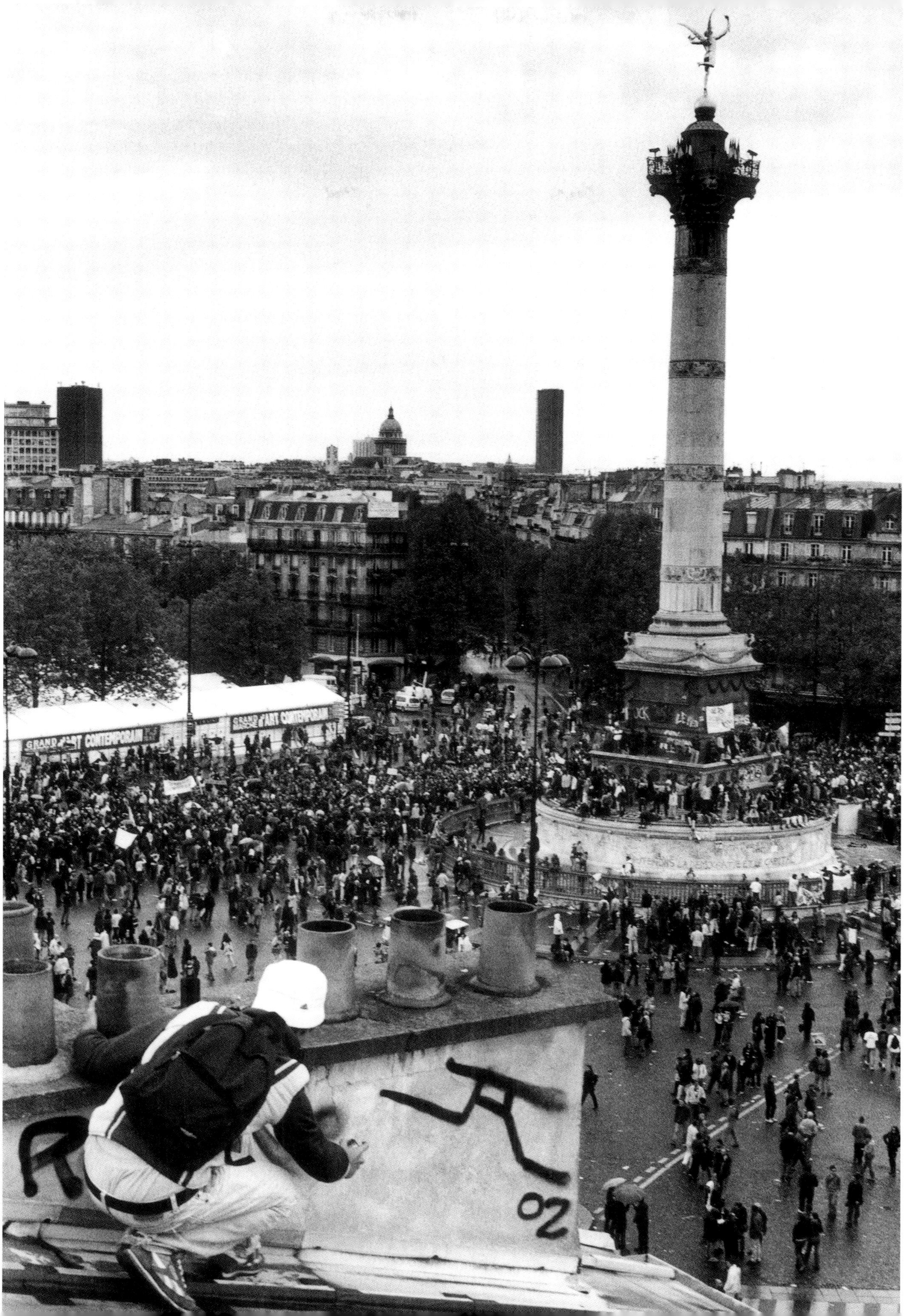
GRAND
ART CONTEMPORAIN
D'ART CONTEMPORAIN

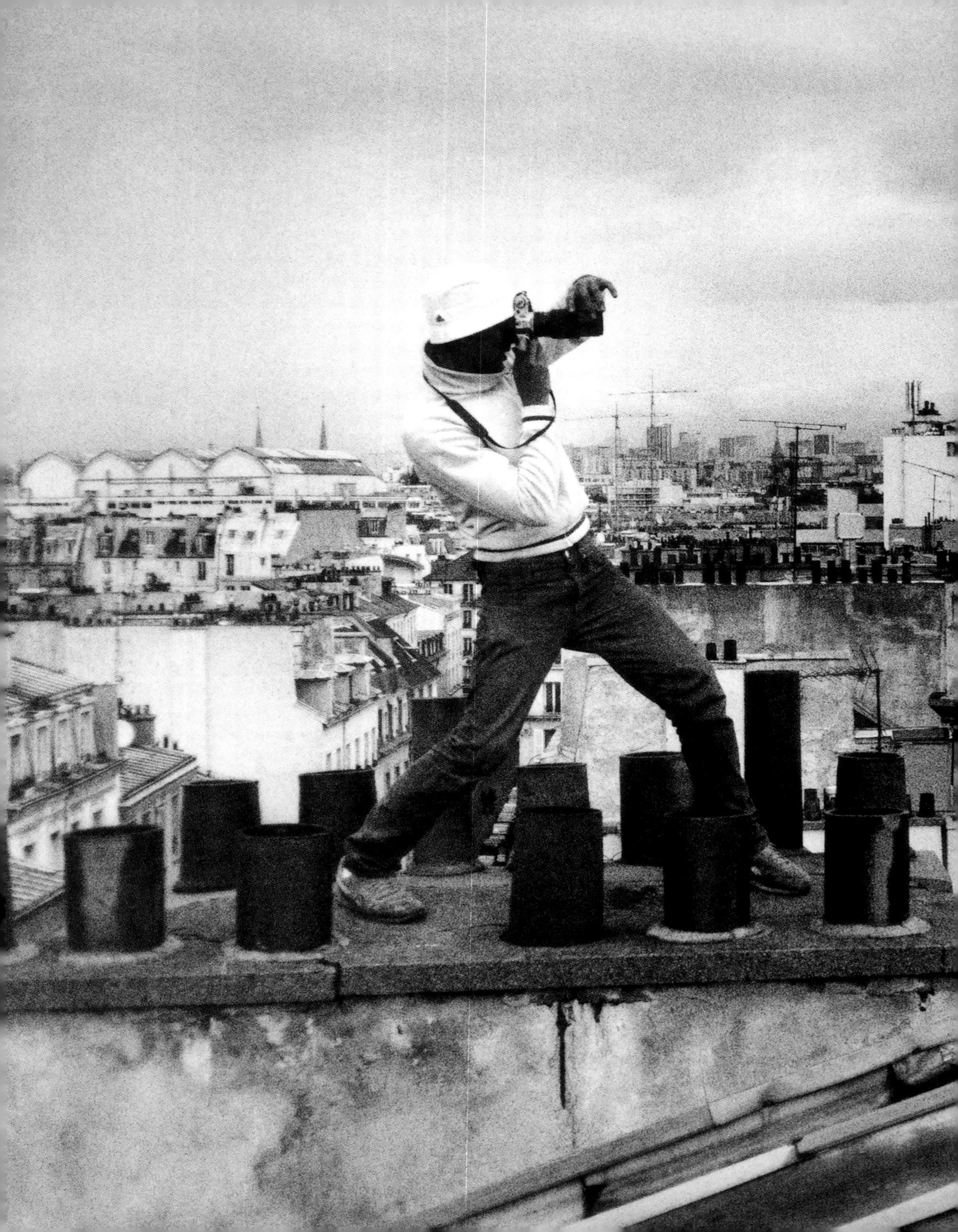

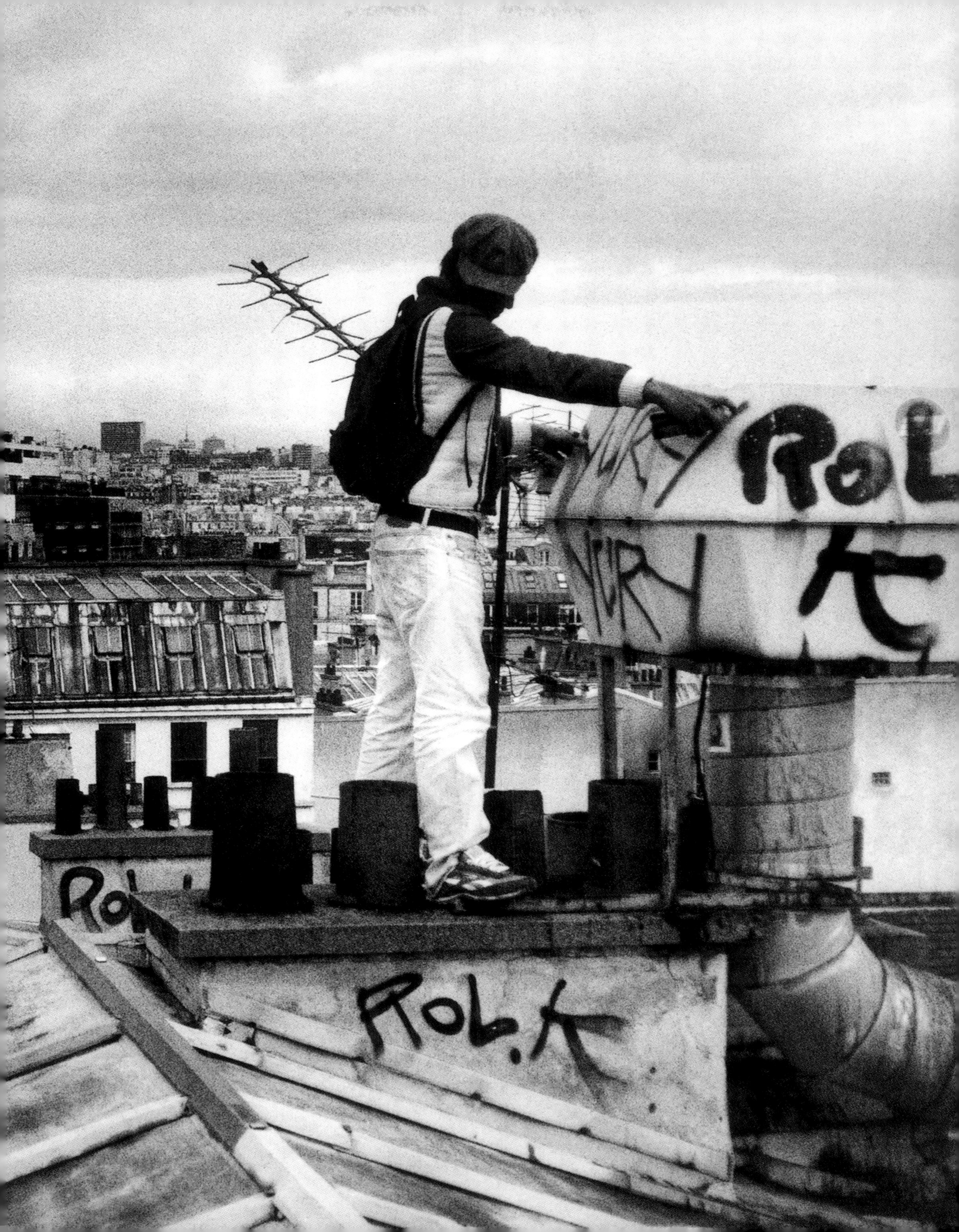
Rol.K

while the others speedily crafted more lavish, wild compositions that filled him with admiration. Because French law considered unauthorized marking of buildings and trains a crime, and the police tracked youths guilty of such activity, graffiti artists developed strategies to disguise themselves and avoid arrest. They worked in the dark, wearing hoods, hats, or reversible jackets to change their appearance and maintain anonymity, or operating casually—posing as workers who belonged on the crowded street. Nonetheless, arrests happened. One time, late at night, an underage JR was arrested for tagging a friend's lycée. His parents refused to pick him up at the police station that night, and the police simply released him. JR got the feeling that this "crime" was not very serious.

Entranced by the subculture but still far from being a connoisseur, JR would sit by the train window on the ride into Paris, scanning railcars and tracksides for new graffiti. At about 15, he left the suburbs to live with cousins in Paris. He suddenly realized he was light years behind the city's graffiti artists. In a 2021 interview with Fabrice Bousteau, editor in chief of *Beaux Arts Magazine*, and Hugo Vitrani, a curator at Palais de Tokyo, JR referred to his younger self as a mere "tagger from the sticks" without a developed style.[1]

He soon bought the 2000 book *Kapital: Un an de graffiti à Paris* by Gautier Bischoff, ECR, and Julien Malland, a seminal volume on Parisian style writing, replete with artist statements. However illegal the pursuit, if the graffiti artist

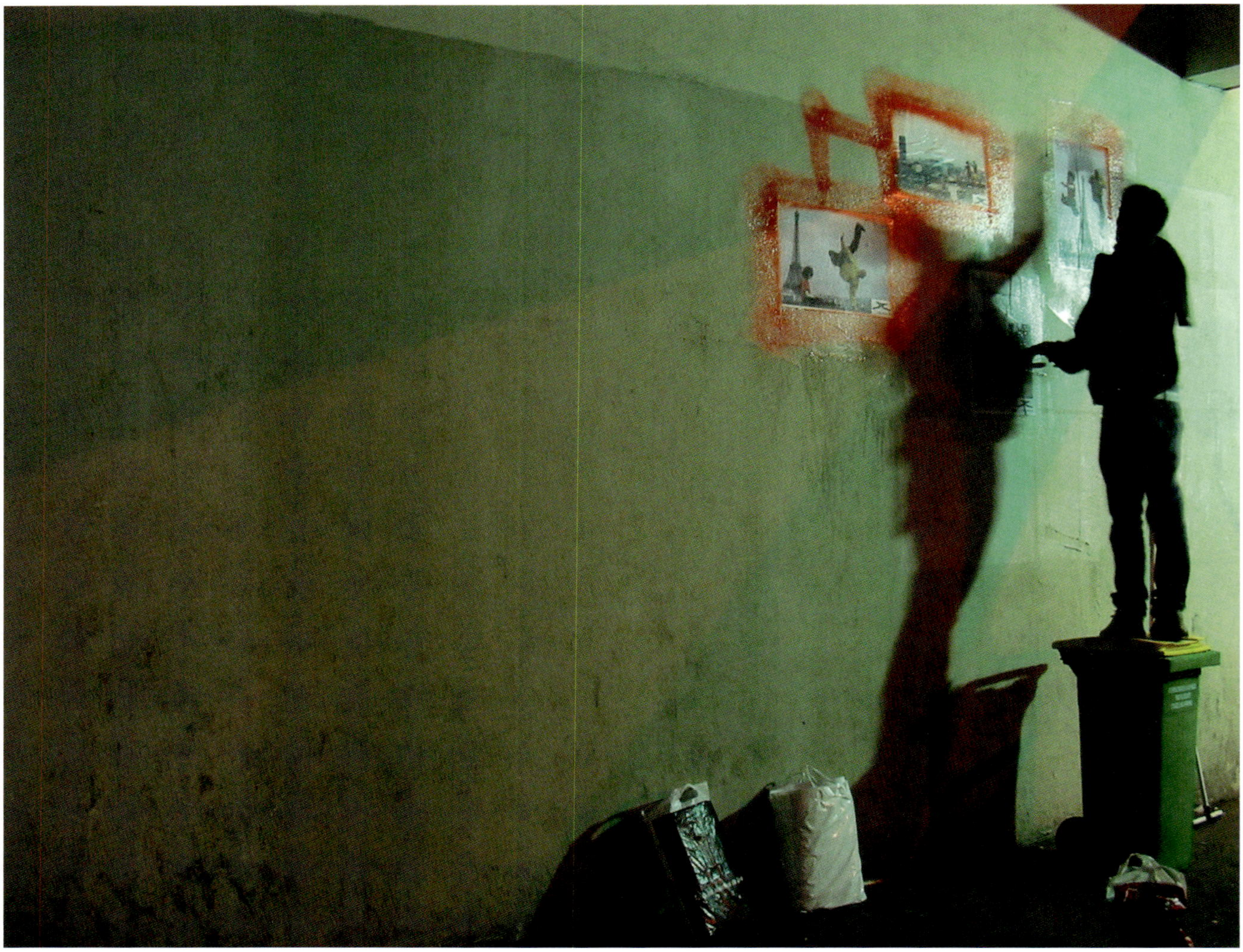

stood out, cultural critics could recognize them as a full-fledged artist capable of visually distinctive work.

One day soon after his self-realization, JR was waiting for a friend at the *métro* at the Charles de Gaulle–Étoile RER station, the regional light rail link between the suburbs and Paris. The friend was late, and after several trains passed, JR noticed a bag had been left behind that no one had returned to repossess. He looked inside, saw a film camera, and took it. It was a used Samsung, and it had a powerful flash. JR didn't know anything about photography, but the serendipity of finding the orphaned camera was enough to make him start taking pictures. He absorbed the newfound tool into his actions. JR realized he could still participate in the adventure that was graffiti by using the camera, so he made his choice. With his newfound camera, he focused on the fraught atmosphere of the graffiti scene, where artists intent on making their mark took risks alongside oblivious pedestrians and commuters. Without revealing their faces, he homed in on their interventions and their choices of location—a well-chosen location was everything to a graffiti artist. JR turned his attention to the daring flow of artistic action and process rather than the static finished work. He befriended and documented those he considered "greats" and "legends"—"the kings of Paris."[2] ROL.K and the inventive O'Clock were two individual graffers he followed and photographed in Paris. JR printed his developed photographs as photocopies in A4 format (similar to US letter size) and distributed them upon request to his friends, the artists, as mementos.

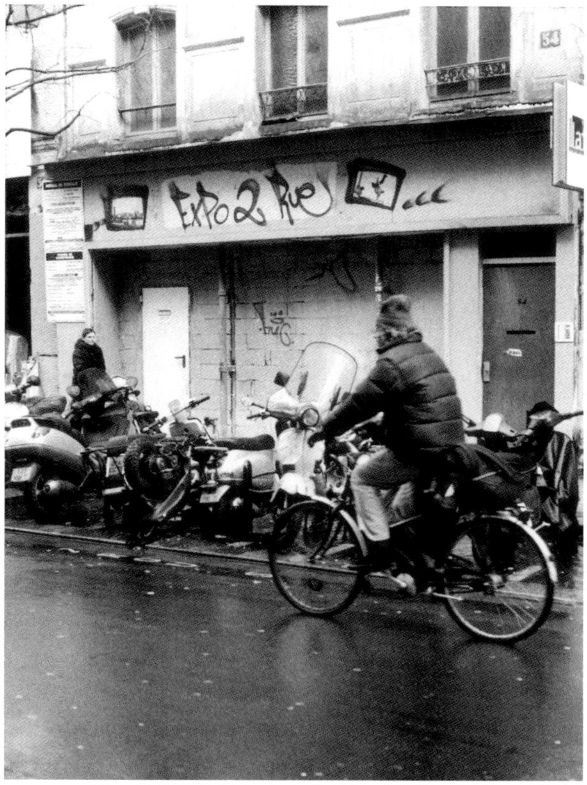

Then, to exhibit the photos more publicly, he took over spaces reserved for advertisements or maps in the *métro*, replacing them with his A4 photocopies—unfastening the frame, covering the advertisement with his own work, and refastening the display. Sometimes he pasted a group of his photocopies directly onto a wall on the street. This tactic of printing posters and displaying them in public spaces, known as flyposting (along with the related sticker technique), had become part of graffiti artists' repertoire, having been established in cities since the 19th century, originating from the wheat-pasting of circus and advertising posters and political propaganda. Unknown to JR at the time, a group of French artists, the Affichistes, had established the technique of *décollage* in the 1960s, using layers of old street posters as their medium. The Affichistes saw the accretion of wall-pasted posters as an expressive revelation of fragmented realities and ideas. Tattered posters might evoke nihilism, the bygone, or simply the archaeology of the everyday. Affichistes selectively removed sections of pasted wall images from the street, framed them, and then brought them into galleries or museums as works of art.

In contrast, JR envisioned his museum on the street itself. He emphasized the exhibition nature of his wall-pasted photocopies by quickly spraying red frames around them, sometimes connecting the "framed" images with lines, as if they were visual "stations" on a *métro* map. He chose red for its contrast with the black-and-white copies; at the end of the spray, he held the can in place to concentrate the paint, allowing it to drip down like blood, and to make the painting look wet, fresh.

He labeled such street exhibitions *Expo 2 Rue*, signed with his JR symbol (pp. 18–20). By combining photocopies with spray paint, he was able to use

Expo 2 Rue, 2001
Paris, France

OPPOSITE
Expo 2 Rue, 2003
Pasting, Paris, France

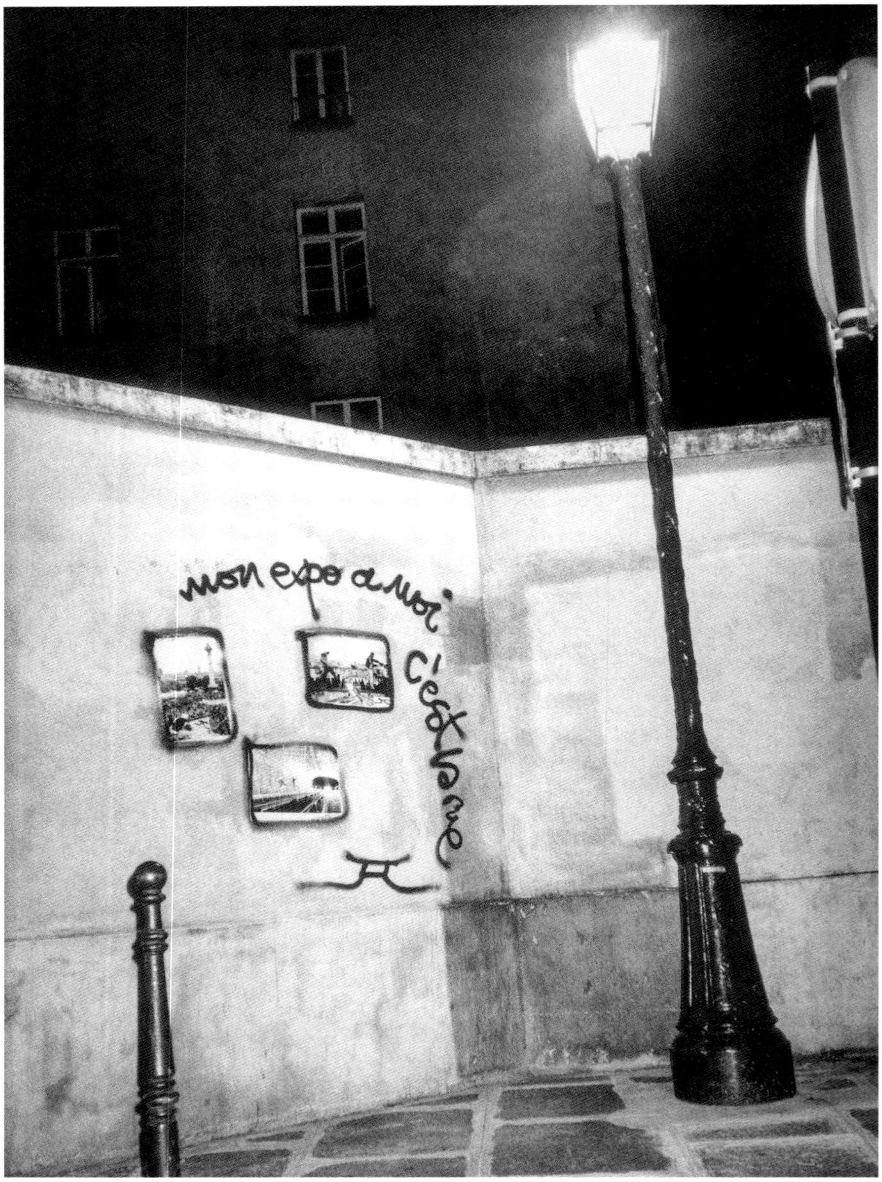

Expo 2 Rue, 2001
Paris, France

OPPOSITE
28 Millimeters, Portrait of a Generation, 2004
Hold-up pasting
Les Bosquets, Montfermeil, France

FOLLOWING SPREAD
28 Millimeters, Portrait of a generation, 2004
Hold-up pasting, Ladj Ly as seen by JR
Les Bosquets, Montfermeil, France

minimal equipment. He never asked for permission to paste on a wall and even did it in broad daylight in areas of the city thick with pedestrians, who inadvertently provided him cover. When the pasted images wore off or were removed, his tag and the sprayed lines of connectivity remained as witnesses to his intent to create a picture. He was still there. JR noticed that people on the street stopped and looked at the photos in their red frames, drawn by the combined mediums, while most just walked by the spray-painted tag or the photos alone.

In an interview about the project, JR said, "When I started papering Paris with my *Expo 2 Rue* … I worked alone—with my posters, my plastic bag, my reversible jacket—and I wandered around the city calmly, never getting arrested, even the time I put up images on the Champs-Élysées, on December 24 at 6:00 P.M."[3]

One problem arose: JR desired a more ambitious scale for his photocopied photos. The city's huge commercial advertisements dwarfed his photocopies. Even when he combined several A4 sheets to form a larger rectangle, to him, the effect remained weak. At the time, only the black and white of his photocopy technique set his pastings apart from the colored shouts of advertising. He needed to introduce scale as an element.

Around 2002, while coming down from a roof, JR met members of an informal art collective named Kourtrajmé (French slang for "short film"). Founded in the northeastern Paris suburb of Clichy-Montfermeil, Kourtrajmé made short films, music videos, and photography. JR connected especially with a like-minded young man five years older than he, Ladj Ly. A French national of Malian descent, Ly lived in an isolated housing estate in Clichy-Montfermeil known by the unlikely name of Les Bosquets, meaning "The Groves." Ly introduced JR to this neighborhood, home to many immigrant families. Ignored and neglected, Les Bosquets retained none of its original identity as a garden city or greenbelt when it had been planned as a middle-class suburb. An aspiring filmmaker himself, Ly wanted JR to photograph the place as it looked now. Covered with graffiti and dysfunctional, the housing projects in Les Bosquets arrested JR's attention. In 2004, he photographed local teenagers and younger kids who were happy to be seen, cut up for the camera, pose, laugh, and have a good time, thus beginning his acquaintance with the people who became the subject of his series "Portrait of a Generation" (pp. 21–28). Sometimes the two friends, JR and Ly, recorded each other with their cameras simultaneously, in the moment, each young man busy with his own type of camera. This was fun and felt right but, for JR at least, didn't yet stem from an ambition to become a professional. JR, just 21 years old, supported himself by working physical jobs like handling baggage at the airport or moving heavy items for antique dealers. Photography he did for the love of it.

The photo sessions in Les Bosquets and another neighboring housing estate, La Forestière, in Clichy-sous-Bois, shaped his thinking and sharpened his editorial eye. JR would choose the best photograph from those sessions for his first large-scale pasted photo. This unposed photo captured Ly turned toward and filming JR. In JR's photo, Ly shoulders his video camera, standing nearly centered before of a line of six or seven young kids, who display a variety of attitudes, moods, and hand gestures (pp. 21–23). Ly becomes the group's focal point and front man. The group creates a cohesive structure that suggests the silhouette of a sagging Greek temple with a sloping roofline—an aesthetically powerful

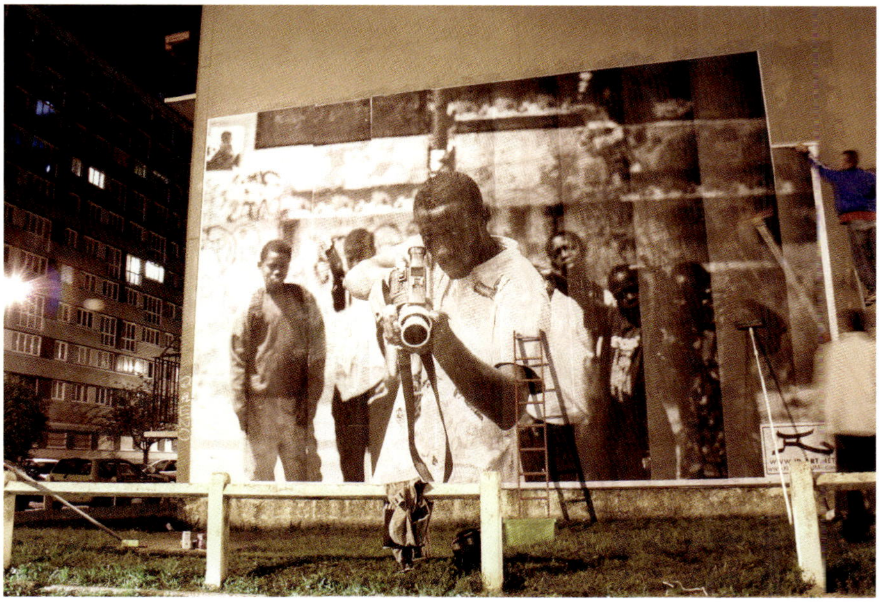

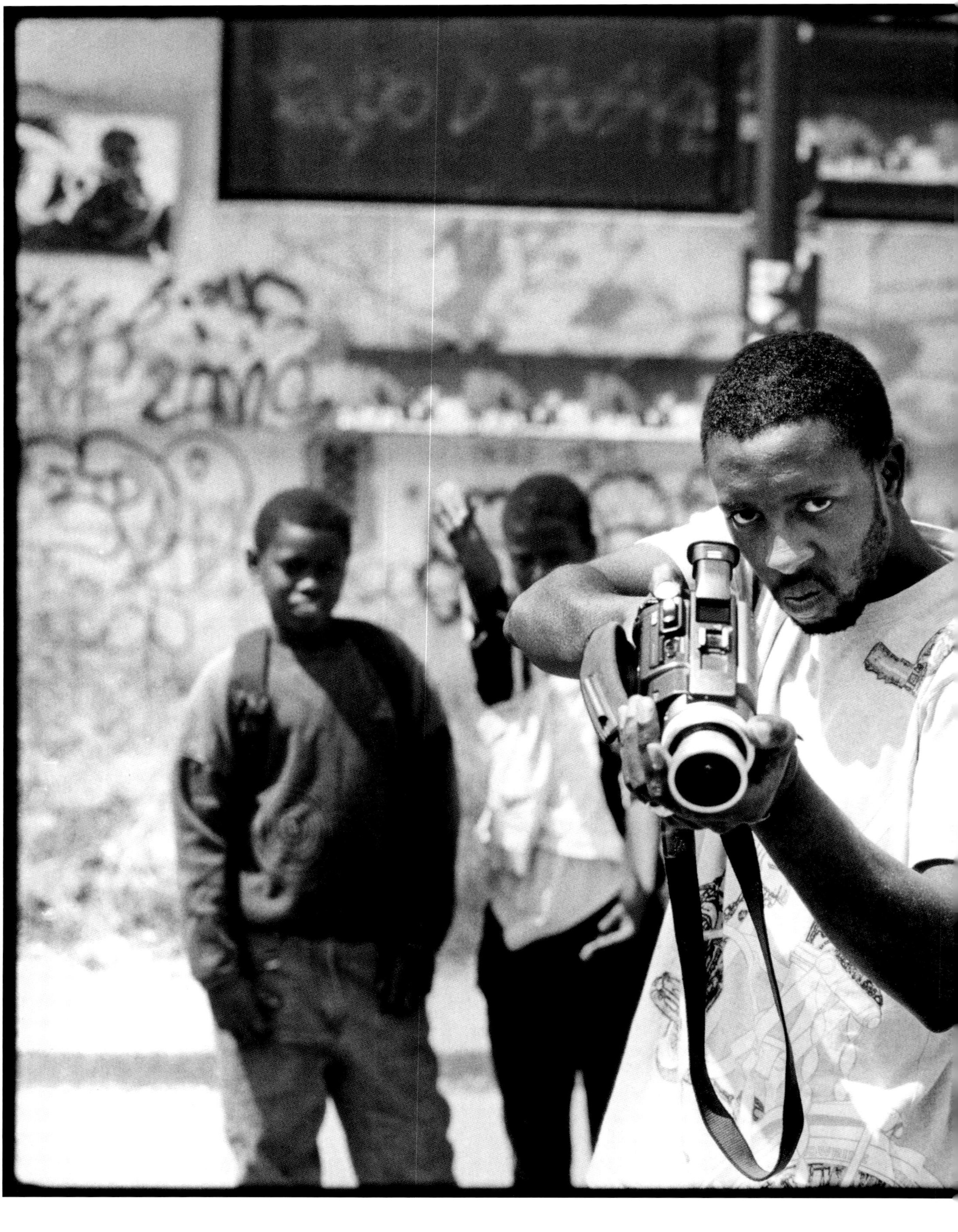

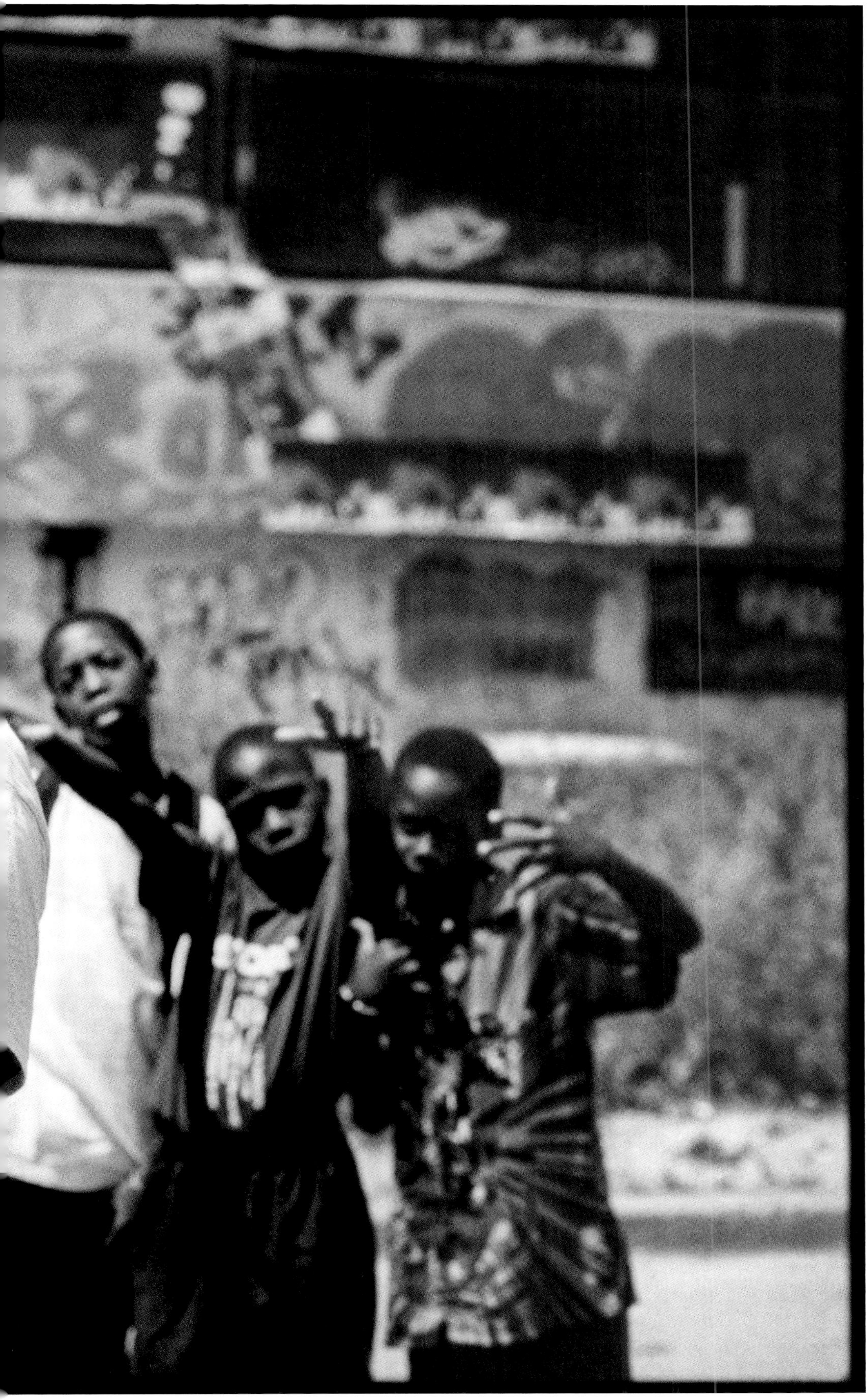

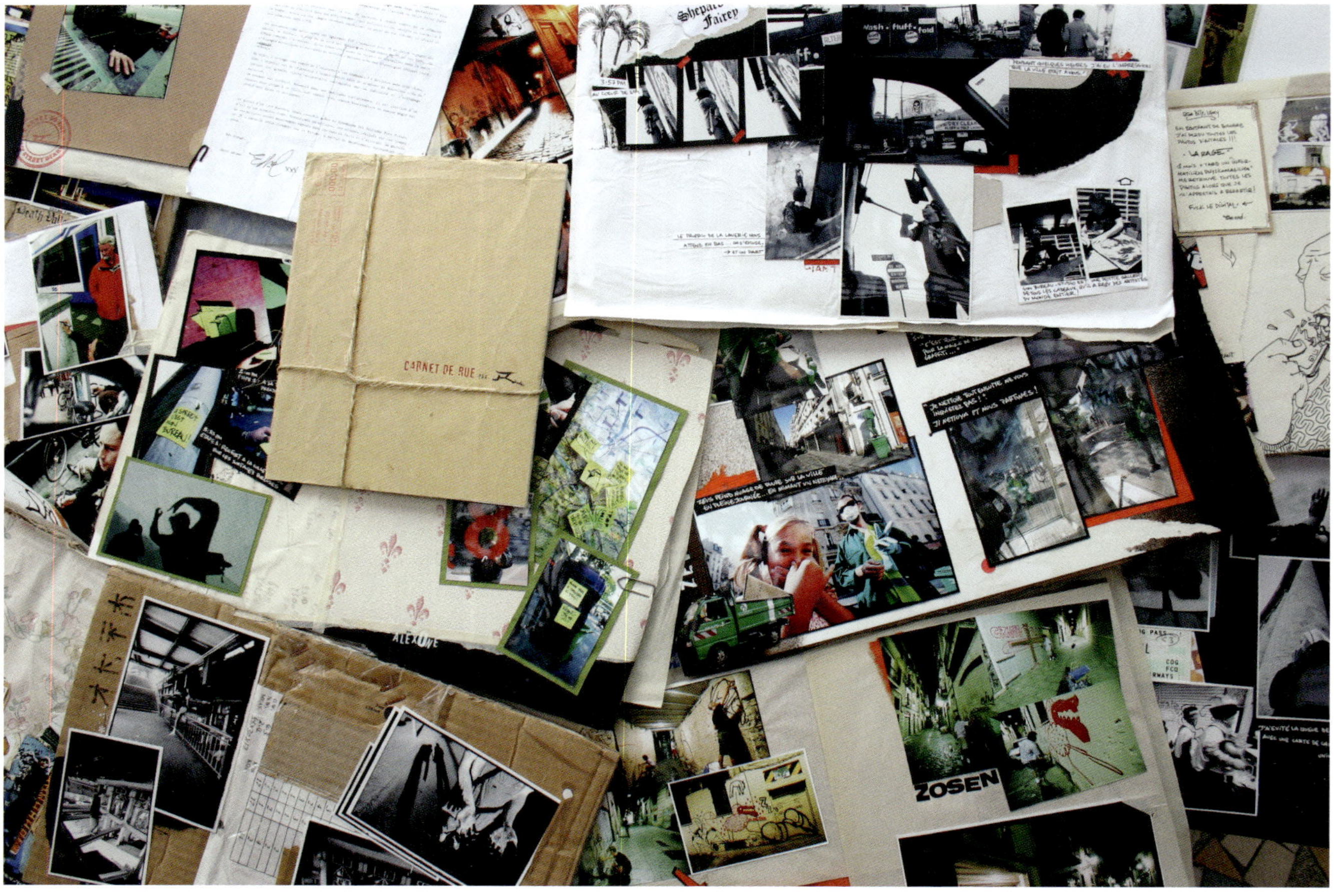

Original boards for ***Carnet de Rue***, 2005

OPPOSITE
28 Millimeters, Portrait of a Generation, 2004
Zid, contact sheet

FOLLOWING SPREAD
28 Millimeters, Portrait of a Generation, 2006
"Kärcher" series, cleaning of the exhibition in Paris city center, n° 3, France

image. A vertical line divides the image, slightly off-center, formed by the dark pole in the background, Ly's head, his dark-lensed video camera, and its hanging strap. Every element of the composition directs attention to Ly's expressive stance. JR's chosen photograph, one of many made that day, pictures a dynamic, seething, and unconquerable group. Because of the length of the lens and Ly's posture and expression, the camera resembles a gun, and the scene a holdup. Ly, the filmmaker who used his video camera to film his neighborhood and document police interactions with its residents, here played the role of a gangster for JR's camera (pp. 22–23).

By then, JR had moved on from his first found camera to a 28mm Canon FTb, a hand-me-down from his girlfriend's grandfather and still a film camera. The sessions in Les Bosquets and La Forestière produced many pictures. How to show them? The walls of the high-rise housing estates beckoned, though with no official invitation. Pasting those walls with pictures of the people who lived there felt like a natural next step.

Increasing the format from an A4-sized print was crucial. JR tried and rejected stenciling, a technique used by artists like Blek le Rat, Banksy, and Shepard Fairey. He knew that large photocopies like the kind used in architectural offices would allow him to assemble one large image from multiple strips. A printer in the 12th arrondissement helped him refine the technique, and JR and helpers pasted the resulting exhibit, which they called *Clichés du ghetto* (2004):

> We had to first deconstruct my images into 90 cm-wide strips that could then be reassembled to create XXL formats that wouldn't cost anything except for the price of the paper and the ink. The printer had never done

> that before. … As soon as I had enough funds, we started printing Ladj's *Hold-Up*, 6 x 8 meters, and the others 4 x 3 meters. We went to the Leroy Merlin hardware store for the gear we needed to paste these photos: we transformed the telescopic handles used to clean swimming pools into giant brooms.
>
> The first pasting operation took several nights, we didn't know what we were doing, the strips kept falling off as we pasted them, we mixed up the order of the strips—we were learning!…We then organized an opening to reveal these photographs that were all over the neighborhood of Les Bosquets…The exhibition was called *Clichés du ghetto*… A crew from France 3 came and fortunately didn't film my face—I hadn't yet come up with the hat and sunglasses look that lets me remain totally invisible once I take them off. The journalists interviewed the young people in the neighborhood, all of them happy to finally be visible, to be seen, to be heard.[4]

Although the opening of *Clichés du ghetto* was actively publicized, with widely distributed invitations and a map that indicated how to get there by mass transit, the audience mostly came from the abandoned neighborhood itself. The trip from Paris was long and included rail, bus, and a 15-minute stretch by foot; the lack of direct rail connection to Paris had always been the area's problem. Paris remained largely oblivious to the artistic effort. The mayor of Montfermeil lodged an official complaint against JR for defacement.

Feeling somewhat endangered, JR decided to accept an offer from the publisher Édition Free Press to make a book about graffiti artists throughout the world. The opportunity would remove him from trouble in France and provide new experiences and input. He traveled for a year, from September 2004 to September 2005, making friends, collecting material, and photographing actions in communal and public spaces in New York, Los Angeles, Berlin, Amsterdam, Brussels, Madrid, Barcelona, Milan, Rome, and Bologna. The book was published in 2005 in French and English as *Carnet de rue*, which translates roughly as "Street Notebook." An unpaginated artist's book in zine format, it has a very tactile appearance, imitating a twined package through photos on its front and back covers (p. 24). Its pages show photos taped down with torn masking tape, collaged travel tickets, and other ephemera, as well as pasted handwritten labels with explanations and comments. *Carnet de rue* stood as the first of what would become an important medium for JR: printed books.

The first page of *Carnet de rue* features a "taped" photo that shows a hooded JR descending into the underground—he is about to disappear for a while. Through his pictures and design, he promises not to forget his friends at Les Bosquets. JR took a roll of the photocopied Les Bosquets photographs with him to paste while abroad, and faces familiar from Montfermeil appear on walls in New York as soon as he arrives there, as further documented on the book's next pages.

Images of genuine affection, friendship, and shared social occasions proliferate in *Carnet de rue*. As a scrapbook of the artist's travels and the initial human contacts that provided further human contacts, the book shows how artists take action on building walls, how bicycles can be used as ladders. We also see children, a dog, tables set with delicious and economical meals that inevitably feature pasta, and a graffer holding the hand of his neatly dressed, white-haired grandmother, whom he may be walking to church. The main message of the book: There is fun to be had with good people while—yes, illegally—making and presenting images, often quirky or heartwarming, in the public realm

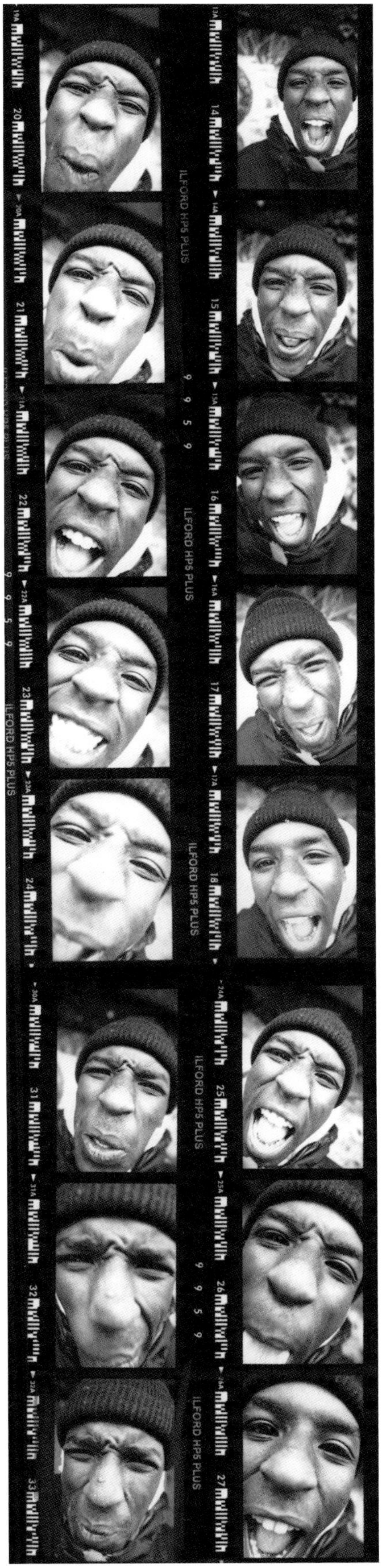

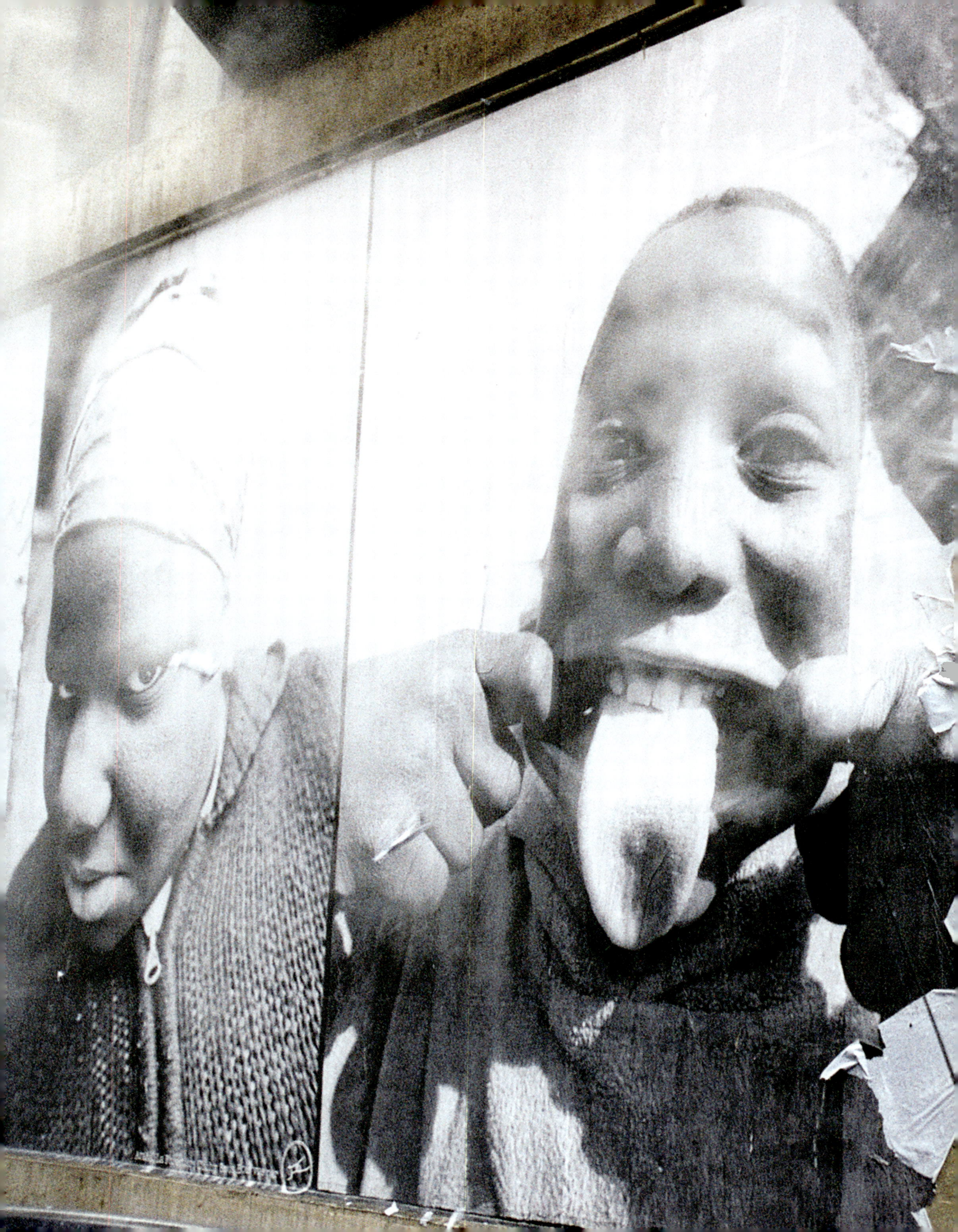

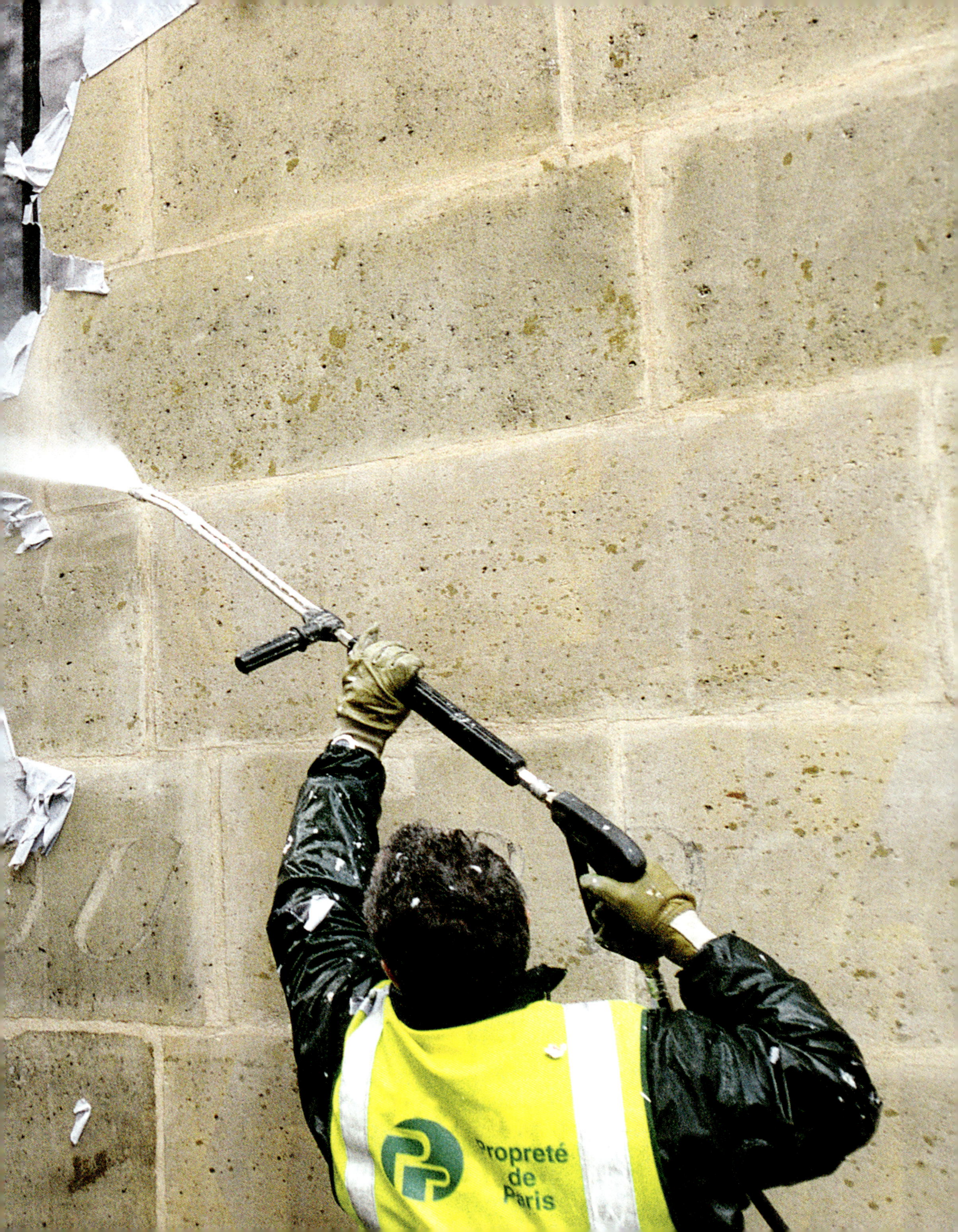
Propreté
de
Paris

28 Millimeters, Portrait of a Generation, 2004
Araba, Paris, 6th arrondissement, France

OPPOSITE
Les Enfants d'Ouranos #25, 2023
Ink on wood, 183 x 123 x 6.5 cm
(72 x 48 ½ x 2 ½ in.)

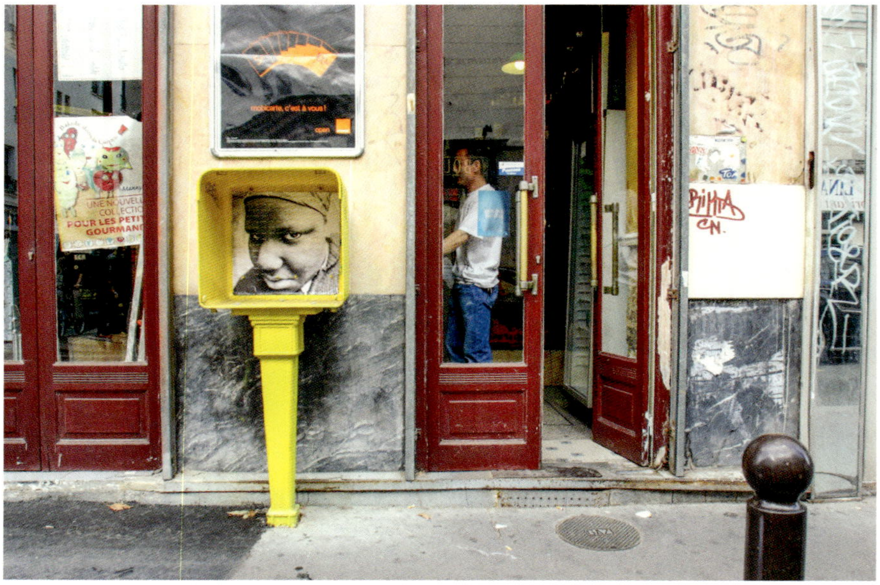

through diverse techniques. In essence, *Carnet de rue* already revealed JR's future approach to art.

When JR returned to Paris in 2005, two things stood out. First, he had a renewed appreciation for his own technique of strip-pasting deconstructed large-scale paper portraits. Second, he knew that foregrounding communication, collaboration, and documentation would make his work flower. The internet made it easier than ever for JR to connect with others, even internationally, by email and through images posted on his website. It also helped that flights had become inexpensive. Google Earth made the surface of the planet navigable for the eye.

While JR was traveling for *Carnet de rue*, his Les Bosquets images remained up in the neighborhood, visible on the internet, and some tourists even visited them. The images were later removed: French Interior Minister Sarkozy at the time (before he was president) vowed to clean the suburbs with powerwasher known as a *kärcher* in France (the city worker is removing the pasting with a kärcher, pp. 26–27). Just after he returned in 2005, riots broke out in Les Bosquets. JR saw the large pasting of his contact and friend Ladj Ly behind a flaming car in a news report on television. As it turned out, three young boys pursued by the police hid in an electric company substation at exactly that location and two of them had been fatally electrocuted, triggering riots that spread throughout France. Law enforcement's embedded biases against the community had resulted in fear, distrust, and panicked avoidance behavior, causing the young boys to become victims of institutional racism. The Clichy-Montfermeil neighborhoods became impenetrable to the press, who remained at a distance with their telephoto lenses. A large press agency contacted JR to take news photographs of the people burning and destroying their own streets, their neighbors' cars. They hoped to gain access to such images through Ly. JR and Ly refused to comply, seeing it as disloyal and extractive of the social inequities at the heart of the riots. In that moment, it became clear to JR that he had made his choice to become an artist, not a photojournalist.

In 2005, in response to the unrest, JR doubled down on the problem of stereotypes, social closeness, and distance. He immediately continued with his series "Portrait of a Generation" (2005, pp. 25–28), for which he used his 28mm camera to take close-up portraits of faces from the affected neighborhoods. He stood just inches away from his subjects and thrust his lens into their faces, close enough to hear them breathing, packing their faces completely into the frame. He asked them to embody a caricature of themselves—the fearsome person the media and the rest of Paris expected them to be. They reacted with contorted faces and grimaces, or looked up threateningly. The 28mm lens distorted those portrayed further as the center of their faces bulged outward. JR pasted the enlarged pictures in the neighborhood, but, more aggressively, also took them into the heart of Paris, pasting them on walls throughout the city. JR included the names, ages, and addresses of the people portrayed on each "Portrait of a Generation" street-pasted image. Because of that, it was possible for anyone who could read to go and find the person in the photograph, talk to them, start a dialogue.

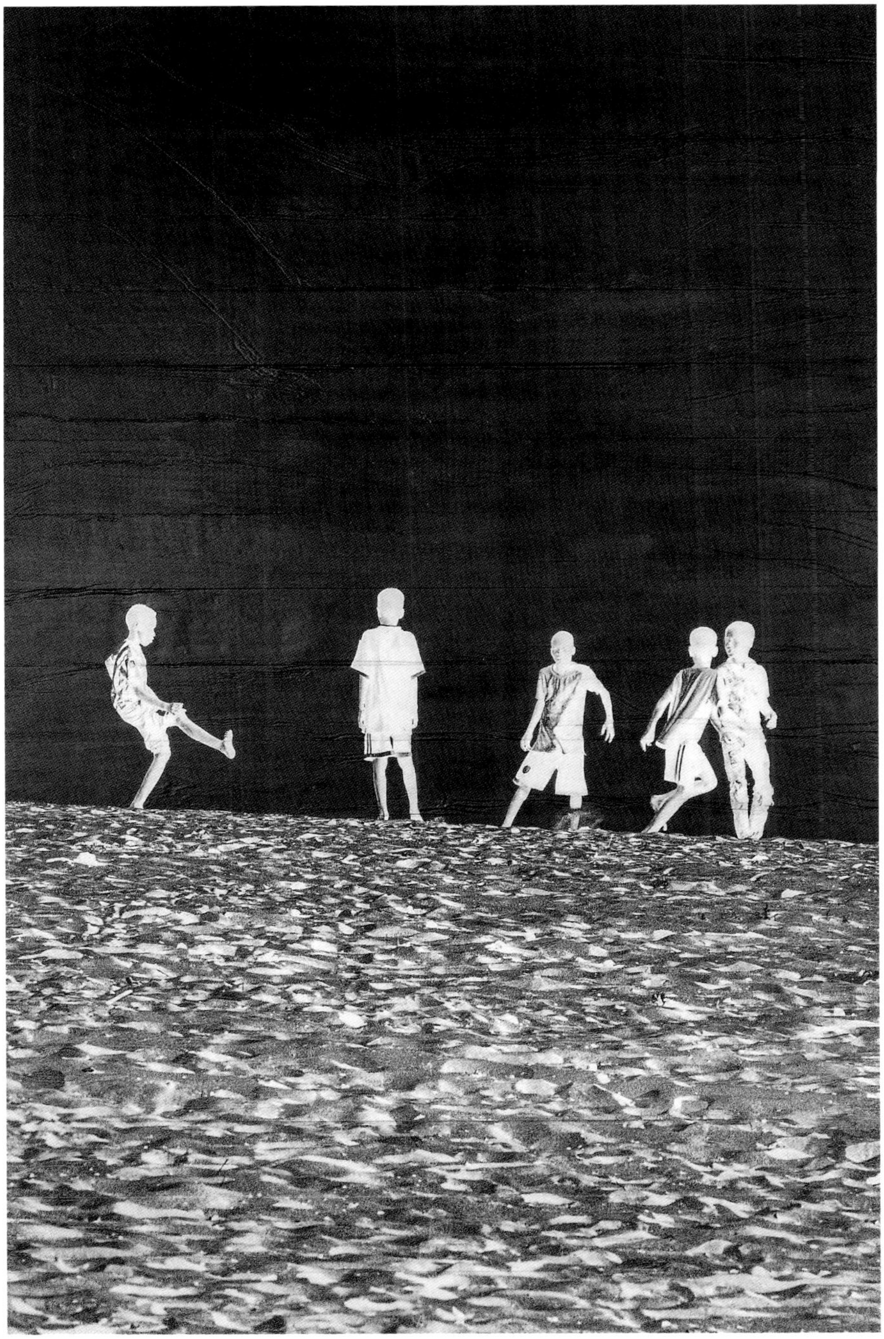

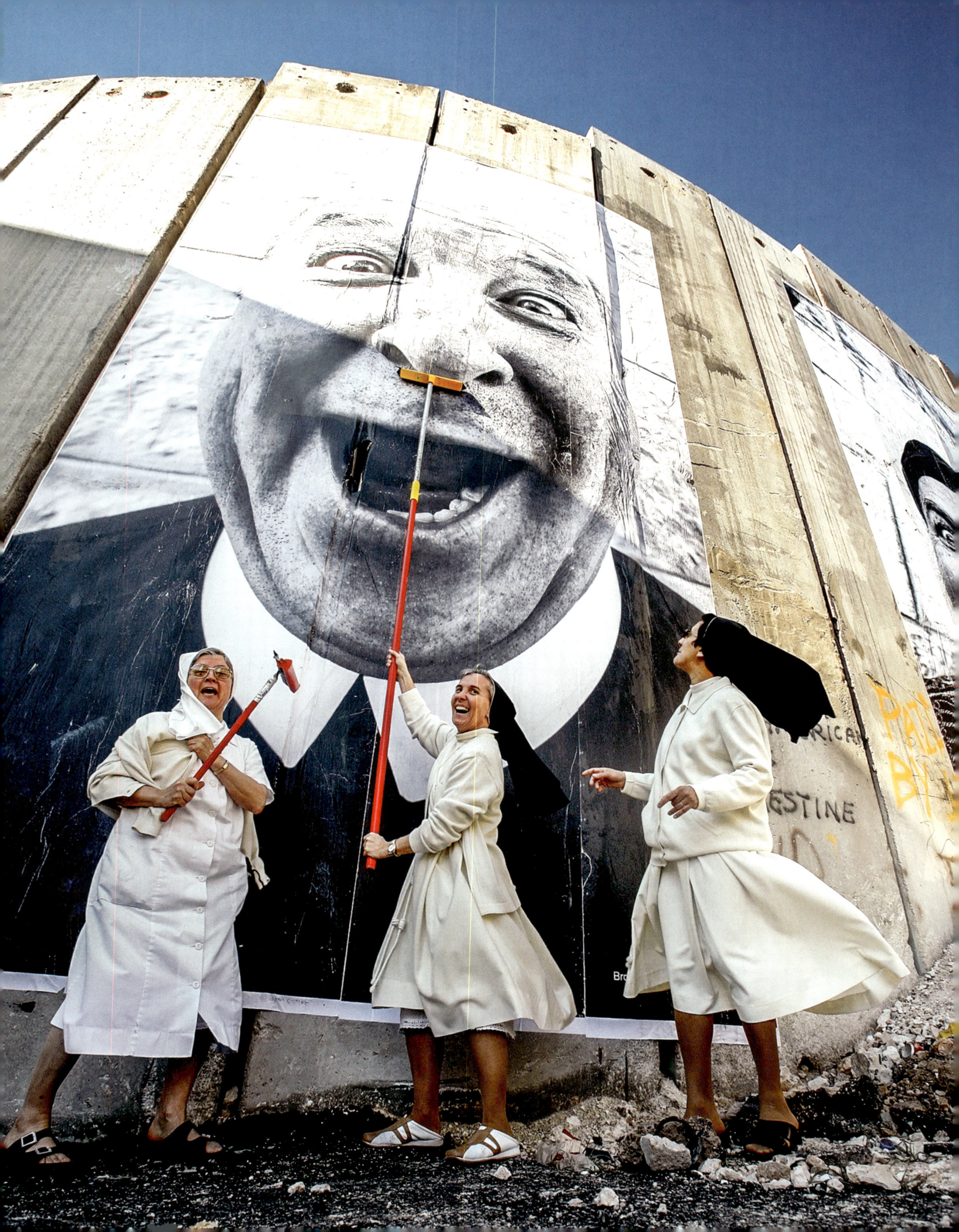

Action, Action, Action

Who really knew what they were talking about when they voiced an opinion about conflict in the Middle East? In 2007, the immigrant community around JR buzzed with discussions about Israel and Palestine. The gulf between Clichy-Montfermeil and Paris had taught him about how destructive stereotyping can be. When his friend Marco Berrebi, who spoke Arabic, suggested they go see for themselves, JR, just 23 years old, acquiesced, knowing their French nationality would allow them to travel freely. He brought his camera. The idea was: take portraits, talk to people. The enterprise, which he would title *Face 2 Face* (pp. 31–33), became the first action that took him abroad.

The concept developed from chance conversations with two taxi drivers, one Palestinian and the other Israeli. Both taxi drivers had the lowest opinions of each other as abstract, unknown entities. They both thought any professional counterpart of theirs (or anyone else, for that matter) on the other side of the West Bank barrier would be hostile, unhelpful, and unlikely to assist JR with an art project. Despite their proximity, JR came to believe they were simply unable to see each other. In that moment, the artist decided to pair large-scale portraits of professionals from both sides of the conflict. He started with the taxi drivers he had met, and then found teachers, hairdressers, students, athletes, police, religious leaders, actors, and more. He imagined paired portraits pasted adjacently, in huge black-and-white images that faced the viewer head-on. Remarkably, sets of Palestinian and Israeli people did agree to be photographed as examples of their professions, even when JR asked them to play and make faces that looked as grotesque as they imagined their counterpart on the other side to be. The photos didn't give any visual hint as to what the portrayed person did for work, except for the religious leaders, who wore their traditional garb. JR took the photographs from very close, as he had done in the second phase of "Portrait of a Generation," with the 28mm lens that distorted faces. Some of the photographs looked scary, others silly (p. 33). The project was able to proceed to the pasting phase. JR papered the large photographs onto walls in eight Israeli and Palestinian cities, including Bethlehem, Tel Aviv, Hebron, and Ramallah, and, illegally, on the West Bank barrier itself (pp. 31 and 33). JR requested permission

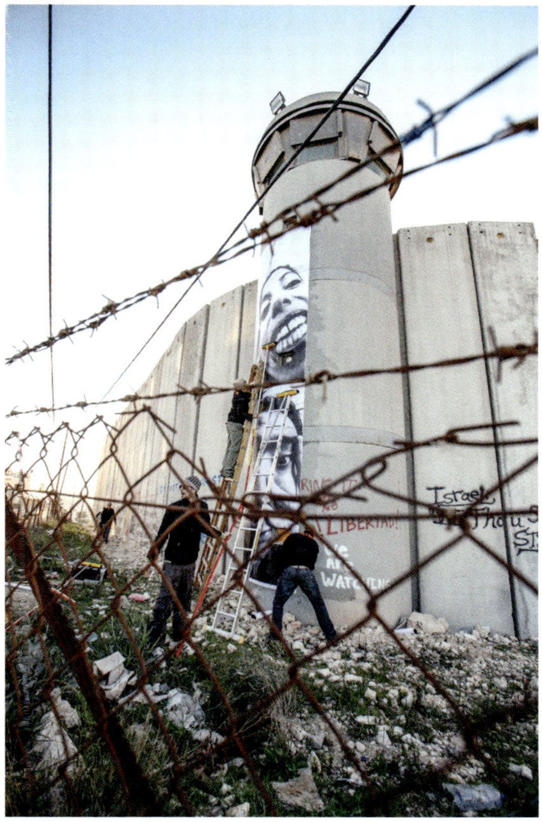

28 Millimeters, Face 2 Face, 2007
Separation wall, mirador, Palestinian side

OPPOSITE
28 Millimeters, Face 2 Face, 2007
Nuns in action, separation wall, security fence
Palestinian side, Bethlehem

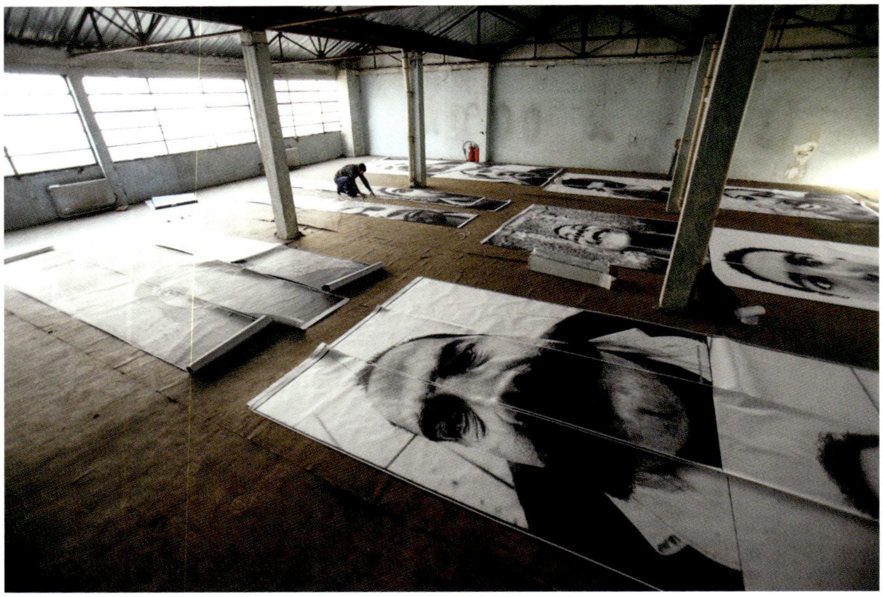

28 Millimeters, Face 2 Face, 2007
Preparation before the pasting, Paris, France

28 Millimeters, Face 2 Face, 2007
Separation wall, security fence, Israeli side
Abu Dis, Jerusalem

from inhabitants to paste on the outside walls of their houses, but not from government officials. Soldiers sometimes intervened and, at least once, JR was taken into some station, only to be released shortly after. The pastings were not approved, and even though JR received an order to leave the territory, he still remained and continued working. People who lived with paired faces pasted on their buildings were often compelled to explain the art project to passersby. As JR said in the short film interview about this action posted on his website, after he left the scene, the people living with the work became the spokespeople for the project.

Oftentimes passersby who fell into conversation with JR as he pasted could not correctly identify which person was Israeli and which was Palestinian. While pasting near the Church of the Nativity in Bethlehem, West Bank, Palestine—the oldest major church in the Holy Land—JR needed a taller ladder. A local generously fetched a very long, ancient wooden ladder from the church to enable him to complete the work. As he leaned the ladder against the wall, the contrast between its unknown age and the ephemerality of his action was not lost on the artist.

Of course, a video camera recorded this action. Documenting all stages of the work is part of the process and its future consumption. A feature film made about this project, *Faces* (2007), directed by Gérard Maximin, includes interviews with a rabbi, a priest, and an imam, whose humorous portraits contrast with their reflections about respecting all persons. Broadcast on television in Palestine and Israel, and in the Arab world, *Faces* may have raised some eyebrows or softened hearts, though the film, like the actions it portrays, had a negligible effect on any conflict. It's difficult not to be won over by the film's grasp of the personalities involved, the sheer chutzpah of the *Face 2 Face* endeavor, the suspense of the pasting, and small moments, like a shot of giggling nuns holding the paste broom up under the nose of a priest they recognize to give him a Charlie Chaplin moustache (p. 30). In JR's documentary photograph and the feature film, they get to prank the priest forever.

In what established itself as one of JR's habitual working methods, for *Face 2 Face,* JR used photography both to orchestrate the action for a "first generation" of participants and street viewers and to fix the action so it could be presented and explained to later audiences not on site. As an artist who worked in real time and specific places and situations, JR instinctually joined other contemporary artists using participation and social relations as their medium in open-ended processes that often did not produce art objects. Art historians and critics have written about this development in the visual arts: Those interested in reading more could start with Claire Bishop's 2012 book *Artificial Hells: Participatory Art and the Politics of Spectatorship*.

"Each time I've seen walls that have caught my attention, they would stick in my mind. I would even dream about them."

THE NEW YORKER (2017)

Appropriately, JR's art foregrounds the portrait, often only a face, or part of a face. For him, people are big. Marrying the human face to a building facade may cause disturbing, playful, or profound effects. The artist's editorial choice of image from a photo shoot and his choice of pasting location (which could include stairs, courtyards, or the bottom of an empty swimming pool) united in aesthetically impactful ways. He recognized that buildings, neighborhoods, and locales impose not only form but also meaning on a project. Through their expression, color contrast, and scale, the distinct black-and-white pastings hold their own and achieve undeniable physical presence on the walls that lend them texture. As they decay, the tattered pastings have friends and foes. Some people appreciate their aging, others tear off a strip to keep, and some voice objections to the messy shreds. Like the caterpillar that turns into a butterfly, the pastings hang on, munching for a while (people meeting, working, talking, thinking) but then complete their metamorphosis and flutter away.

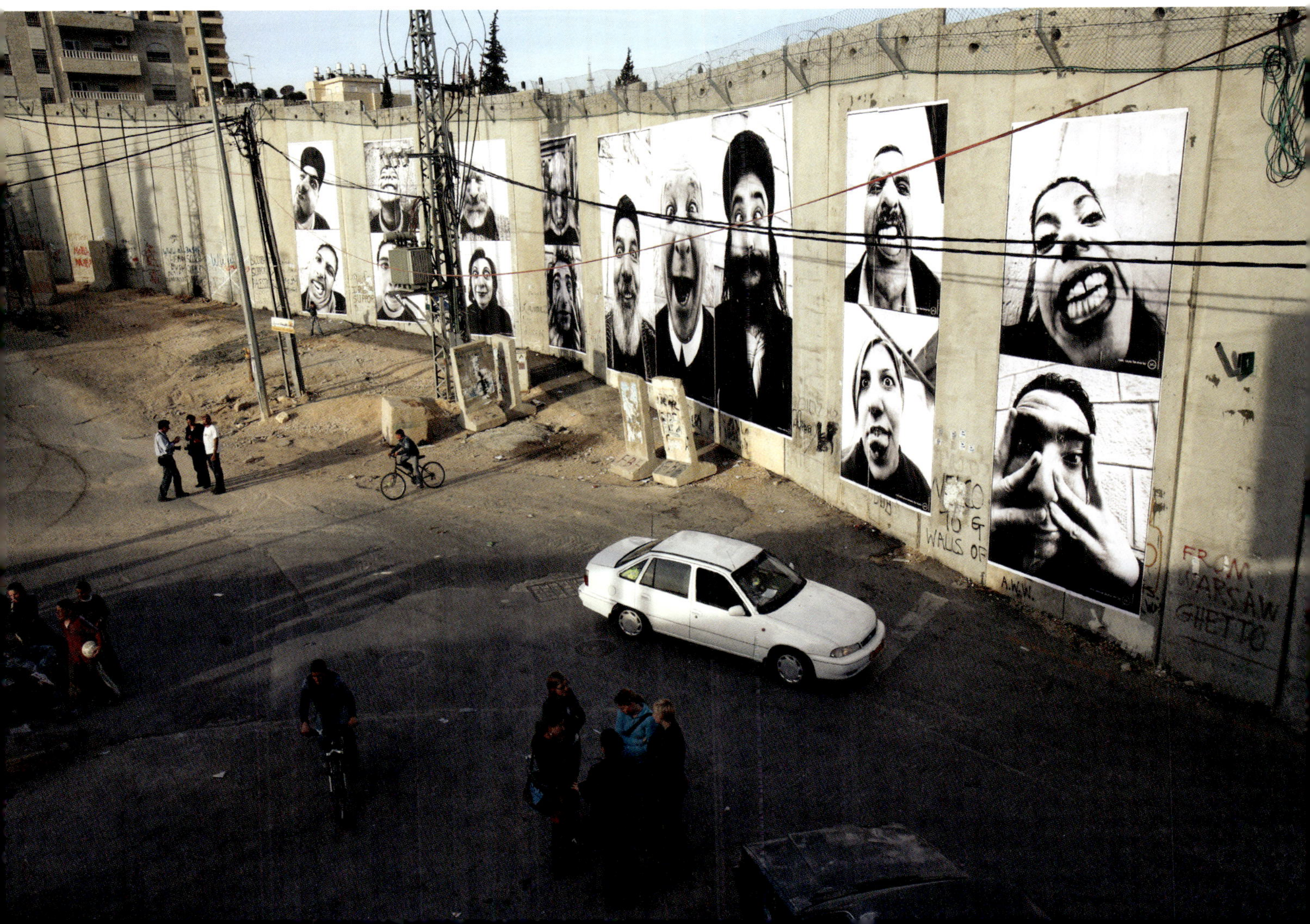

BELOW AND OPPOSITE TOP
28 Millimeters, Women Are Heroes, 2009
Action in Kibera Slum, general view
Nairobi, Kenya

OPPOSITE BOTTOM
28 Millimetres, Women Are Heroes, Rispah Atemba, Kenya, 2008
Black-and-white print on paper, pasted on wood, matte varnish,
200 x 137 x 12 cm (78 ¾ x 54 x 4 ¾ in.)

After working in the Middle East, JR's desire to travel to new places led to his project "Women Are Heroes", which started in 2007 (pp. 34–41). The large international project was made up of actions that took him and his team to Kenya, Sudan, Sierra Leone, Liberia, Cambodia, India, and Brazil. The artist was still very young: In 2007, he was only 24 years old. For this project, he chose wounded societies—communities in severe distress, where one would not necessarily expect art to be the most immediate need. The individual actions foregrounded women, who, despite being the mainstays of their communities and families, were often the first victims of crime and conflict, political dogmatism, and religious fanaticism. The action spoke to local men who helped JR paste the women's photos; the women literally gained size and presence in their eyes. Books documenting local participants and JR's action were distributed within each individual community as keepsakes. In addition, JR produced a comprehensive volume, also titled *Women Are Heroes* (2012), which documented all the actions together. A 2010 documentary feature film of the same name shows the projects unfolding.

In 2007, JR traveled to the shantytown Kibera, the largest slum in Nairobi, Kenya, to take pictures of women for the project. Kibera became a center of social unrest after contested presidential elections that same year. JR used his 28mm lens again, achieving proximity and distortion, but the images were used differently this time. The shantytown's housing density meant that rooftops offered a significant imaging plane. When he returned in 2009, the artist had

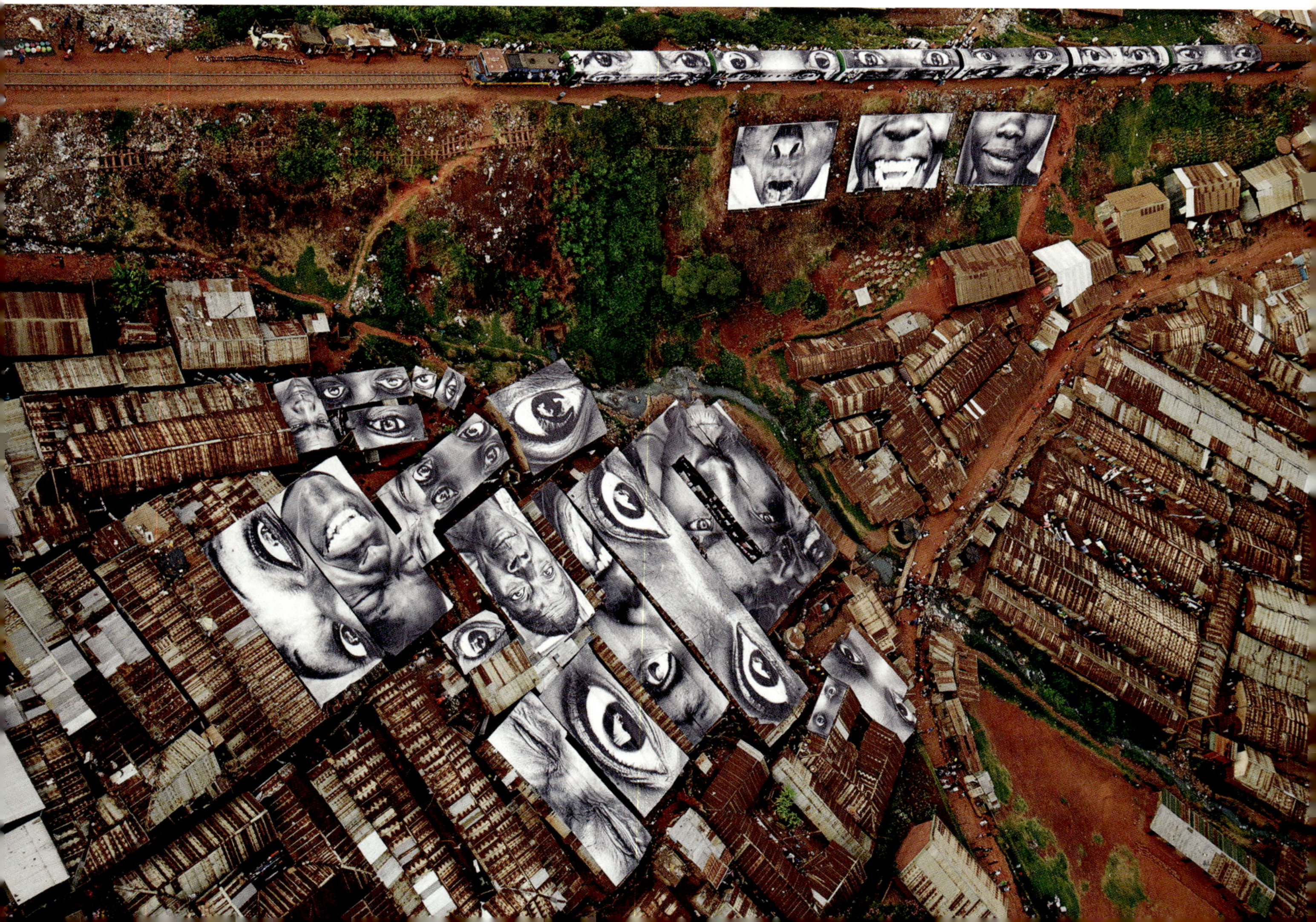

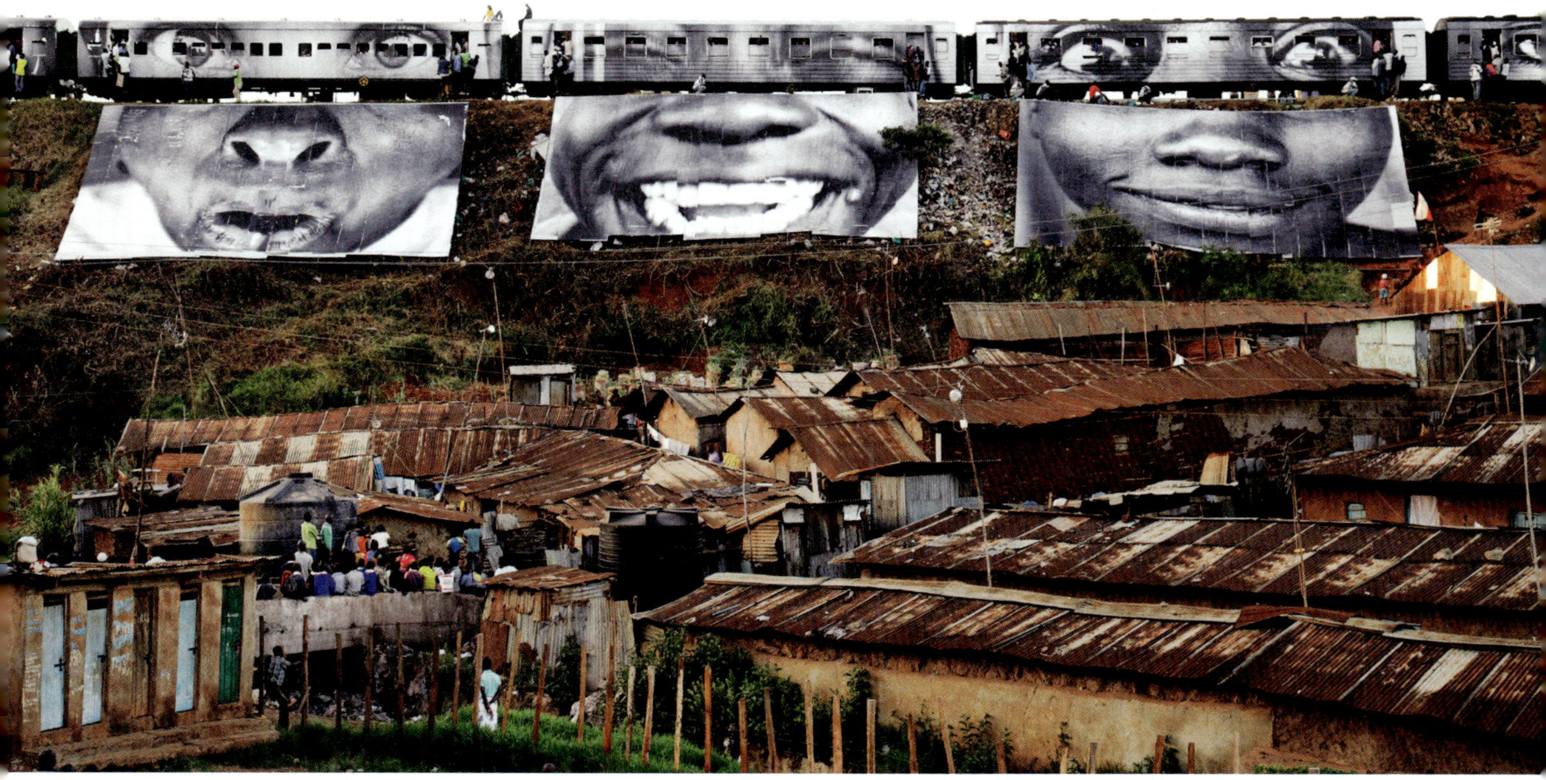

changed his medium to vinyl tarps, which also waterproofed the Kibera roofs, thereby contributing to the community's well-being. The roof tarps were printed with his black-and-white photos of the women's faces and eyes. Eventually, *Women Are Heroes* covered 21,528 square feet of rooftops in Kibera; the tarps turned out to be highly desirable to the families, and they requested them. In the aerial photograph *28 Millimeters, Women Are Heroes*, action in Kibera Slum, general view, Nairobi, Kenya (p. 34), the artist employs line, geometry, color contrast, and a touch of the surreal to create an arresting documentary image.

While in Kibera, JR conceived a playful, kinetic landscape composition using a hillside and a local working train (pp. 34–35). He pasted the train with three sets of eyes. On the rail-adjacent slope, he laid corrugated roofing panels pasted with six sets of noses and smiles. As the train moved past this location, from a certain point of view, eyes and smiles aligned, forming complete faces for fleeting moments. As the train moved, the faces changed expressions, as different configurations of eyes and mouths occurred, achieving a lively and humorous effect. A young woman spoke about why she lent her face to the project: "I need my photo to be on that train so that everyone in this world or even our country may want to know much about me, who she is, what does she do in her life. I believe I can do anything a human being can do … I have hope in life."

Photography and setting came together in a distinct way when JR continued his project *Women Are Heroes* in Rio de Janeiro (2008–9) in the oldest favela of the city, Morro da Providência. The young artist who loved to travel had been thinking about working in Brazil for a few years, but the difficulties of the locale—violent gangs, drug dealing, the prevalence of guns—had kept him at bay. He became especially interested in Providência when he heard a news story

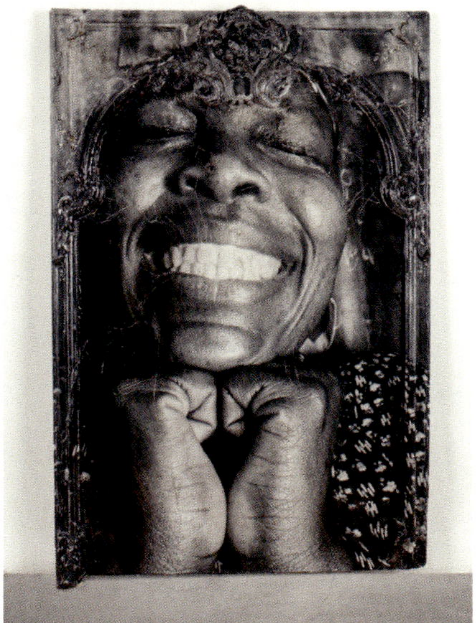

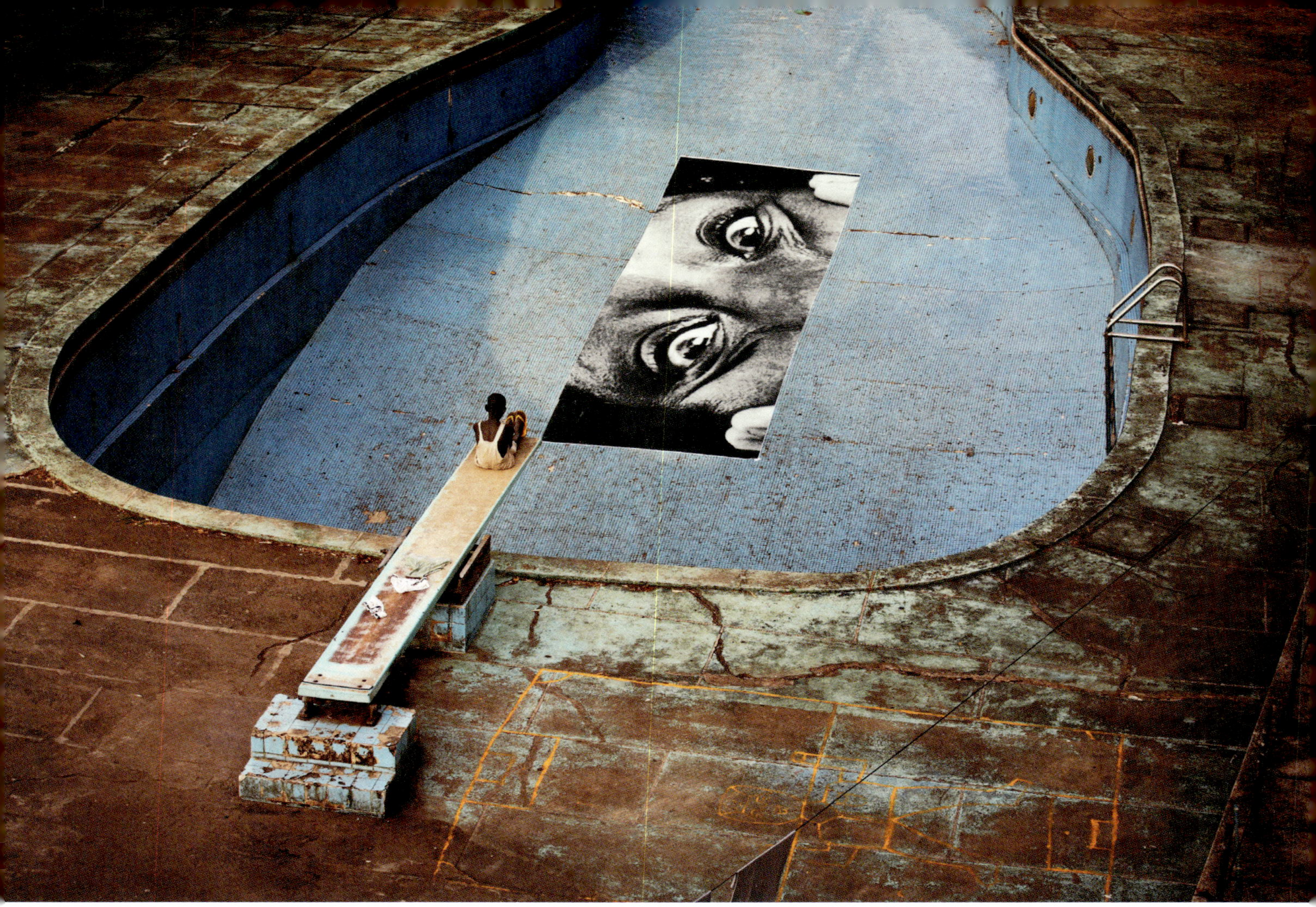

28 Millimeters, Women Are Heroes, 2008
Swimming pool, Intercontinental Hotel
Monrovia, Liberia

OPPOSITE
28 Millimeters, Women Are Heroes, 2009
"Open Eyes" in Phnom Penh, Cambodia

about three boys who were stopped by police on their way to school. The boys lacked identification papers, so the police detained them and handed them over to a rival gang, who killed and dismembered the boys before throwing their bodies into the trash. Although he spoke no Portuguese and knew no one in the favela, the shocking story of the schoolboys, echoing that of the electrocuted innocents fleeing a police chase in Clichy-Montfermeil, compelled JR to fly to Rio de Janeiro.

As JR and his friend and interpreter from Rio approached the favela, they met a local resident, a woman in her mid-40s named Rosiete Marinho. Marinho was a prominent resident with a fierce pride in her community and its expressive and artistic festival traditions. Once she heard JR was an artist from France, she invited him and his friend to return to see her the next day, without backpacks and with examples of his art. If they encountered any trouble along the way, JR had only to mention her name.

The next day, JR and his friend climbed the steps of the favela, where Marinho introduced them to a photographer, Mauricio Hora. Although Hora was initially doubtful, JR convinced him to help with the project by showing him a mock-up of faces and eyes from older projects freshly glued onto buildings in a recent photograph of the hillside. The word *morro* means "hill" in Portuguese, and the favela is built on a steep incline. The building materials for the houses were portable enough to be carried up a hill on someone's back and small enough to fit through narrow streets and stairways. The housing came together over time, with each generation of a family building upon the work of the previous one. An architecture of the improvised, Morro da Providência presents as a mass of contiguous houses of at most three stories. For the French artist, the facades, pocked with small, often grilled windows, appeared from the distance like an interconnected complex of pasteable surfaces.

Hora helped gain permissions from the community. Then JR began to photograph the women for whom gratuitous violence had become a way of life. Using a room in one of the houses of the favela, JR took pictures of two of the mothers and one of the grandmothers of the three young boys who had met their end through the police, and he heard their stories. Other women volunteered to be photographed, as did Rosiete Marinho herself. JR quickly emailed the images to his staff in Europe, with instructions to print them and fly back with them.

"I'm independent, but I don't work alone. I need a team and to be involved in local communities because the projects are immense and one person is not always enough."
JR CHRONICLES (2021)

The largest printing for the action, intended for the longest and widest set of stairs in the favela, featured the face of the grandmother, Benedita Florencio Monteiro. JR shows the elderly woman supporting her head with her left fist and framing cheek with her right hand, as if protecting herself but also drawing strength from within (p. 41). Its placement meant that the image could be seen best in its entirety from the bottom of the stairs, as one paused to ascend, and from within the favela community, not from downtown Rio. The printed strips of paper were pasted onto the riser of each step but not its tread, meaning no one stepped on her face. Nonetheless, traffic wore at the edges of the riser strips. By placing the grandmother's face on this incline, almost as steeply vertical as a ladder, JR made clear his topical reference to recent violence. The favela rose

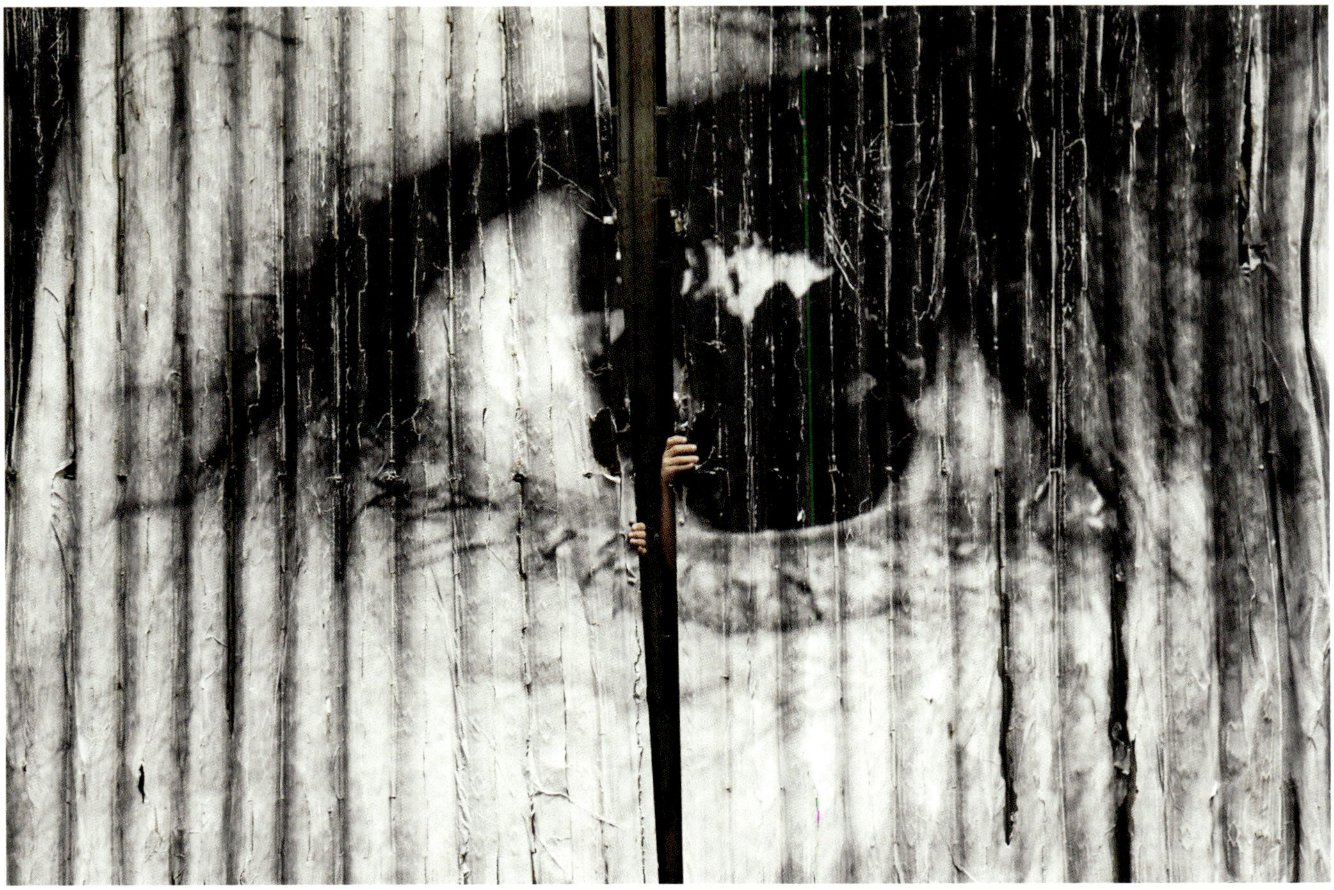

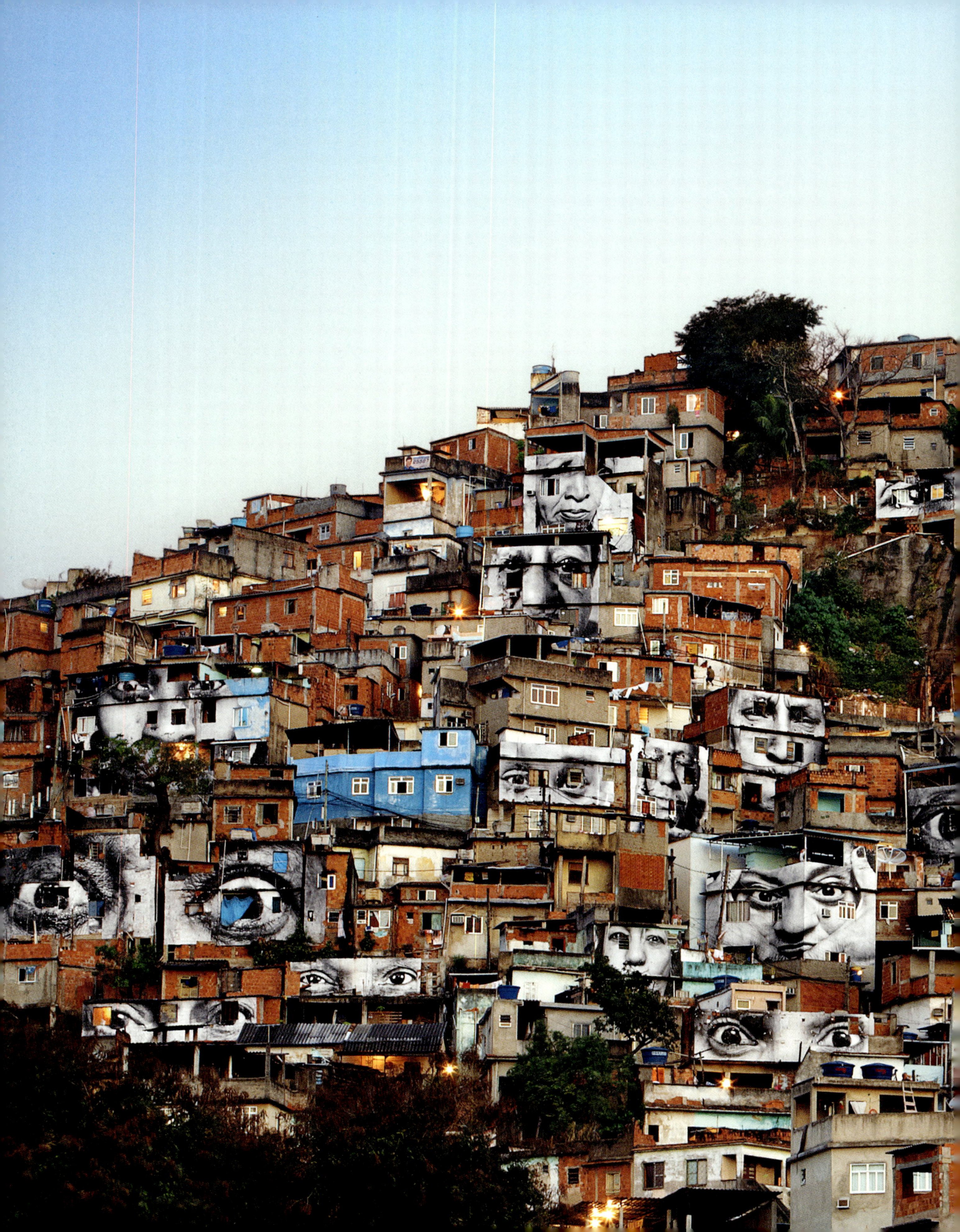

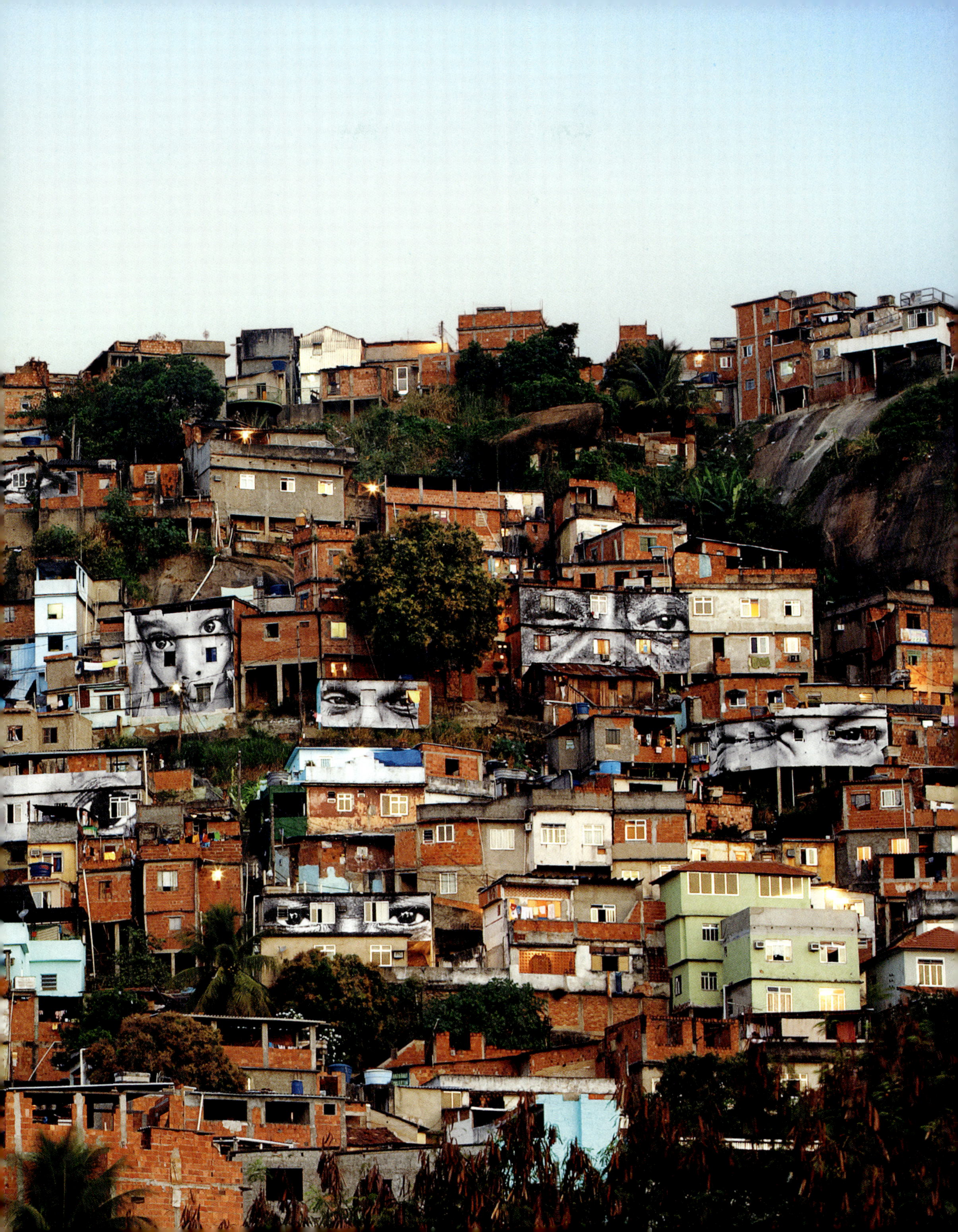

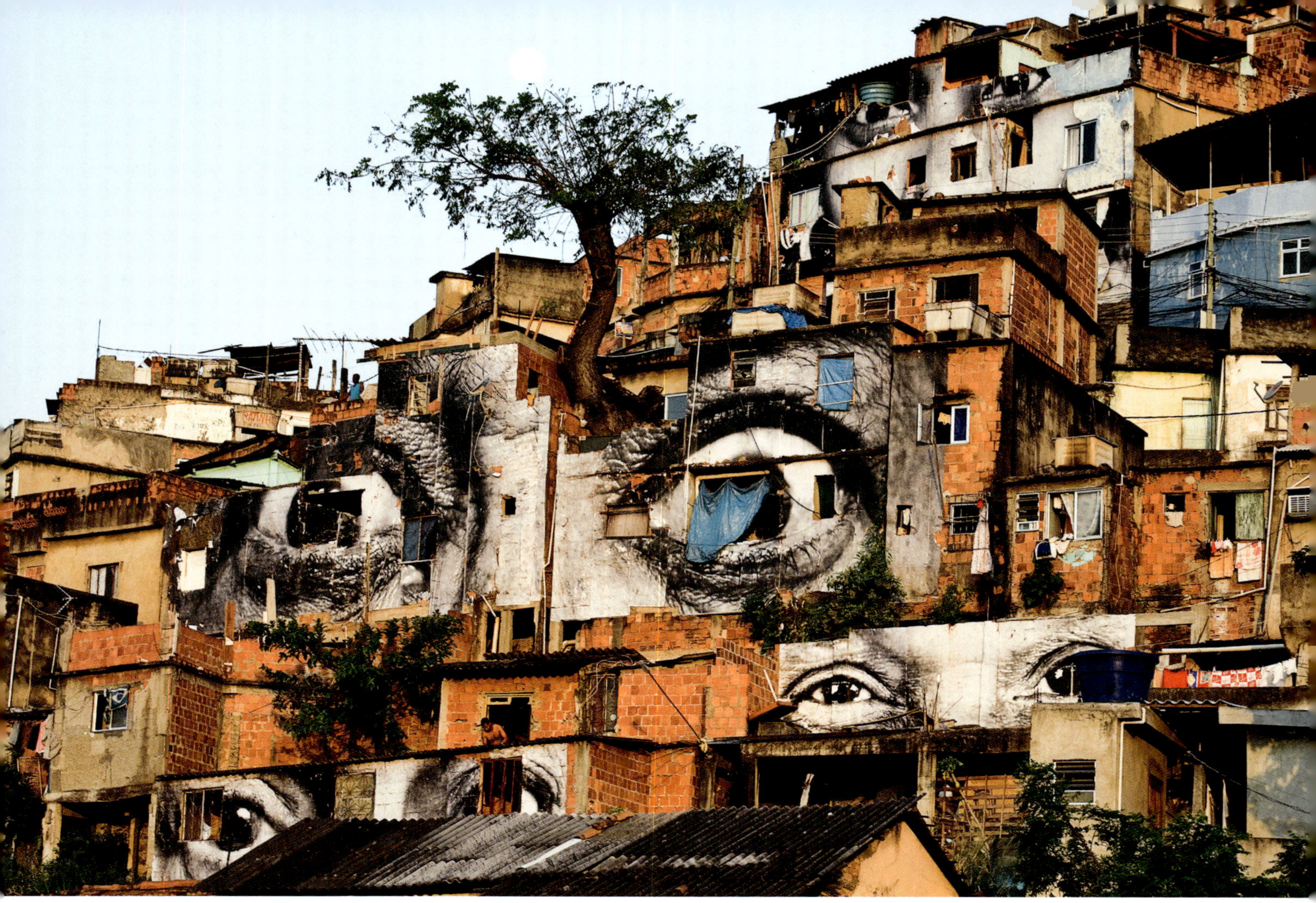

through Benedita Florencio Monteiro. During the stair's pasting, a gun battle broke out between drug dealers and the police, which paused the work for a short while. Ladj Ly, who accompanied JR on the project, caught the noise of the battle on film as the crew took shelter.

One by one, the chosen favela facades were pasted (pp. 38–40). The drug lords did not prevent it. Sometimes just one eye, or a cropped face showing two huge eyes, looked out. No unity of scale homogenized the images. JR enlarged some details fiercely, almost abstracting them. He planned the effects of individual images on walls according to their size, composing the entire living hillside of eyes around those of Rosiete Marinho, who frames her expressive features with her fingers, thumbs up, in an open-heart shape. In a final documentary photograph, the total effect is harmonious. The rectangles of houses hang together as if woven in place, illuminated by JR's images. Evenly cast over the hillside among the red brick and concrete buildings, the black-and-white photographs glow.

Why make such ephemeral art, produced in unsuspecting communities through focused artist planning and without corporate sponsors? Does it matter that, after this art has lived its pasted (usually) paper life, it remains known to posterity only through memory, social media, reproductions of photographs of photographs, the moving pictures of short and feature films, and the rhizoming website of the artist? The artist would say no. Or, not one to be dogmatic, he

PREVIOUS SPREAD
28 Millimeters, Women Are Heroes, 2008
Action in the Favela Morro da Providência, Favela, daytime, Rio de Janeiro, Brazil

ABOVE
28 Millimeters, Women Are Heroes, 2008
Action in the Favela Morro da Providência Favela, tree and moon, Rio de Janeiro, Brazil

OPPOSITE
28 Millimeters, Women Are Heroes, 2008
Action in the Favela Morro da Providência, staircase, Rio de Janeiro, Brazil

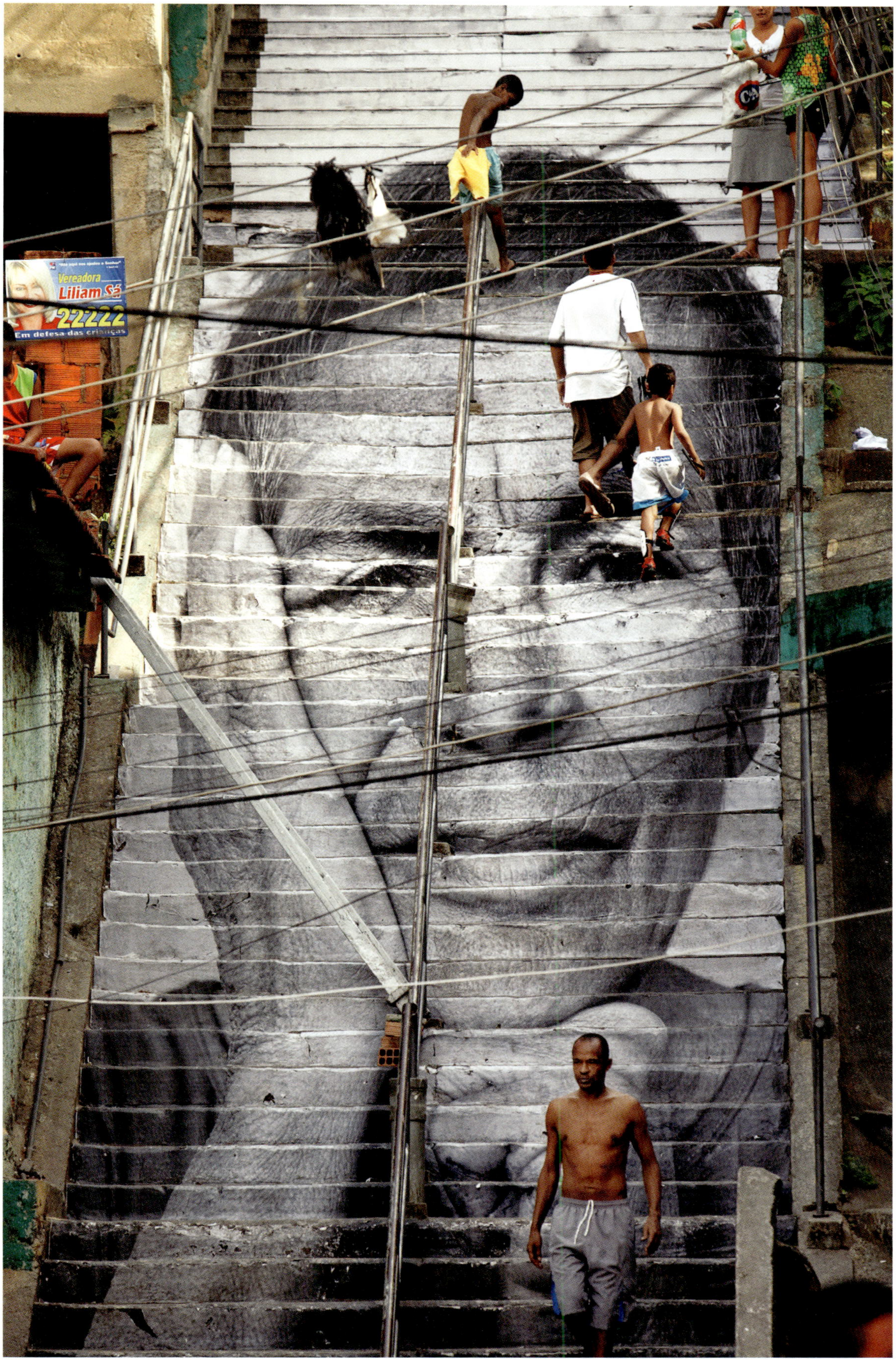
Vereadora
Liliam Sá
22222
Em defesa das crianças

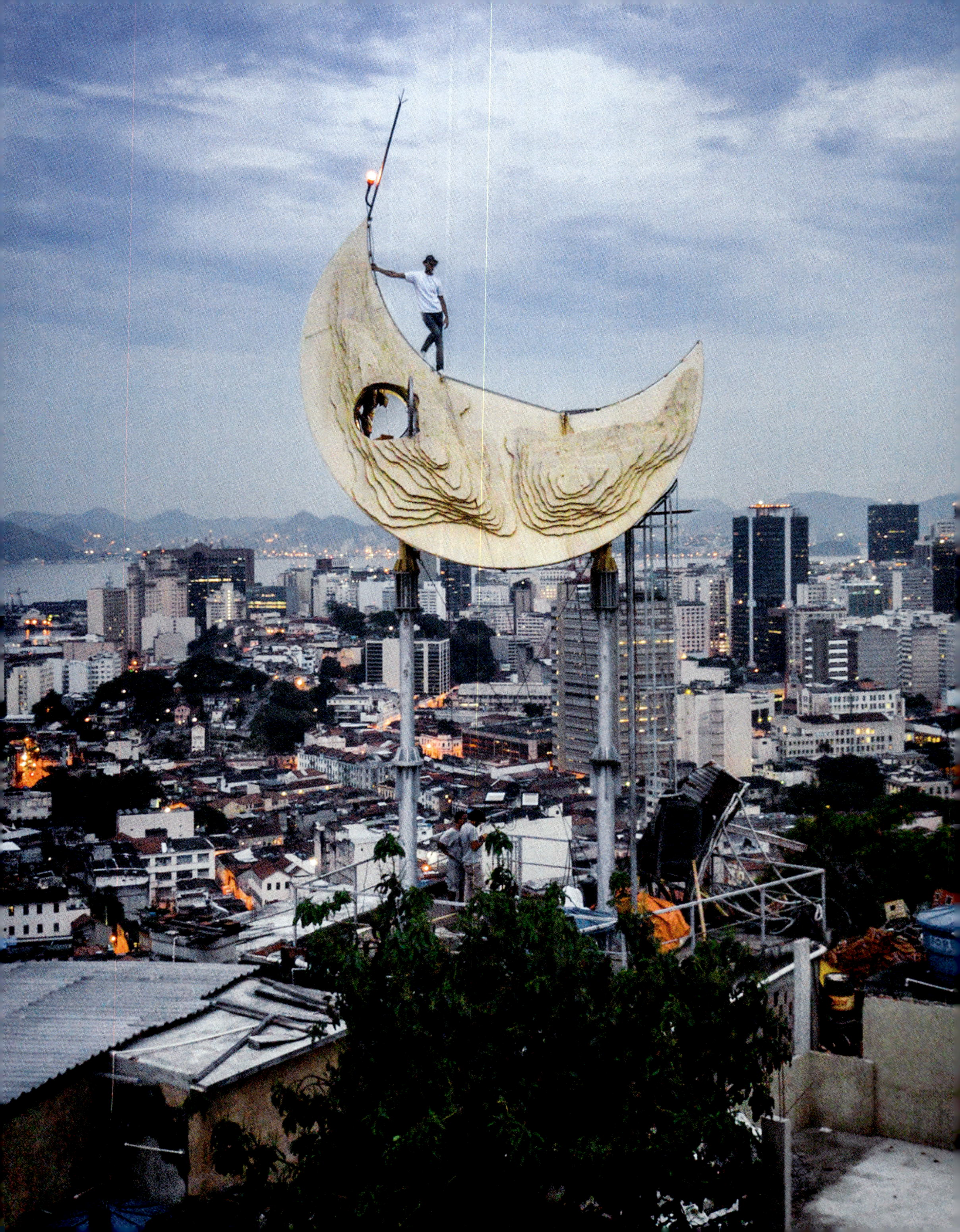

might say, "Let's see." In many cases, a belief in real human positive fulfillment and learning has attached itself like a barnacle to the souls of those involved in JR's projects.

Encouraged by Mauricio Hora, JR purchased a house in Providência to make a community center and school, called Casa Amarela (p. 42), with free classes and cultural programs. The center includes an artist's apartment on its roof, a moon-shaped, one-room sculptural structure that jives with the improvised architecture style of the favela. In 2026, Casa Amarela added a second building to increase its offerings, marking the 17th year the artist has returned to the favela. A new pasting for the project "Inside Out" put many favela faces on the main stairs, which had once carried the single face of a bereft grandmother.

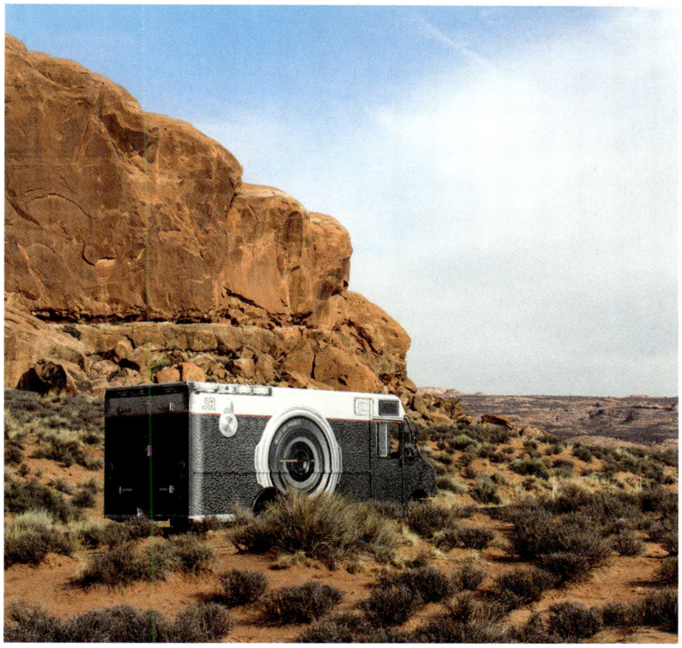

JR conceived "Inside Out" as a working title that could encompass many actions with a truly global reach. The project is ongoing. The idea began in 2011, when he became the first visual artist to receive the TED Prize (Technology, Entertainment, Design). Awarded by TED, this honor recognizes a remarkable individual with a world-changing wish who aims to create long-lasting social change. JR received $100,000 to realize his wish to "turn the world inside out" and ignite change. He wanted to do this through photography—to lead the creation of public art inspired by his own work but carried out by any group of at least 50 members of a community with a good cause. For this project, a group takes the pictures themselves using JR's recommended format and then sends them to JR's studio. After reviewing and approving a statement about their group cause, JR's studio prints the photographs as large-size posters and mails them back for pasting. The community then mixes their wheat paste and gets to work, pasting faces on walls and other local surfaces. Through this process, they begin conversations about their cause or idea. A helpful video on the JR website demonstrates how to mix the paste with flour, cold water, boiling water, a bucket, and a stick.

As of 2026, about 600,000 people have participated in "Inside Out" in more than 154 countries. The actions are documented, archived, and exhibited online. In 2013, a documentary film about the project, also titled *Inside Out*, premiered at the Tribeca Film Festival.

In a self-referential gesture, a large pasting on the National Library of France in Paris (2013) turned the building into a printer spitting out an image. A pyramidal photo booth, built especially for Giza, Egypt, as part of the annual contemporary art show *Forever Is Now II* (2022, p. 44), invited visitors to enter the newly created pyramid for a photograph, then wait as their ejected poster floated down from near the pinnacle, where JR positioned the 16-foot-tall printer output. In Giza, participants pasted their faces on billboards specifically set up for that purpose, not on existing walls, perhaps as a workaround for concerned archaeologists and politicians, so that every participant could enjoy an ephemeral presence and leave their mark through their portrait, even for a few minutes, in an ancient site. *Inside Out* in Egypt—how can it effect positive change? While JR's action arrived as a fun, seemingly apolitical art action, it insisted on the power due to the individual within the state.

Photo booth trucks, both large and small, which are themselves interestingly pasted, help proliferate *Inside Out* actions (p. 43). The mobile photo booth drives into a community, moving between neighborhoods, and brings people into close contact with the immediate printing process. Right after a photo is taken, the

ABOVE
Inside Out Project truck as part of *Dreamers* in 35 cities across the United States, 2008

OPPOSITE
JR on the moon of ***Casa Amarela***, 2017
Morro da Providência, Rio de Janeiro, Brazil
Founded in 2009 by JR and Mauricio Hora

image slips from an output opening into the hands of the portrayed. The ensuing pasting puts them out there! They are large, show their face on the street, and they matter. In some cases, they may ask themselves, "Now what?" The answer is for them to discover.

An "Inside Out" photo booth truck features in the charming film that JR made with Agnès Varda, *Faces Places* (2017). In the film, they travel around the French countryside and take photographs in small towns. Villagers enter the truck through doors in the back that swing open to reveal a little photo studio. The print ejects from the truck's side. All wonderingly admire the large-format images, which get pasted onto walls in their villages, creating discussion. One shy waitress feels overwhelmed to be magnified this way; her boss complains that she, though just a waitress, is now the star of the village. Some children suddenly realize their mother is actually beautiful. Varda, whose somewhat autobiographical first film *La Pointe Courte* (1955) employed the denizens of a small French fishing village known to her from childhood and only two professional actors, expresses herself in *Faces Places* as very happy to be getting to know new faces in French villages this way (p. 47). Introduced to Varda through her daughter, JR found a soulmate in the Nouvelle Vague filmmaker, who, before him, had pictured and told the story of many a quirky, weathered, or angelic individual. She became a mentor who encouraged JR to acknowledge the surreal in his visual compositions. Varda explained art to JR as the place where people meet and where empathy could be fostered. In *Faces Places*, a bystanding mechanic, puzzled, asks Varda why JR has pasted huge photos of her feet and eyes on the

OPPOSITE
Inside Out Project, 2021
1040 portraits
Tower Bridge, London, United Kingdom

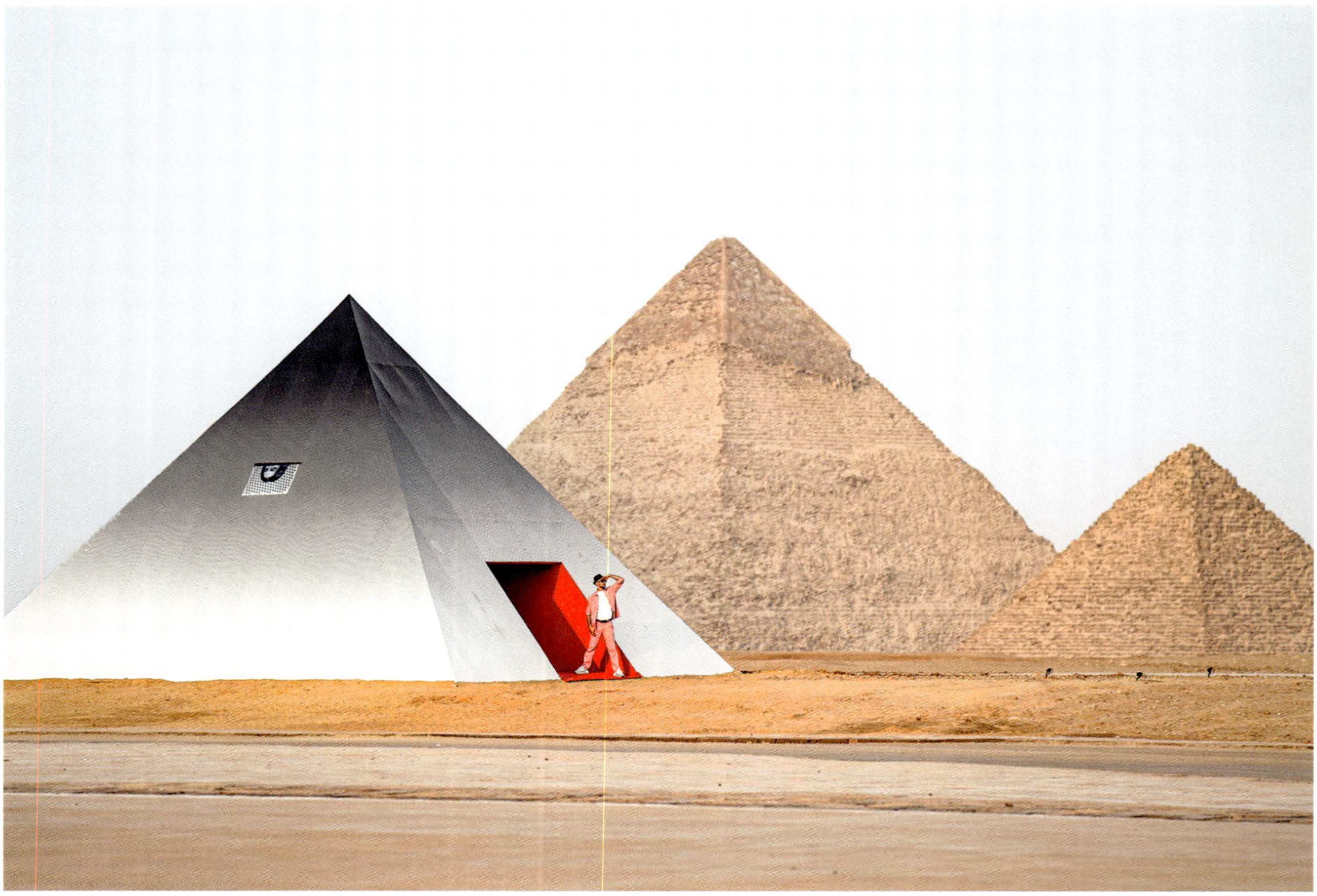

Inside Out Project for *Forever Is Now II*, 2022
Giza, Egypt

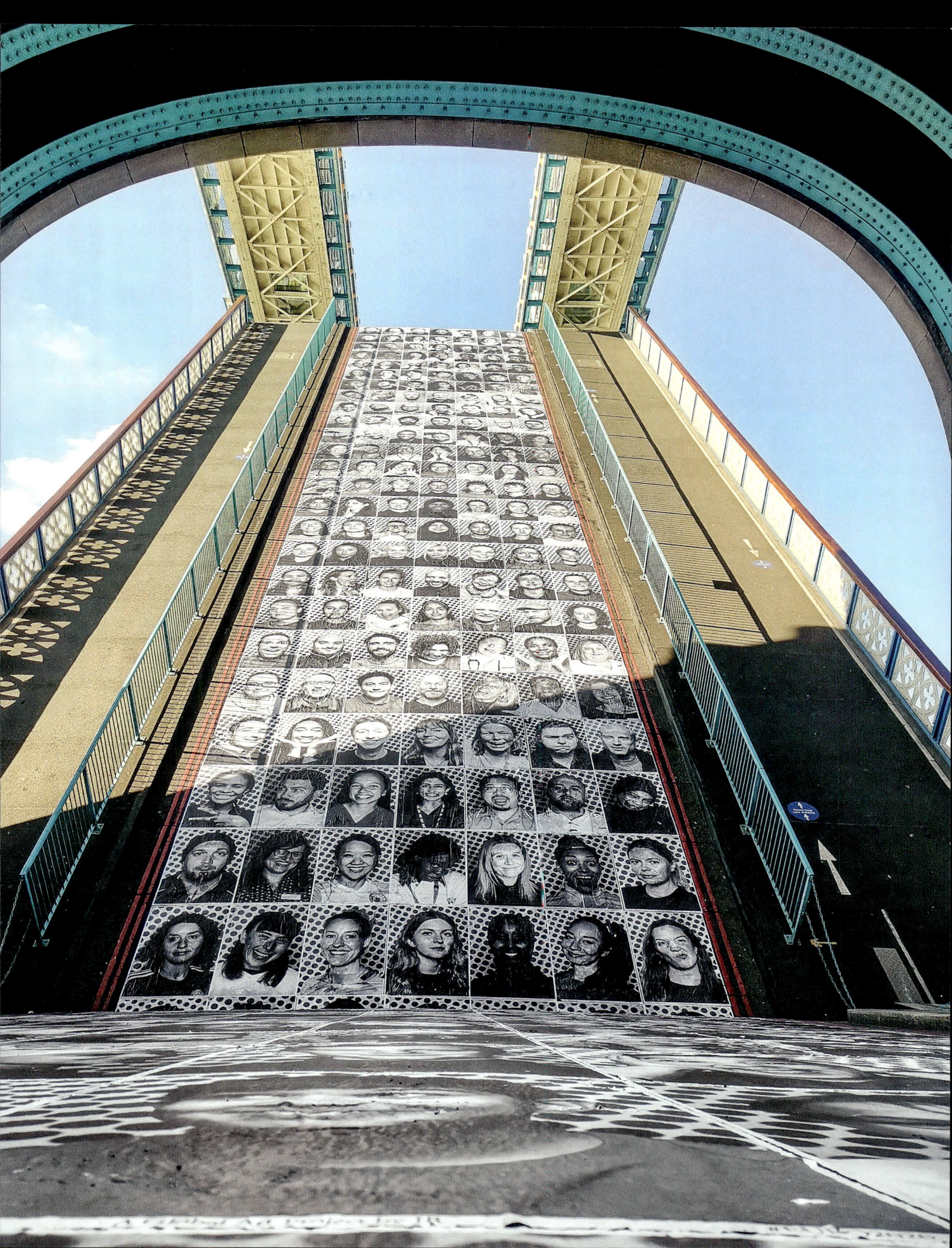

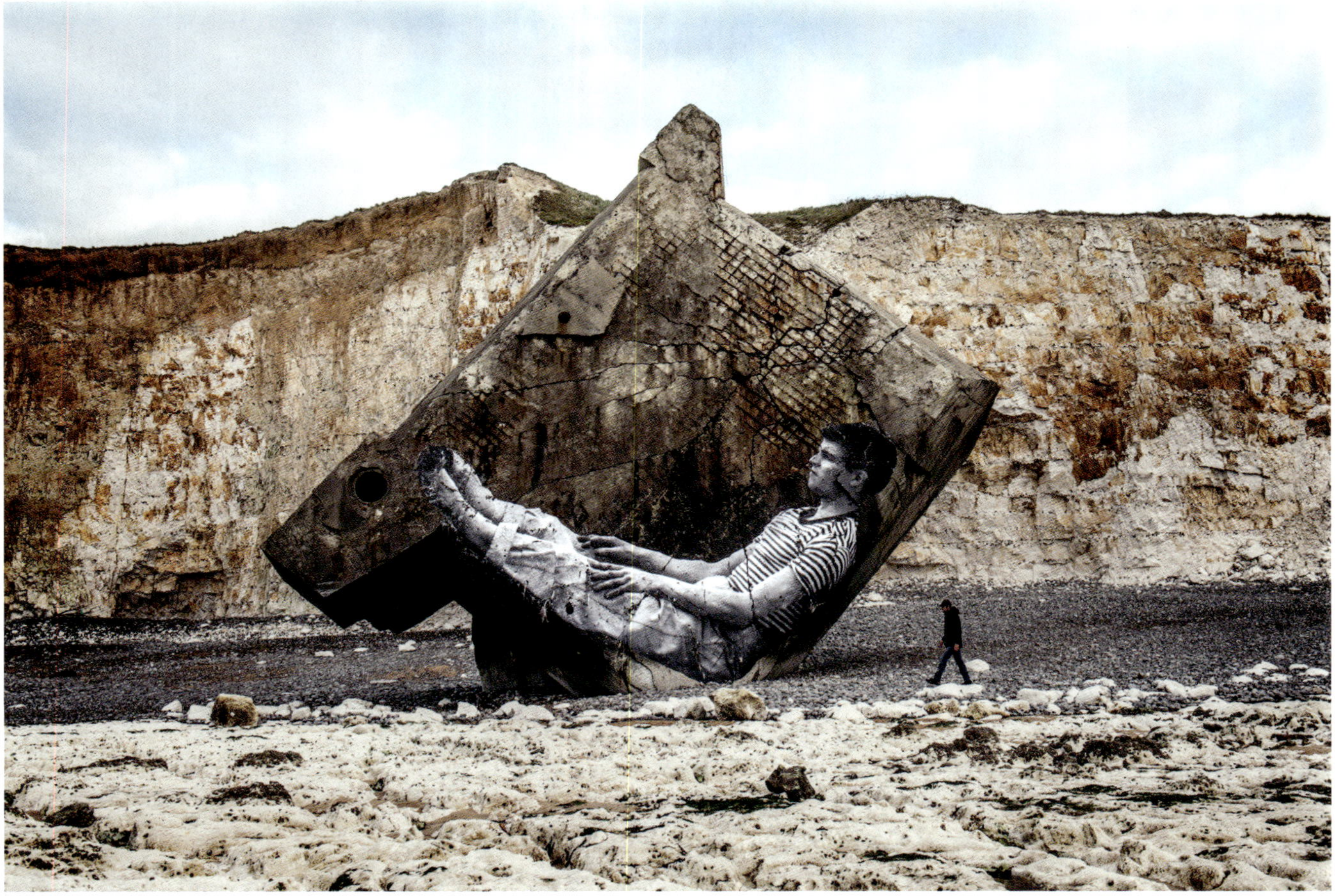

side of a railway car. What was he trying to convey? She answers, "The power of the imagination."

JR worked on a series of projects, titled "Unframed," in which he recontextualized existing photographs sourced from archives, family photo albums, and museums, instead of pasting pictures he took himself. During the filming of *Faces Places*, JR agreed to help Agnès Varda reuse a photograph of an old friend, the fashion photographer Guy Bourdin, by pasting a huge black-and-white copy of her photo on the remains of a decrepit war bunker along the shore (p. 46). The pasted paper image washed away hours later when the tide rose, a poetic visual metaphor for the inability of humans to hold onto each other forever.

AV and JR, ***Unframed***, 2016
Guy Bourdin, 1954, photograph by Agnès Varda, seen by JR. Saint-Aubin-sur-Mer, France

OPPOSITE
Faces Places, 2016
Pasting of postman and its double
Bonnieux, France

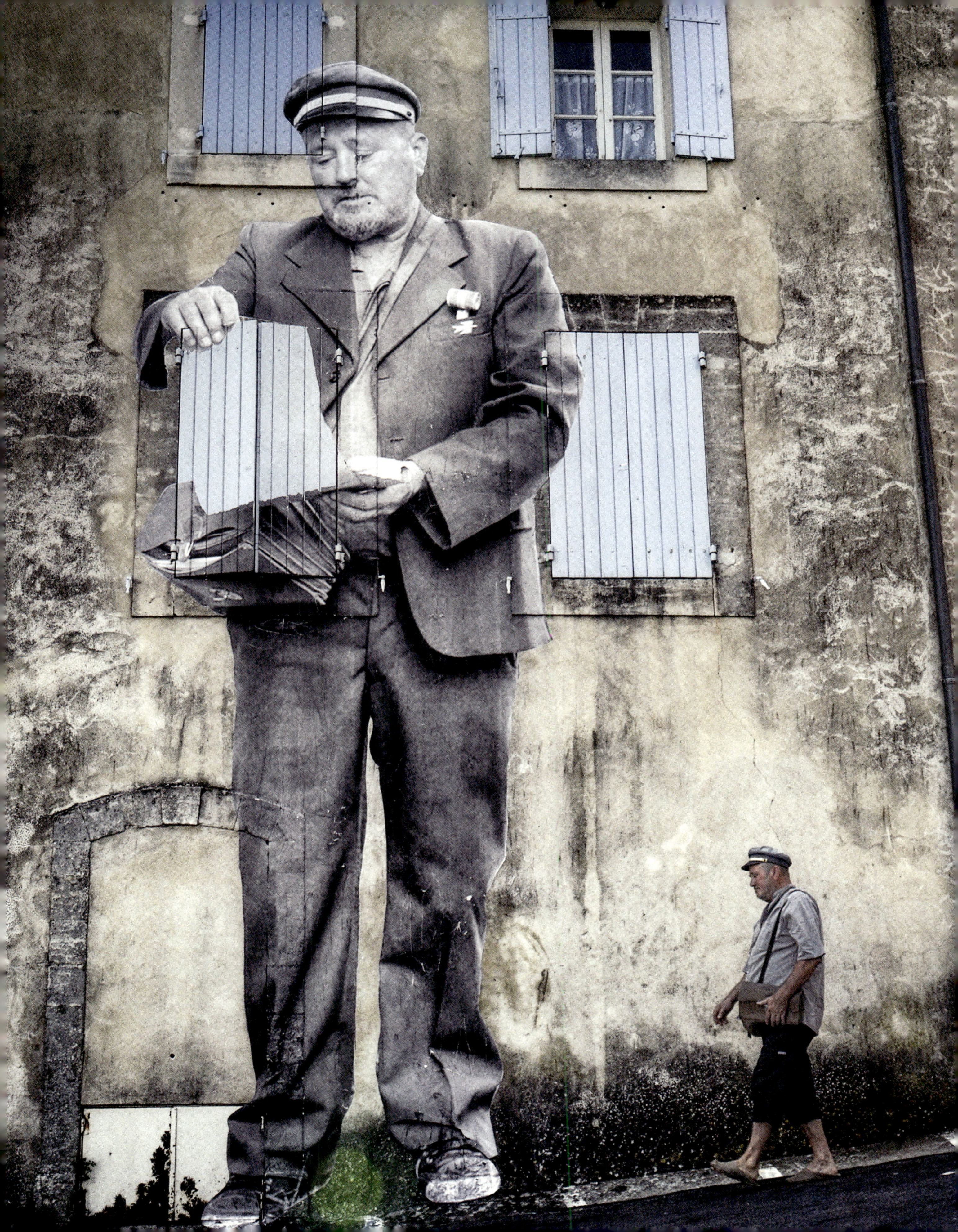

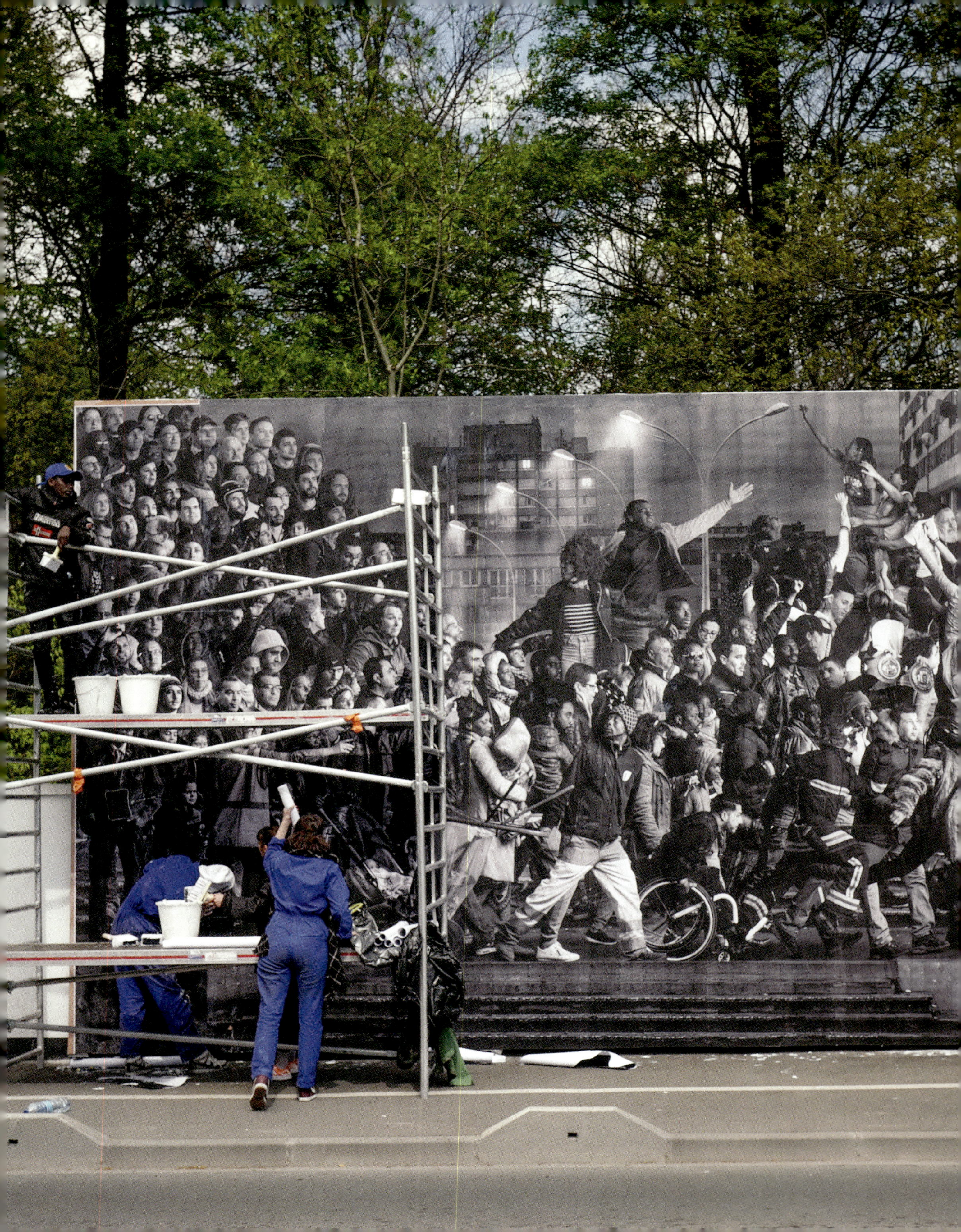

Inside, Outside

One of the methods of working that developed from JR's photography might be called panoramic peoplescapes, exemplified by his "Chronicles" series. Like written chronicles, his photographic compositions in this genre are detailed and historic. JR made his first such work, *The Chronicles of Clichy-Montfermeil* (pp. 48–53), inspired by a mural by Diego Rivera (1886–1957) that he had seen in a book. Rivera's work stood out to JR because he included working class, Indigenous, and revolutionary figures in his public art. One work that particularly caught JR's eye was *Dream of a Sunday Afternoon in Alameda Central Park* (1947, pp. 52–53). In this large-scale work, hundreds of historical Mexican characters transcend time and gather for a stroll through Mexico City's oldest public park, where conflict arises and a shooting occurs. JR started to plan his mural by showing *Dream of a Sunday Afternoon* to his Clichy-Montfermeil friends and asking them who they would be in Rivera's painting. It was not a hard question for them—everyone identified with one of Rivera's figures. JR resolved to do a contemporary mural using black-and-white photography that would represent everyone.

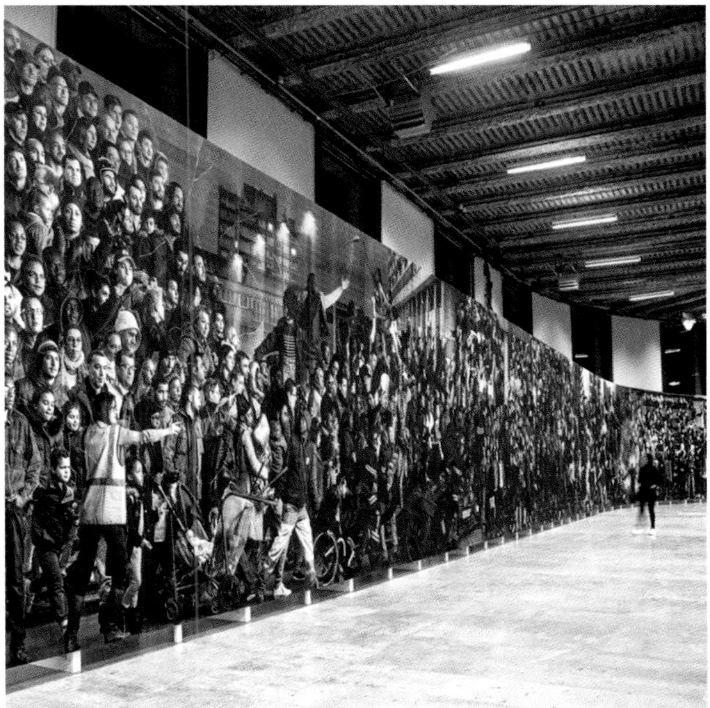

Diego Rivera's murals (and thus also JR's murals) have art historical precedents in ambitious Renaissance and 19th-century historical and biblical paintings commissioned for public spaces like churches or city halls. Early photographers had also attempted to copy the narrative storytelling of history paintings through the tricky technique of combination printing, in which multiple negatives are combined to create a single image. These concocted photographic prints contributed to photography's eventual acceptance into the realm of high art. JR's process for arranging his group scenes, although digital, is not unlike Victorian composite photography. JR photographs each subject individually and sometimes as posed pairs or families. The artificial environment of the green room ensures that lighting and camera distance remain

The Chronicles of Clichy-Montfermeil, 2017
Mural exhibited at the Palais de Tokyo in 18 wooden panels in 2019
Black-and-white print on paper, pasted on wood, matte varnish, each panel 200 x 400 cm (79 x 157 in.)

OPPOSITE
The Chronicles of Clichy Montfermeil, 2017
Installation of the mural, Montfermeil, France

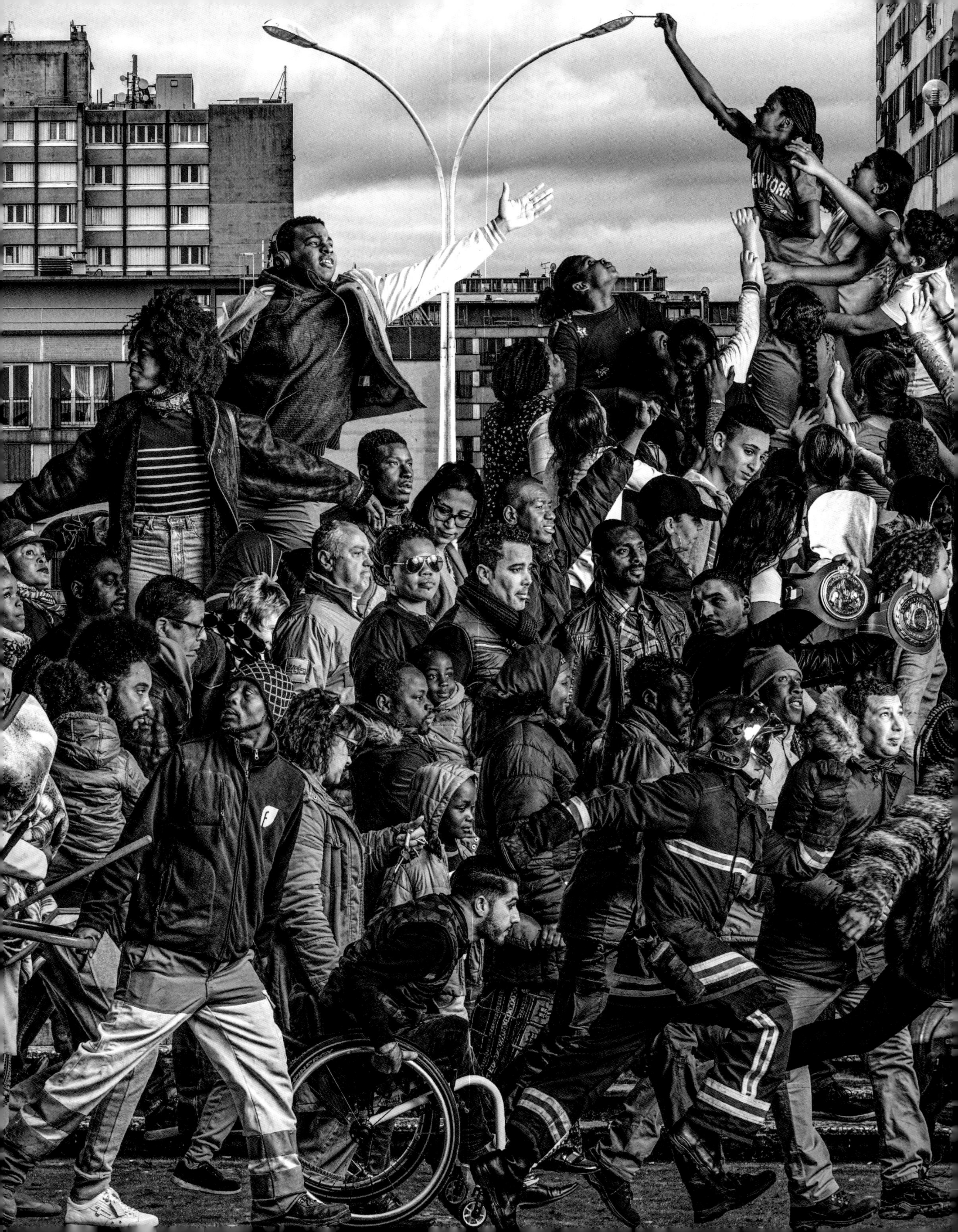

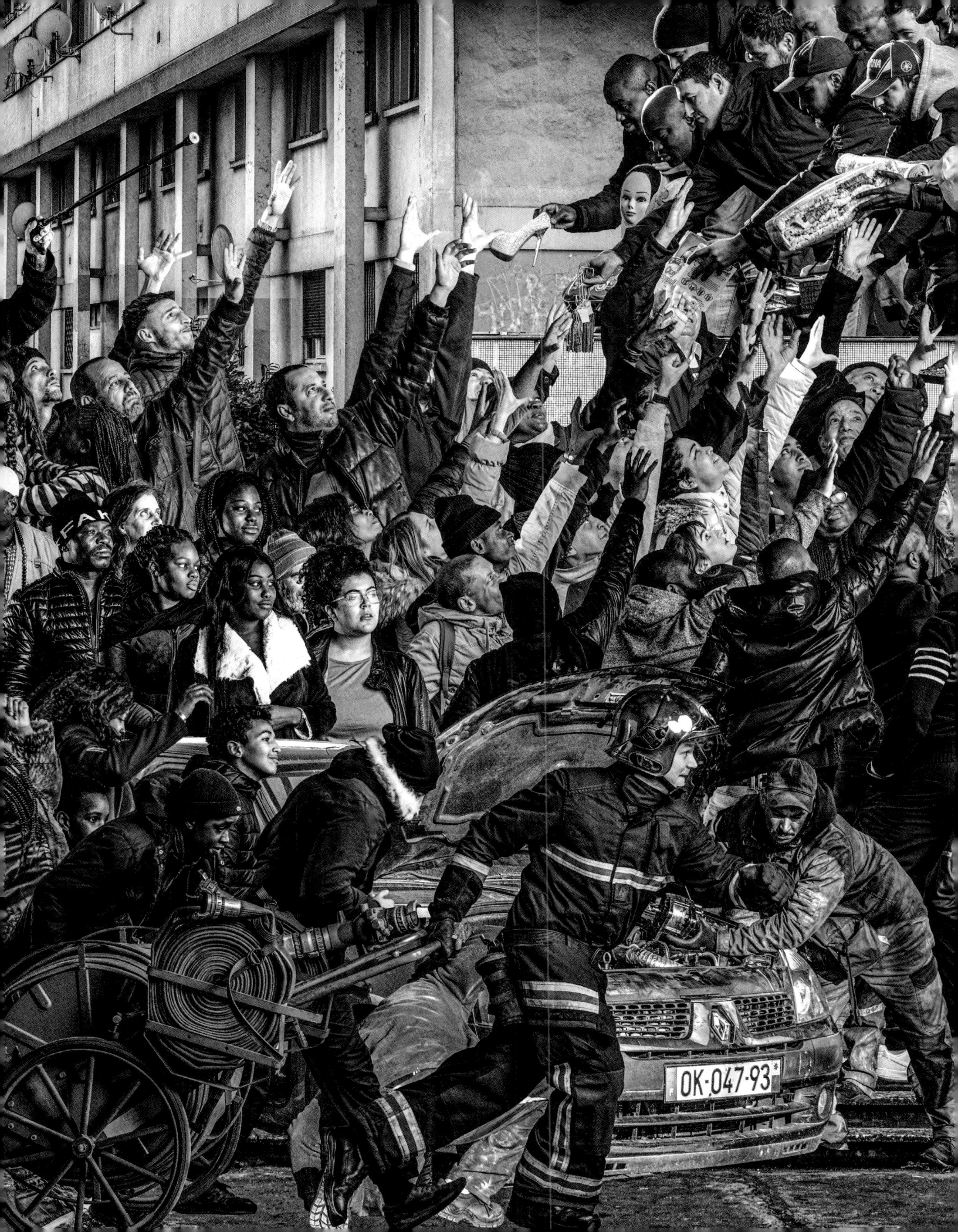
OK-047-93

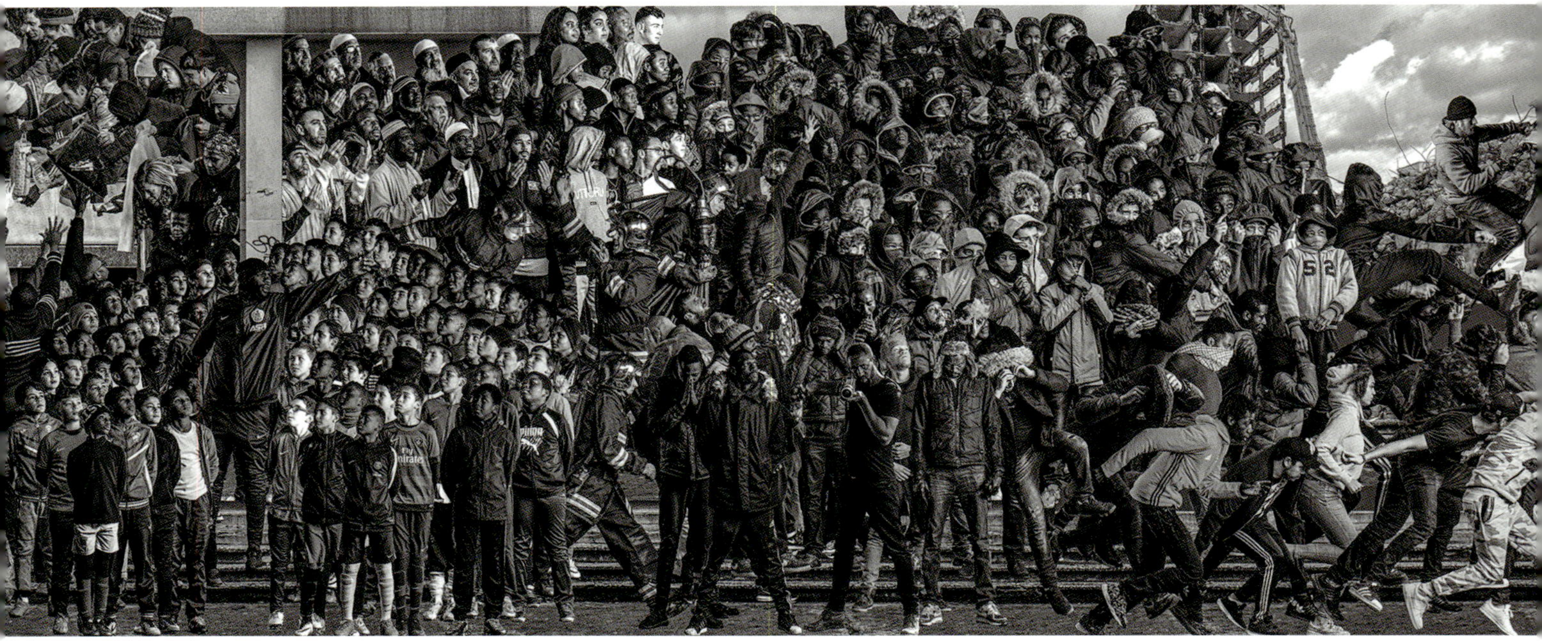

In 2016, 11 years after the riots in Clichy-Montfermeil, JR photographed 750 residents to create a massive photographic collage. The mural shows the tension and anger of the rioting community; JR choreographs the figures into a powerful performance. *The Chronicles of Clichy-Montfermeil* was inaugurated at the Palais de Tokyo in Paris in an opening attended by then-president François Hollande. At Hollande's suggestion, the mural was later installed outdoors in the neighborhood where the 2005 riots began.

consistent across subjects, while also allowing for flexibility when later adjusting the collage background. Each person decides how they want to be shown. JR directs them and maintains artistic control. Finally, he builds each photograph into an evolving composition, working until it feels completed as a compelling scene.

Social conflict lay at the heart of JR's first two murals. His second *Chronicles* composition became the cover of a special issue of *Time* magazine in 2018 that focused on gun ownership in the United States. The third *Chronicles*, however, took San Francisco as its subject. JR had the chance to study Diego Rivera's mural *The Marriage of the Artistic Expression of the North and of the South on This Continent (Pan American Unity)* (1940, pp. 54–55) firsthand at the theater of City College of San Francisco, where it had been installed since 1961. He included references to it in his own mural, reinterpreting some of Rivera's details. JR even included a contemporary woman dressed as Mexican painter Frida

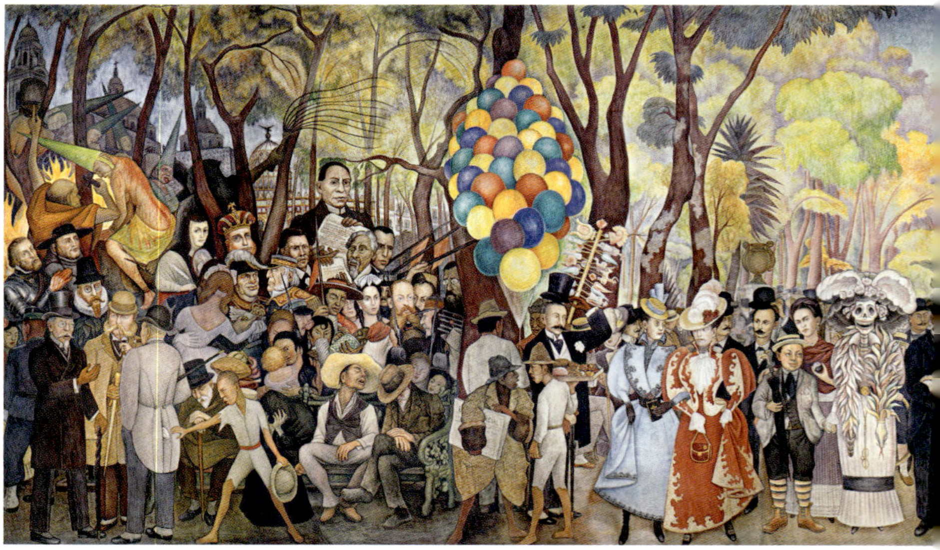

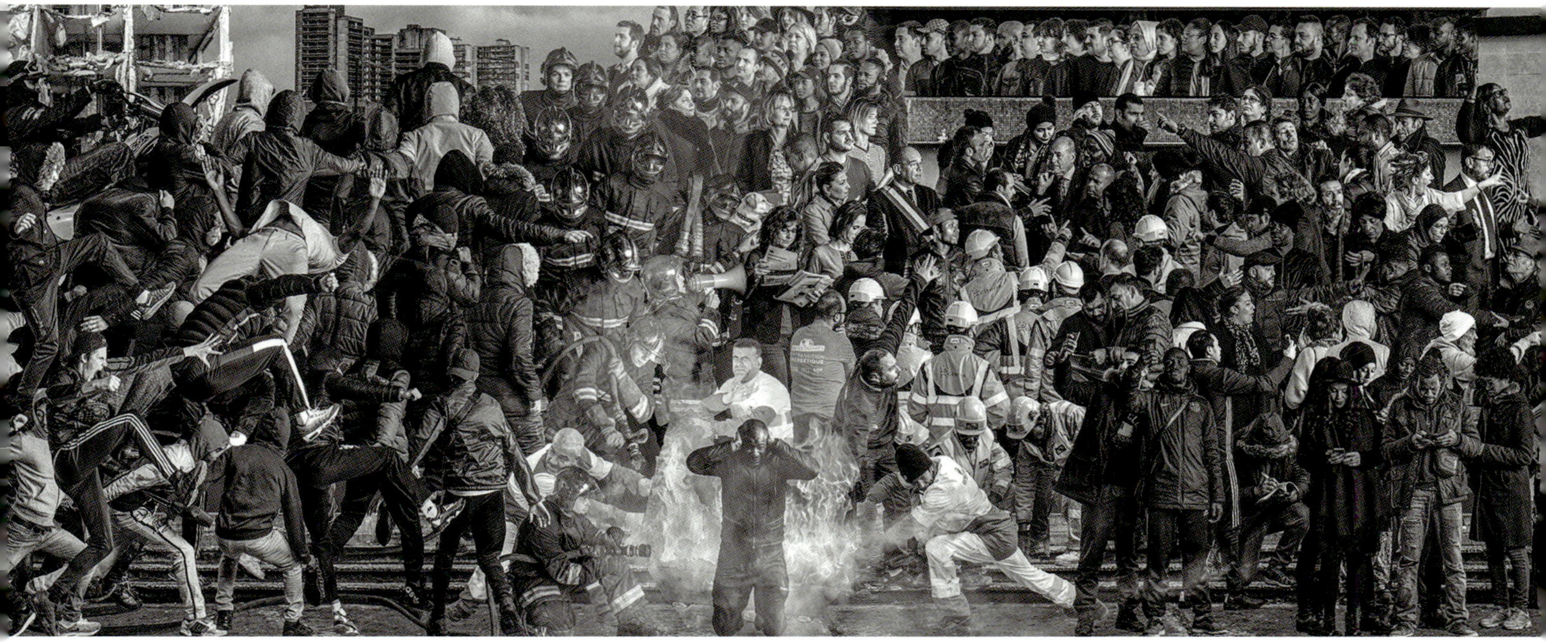

Kahlo (1907–1954), who married Diego Rivera twice, the second time in San Francisco. Like Rivera, JR included himself, too.

The Chronicles of San Francisco (2018, p. 55) was the first of JR's murals to span an entire city, but it was not the last. Other city-based murals include New York (2018–19, pp. 56–57), Miami (2022), Naples (2024), and Kyoto (2024). In the San Francisco mural, everyone is represented: an entire choir, police, ocean swimmers, unhoused people, tech workers, drag queens, artists, and even an art history major. JR's mobile studio, outfitted for the project, moved to 24 different locations throughout the city, inviting passersby to be photographed. He also set up a studio for larger groups. As a result, the team achieved a random but representative selection of 1,206 San Franciscans. The mural exists both as a static composite photograph and a video installation. In the video, participants move in place in individual time loops, making the image come subtly alive with unexpected movement.

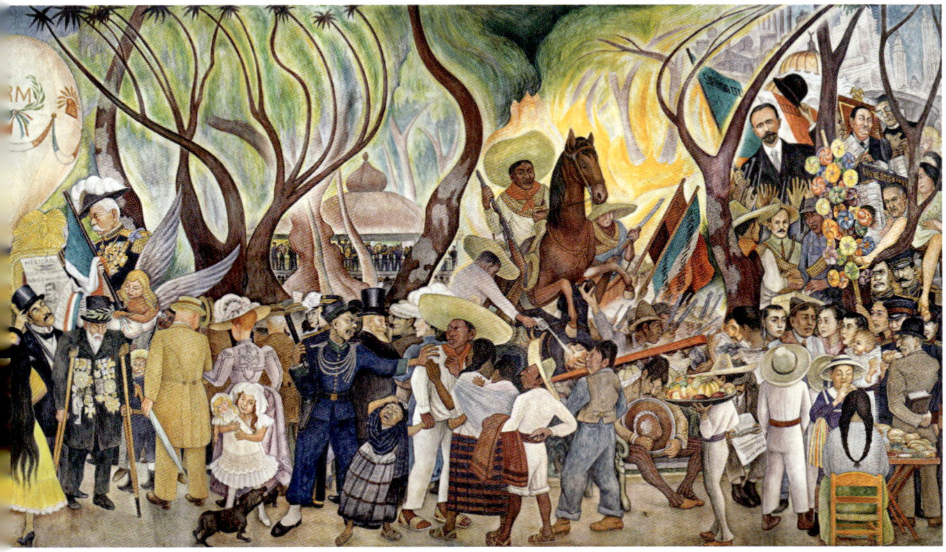

PREVIOUS SPREAD AND ABOVE
The Chronicles of Clichy Montfermeil, 2017
Mural, Montfermeil, France, details

Diego Rivera
Dream of a Sunday afternoon in Alameda Central Park, 1947
Fresco on movable panel, 480 x 1500 cm (189 x 590 in.)
Painted for the Hotel del Prado, Mexico

"Since the visit of Diego Rivera in 1931, San Francisco has had a long muralist tradition. It is a city rich in contrasts, one that features immense innovation and wealth as well as one of the highest rates of child homelessness in the country—which makes it a perfect canvas for this project. When I travel for my different projects, and I visit the local museums, I encounter beautiful murals that represent times I haven't known, realities from another era. Since the birth of photography, that tradition of murals has been lost."
THE CHRONICLES OF SAN FRANCISCO (2019)

JR wanted sound—participants voicing their own stories—to become part of the mural. After having their photo taken, each participant entered a makeshift sound studio to have their words recorded. JR's free augmented reality app JR:murals—which was used to scan any of JR's interactive murals and books—connects the participants' words to their portraits, allowing users to select a face and hear a recording. As the app no longer works, material can be consulted on the artist's website: jrchronicles.net. In an essay about their experiences, the sound recordists working with JR wrote, "Participants shared their struggles with sickness, grief, housing, heartbreak, natural disaster, and money. They also used this space ... to sing, to confess funny secrets, to talk to their loved ones—whether gone, alive, or yet to be born."[5]

As fate would have it, one of the 1,206 people pictured for the San Francisco mural would soon be able to help JR begin another project suggested by a friend: working with inmates in a prison. Gavin Newsom, then the lieutenant governor of California, gave JR and his team clearance when the artist chose a maximum-security prison as the location for the work. He chose it because out of all the prisons in California, as far as he could see on Google Earth, this was the only one that had a concrete courtyard where he could paste. JR thought the pasted yard and the surrounding mountainous desert landscape would make a compelling image when photographed from above with a drone.

The action became known by the site of the prison: Tehachapi. *Tehachapi, the Yard* (pp. 58–61) began with the artist introducing himself and his art to selected prisoners. Many of the men had been imprisoned since they were teenagers, and some had extended their sentences by participating in gang activity while in prison. Some were serving life sentences with no prospect of release. The gang activity and violence within the prison had sometimes encouraged the guards to think of the inmates as animals. JR's idea was to photograph 28 men individually from above while standing on a scaffold. After they were photographed, the men were invited to express themselves in front of a video camera. No prompt questions guided them; they could talk about anything they wanted. This audio was later accessible via the JR:murals app as part of the action. JR took pictures of staff and former inmates, collecting 48 portraits and stories from the prison.

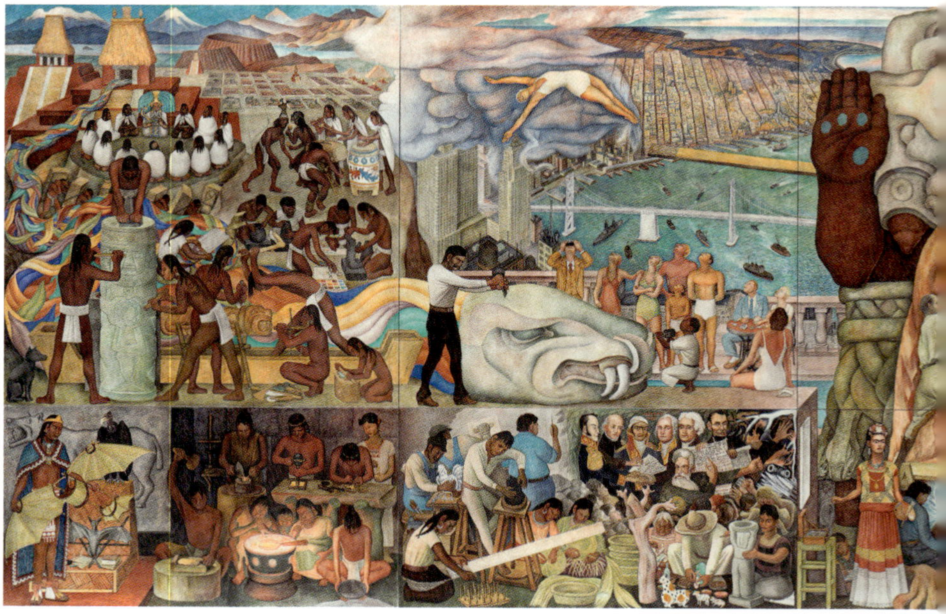

OPPOSITE TOP
The Chronicles of San Francisco, Theater, Lightbox, United States, 2018
Printed duratrans, LED backlight, black steel frame, 70 x 140 x 7 cm (27½ x 55 x 2¾ in.)

FOLLOWING SPREAD
The Chronicles of New York City, 2020
Domino Park, United States

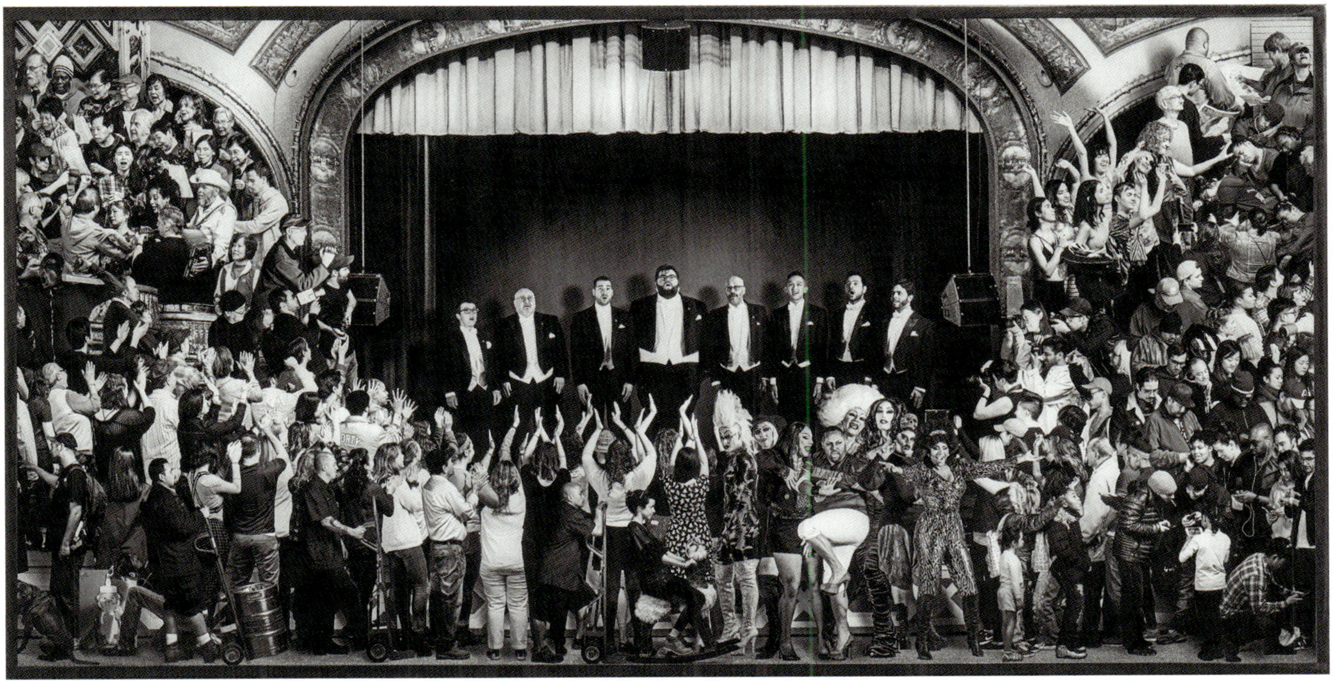

Two weeks later, JR returned to the prison with his composite image, though in pieces. The composition had been turned into 338 strips of 36-inch-wide white paper, each 36 feet long and covered with black dots—the pixelation of the image. The sheets were numbered for assembly purposes. The inmates pasted the strips of paper on the concrete ground with push brooms, assisted by JR's team, some initially reluctant guards, and even family members of some victims. Those pasting could barely imagine what was coming together, since the full composition was most clearly visible from above. From an aerial perspective, the printed dots assembled to form the faces and upper bodies of the inmates, standing shoulder to shoulder as if in a deep hole and looking up. The subjects appear friendly, charming, ready to have a conversation, but also like

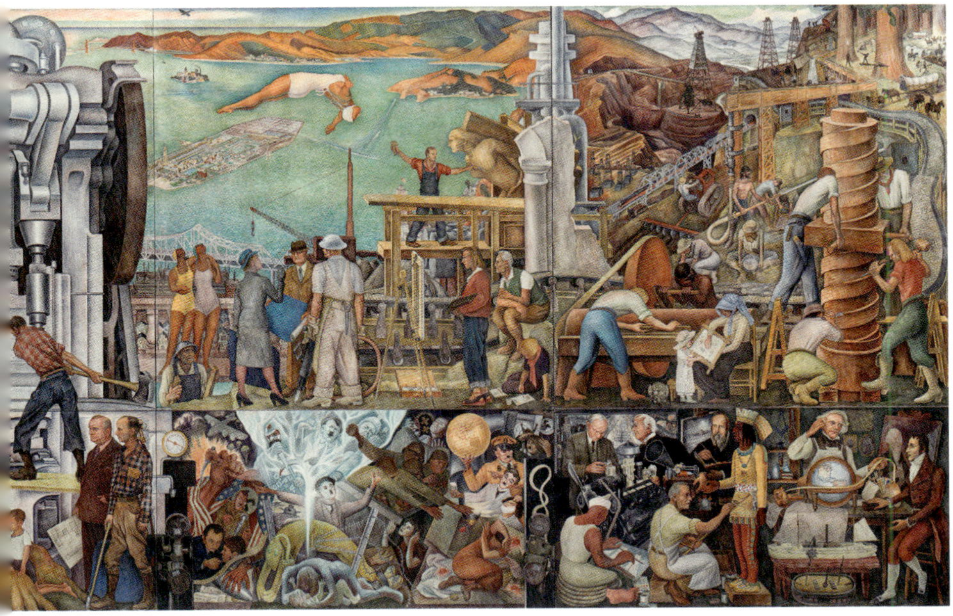

Diego Rivera
The Marriage of the Artistic Expression of the North and of the South on this Continent, also known as *Pan American Unity*, 1940
Fresco on movable panel, 670 x 2247 cm (22 x 74 ft.)
Courtesy City College of San Francisco

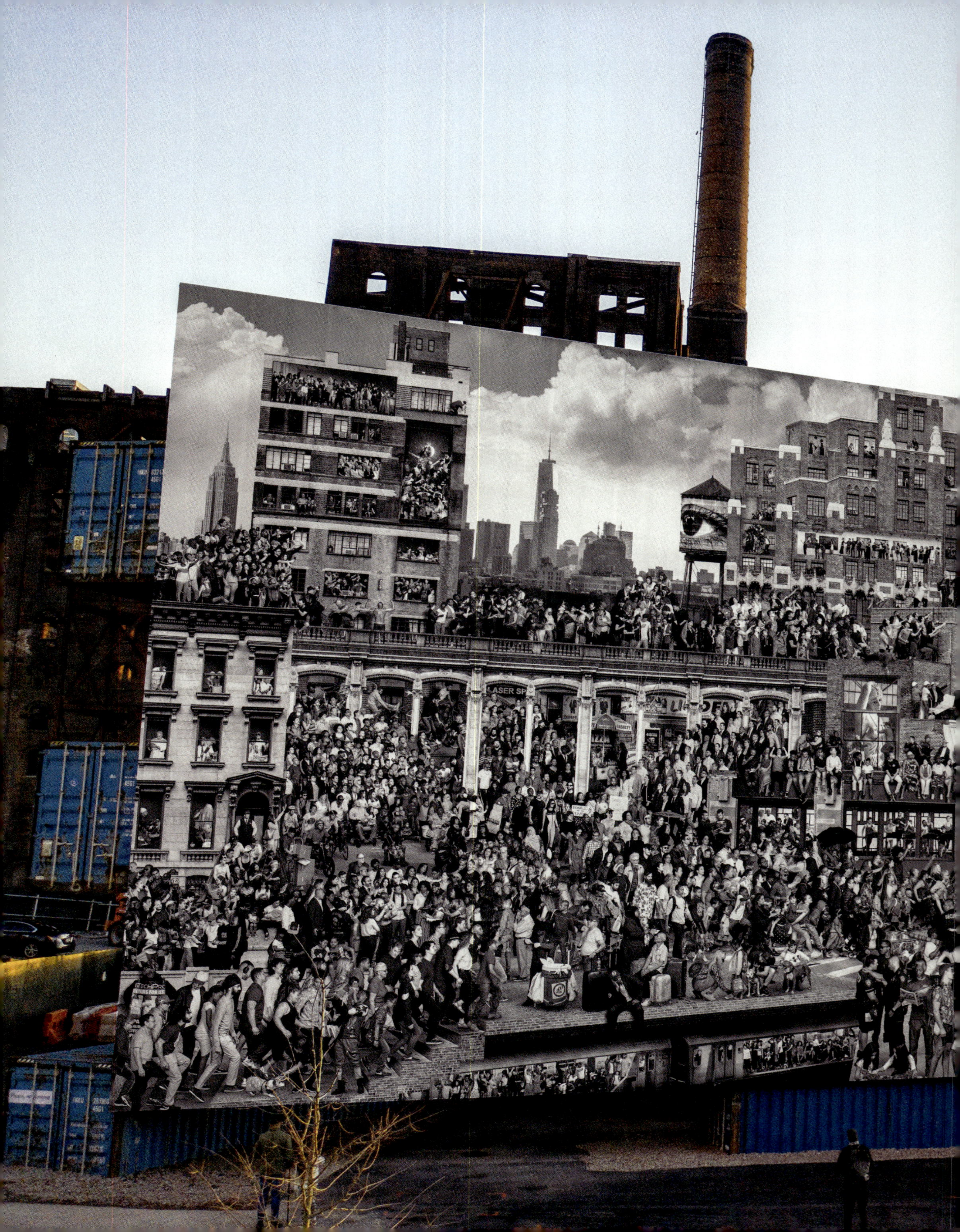

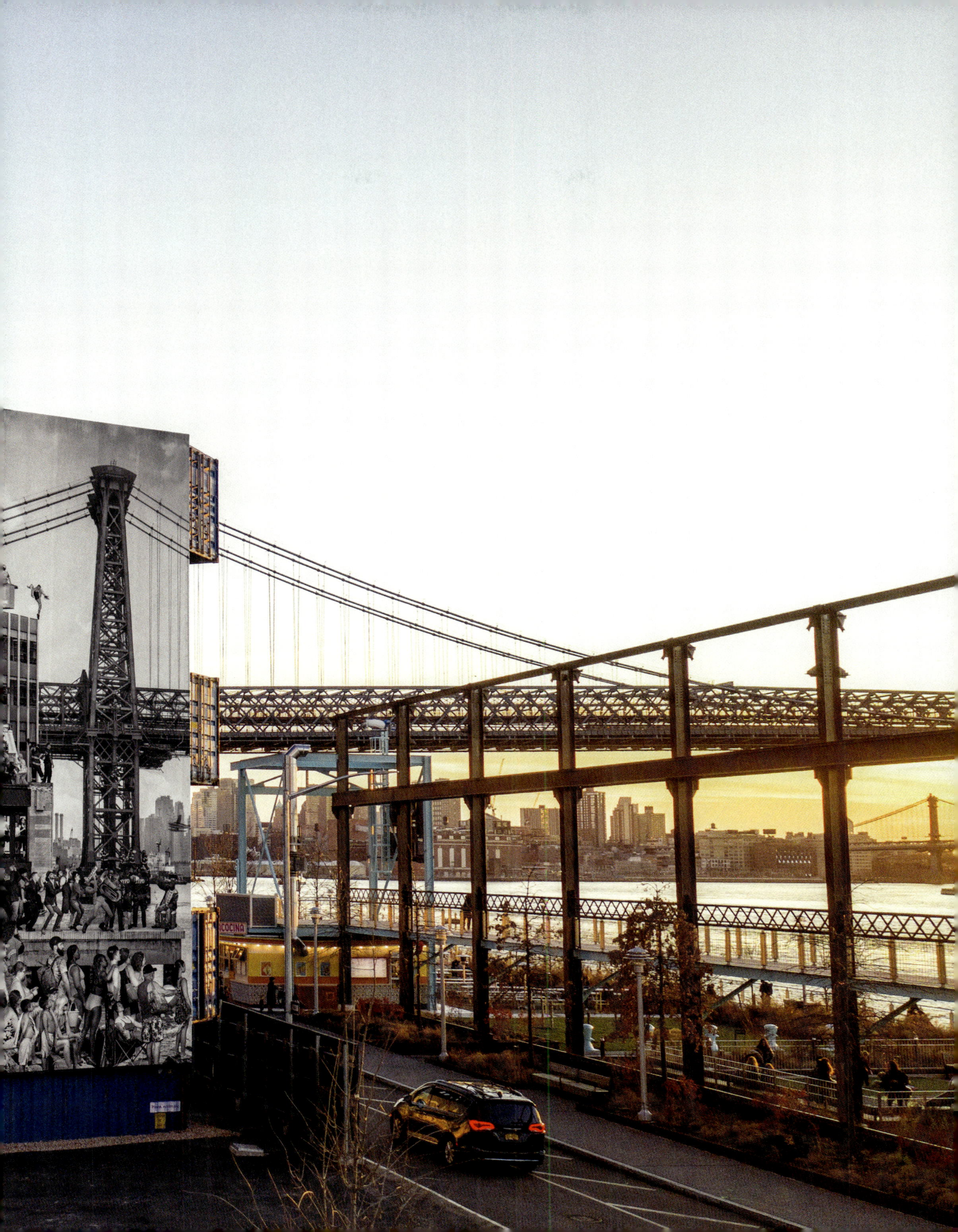
COCINA

OPPOSITE
Tehachapi, 2020
Mountain, February 6, 5:07 P.M., United States

BELOW
Tehachapi, 2022
The Road, Anamorphosis, #2, detail
United States

FOLLOWING SPREAD
Tehachapi, 2019
Aerial view of the pasting in the yard
Daytime, United States

human cargo, concentrically ordered and tightly packed into a five-sided, windowless concrete box. A drone was authorized to fly over the prison to take the picture. Video footage was also shot with a drone.

The Tehachapi pasting broke open the rigid boundaries among the imprisoned men. Some of the guards revised their thinking about the inmates after listening to their stories. Eventually, the pasting wore off and was torn off for mementos, and the courtyard was cleaned. What remained was the memory of working together effectively on a common project. The collaborative work helped inmates believe they could change and that they could get out of prison. An inmate who was full of remorse about his facial swastika tattoo planned to have it removed. Other inmates reconnected with their families, who learned of the pasting through social media and began to communicate with their incarcerated family member through the artist. Humanity began to flow back into the prison environment.

JR returned to the prison for a second pasting on the outer walls of Tehachapi's courtyard; he created a trompe l'oeil effect that made the prison walls "disappear" by pasting them with a photograph of the surrounding mountains. The men then had a view of a dramatic landscape—the one that waited beyond the prison walls.

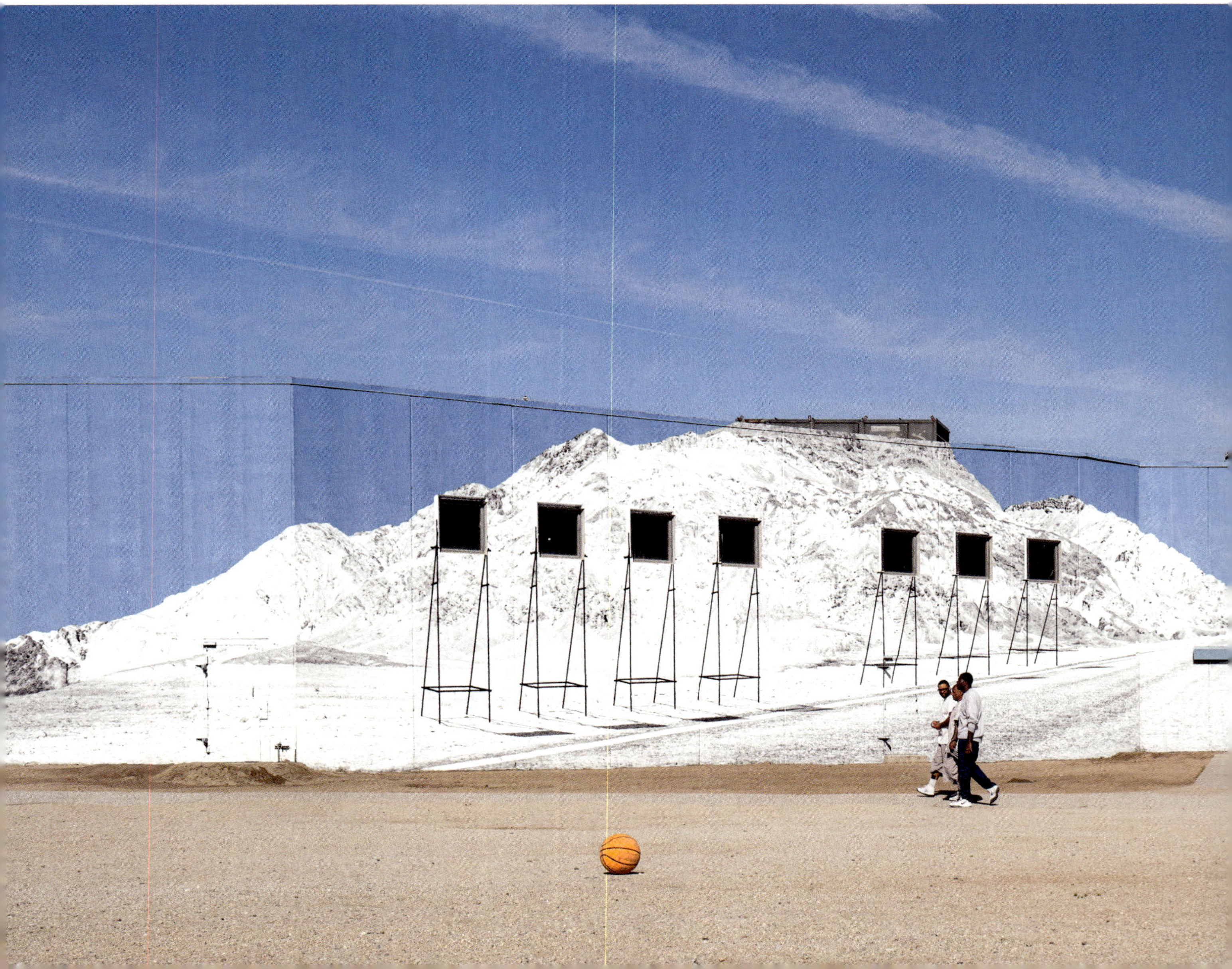

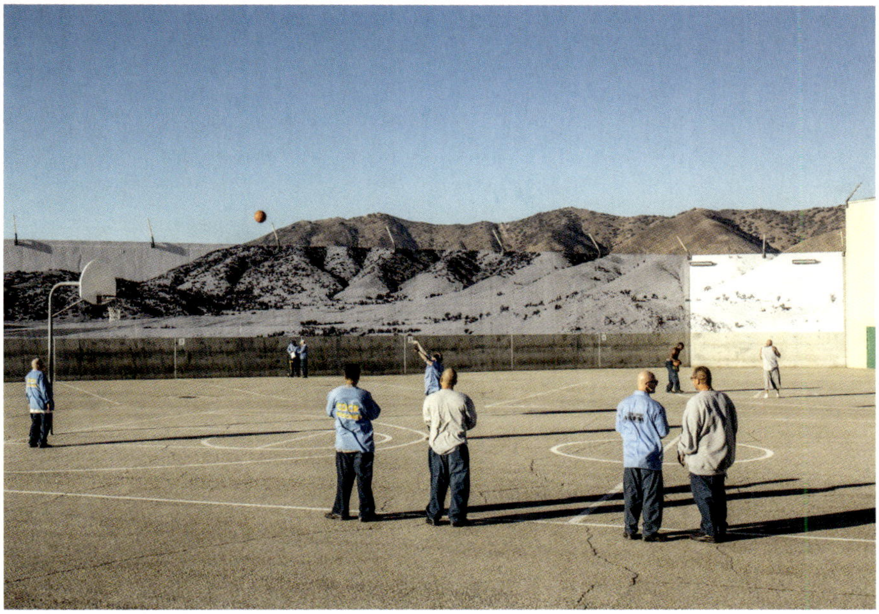

The feature-length documentary film *Tehachapi* (2023) shows the process of the action—JR getting to know the prisoners and photographing them, and his team pasting with them—as well as what becomes of the prisoners afterward. JR won the confidence of the prisoners by shaking their hands and telling them the touching story of his unsanctioned border installation, *Giants*, Kikito (p. 6). Because of their participation in the action, numerous inmates had their security classifications lessened, and some were eventually released. The artist's book *Tehachapi*, published by Maison CF in 2020, features inmate testimonies, letters from inmates to the artist, and photos.

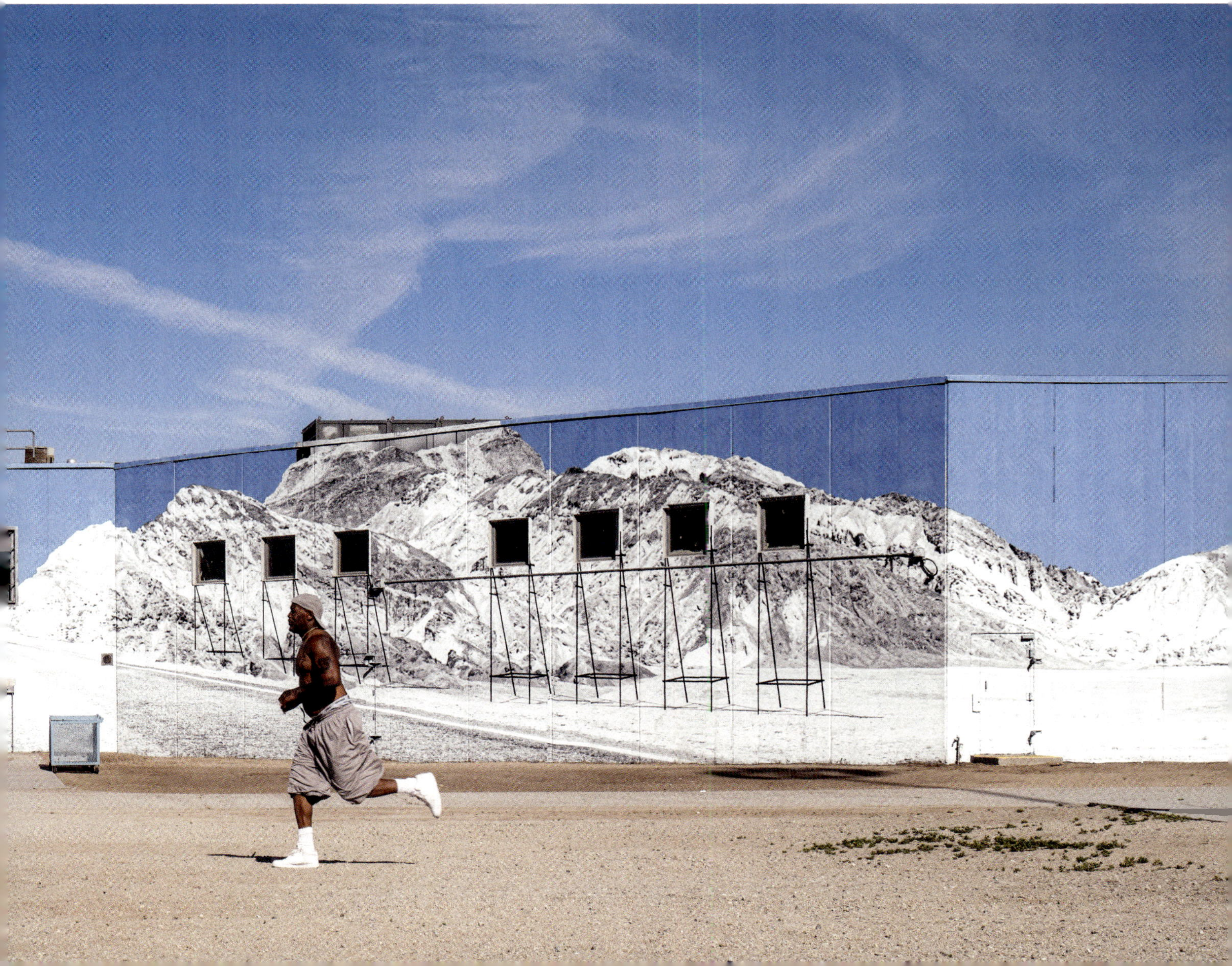

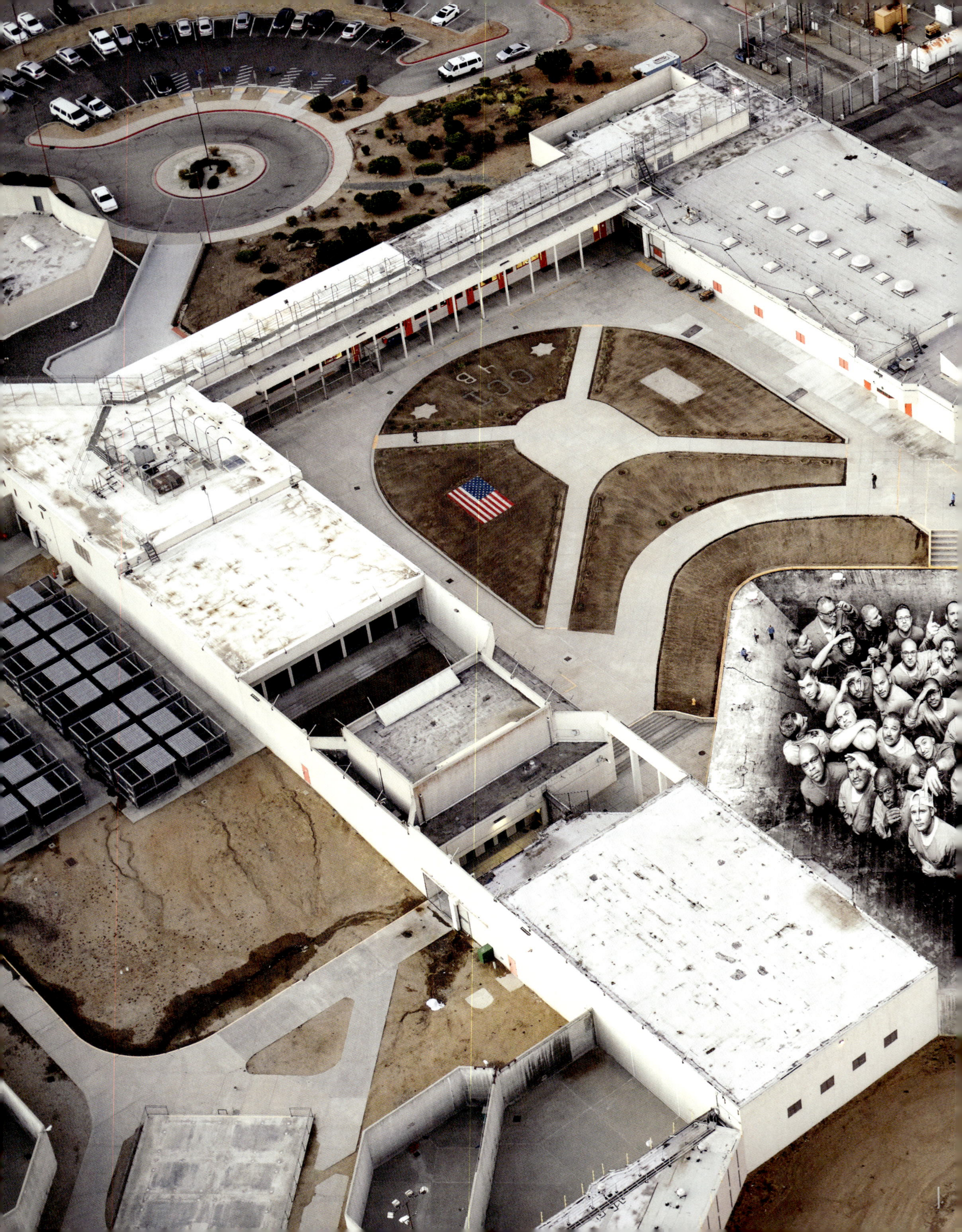

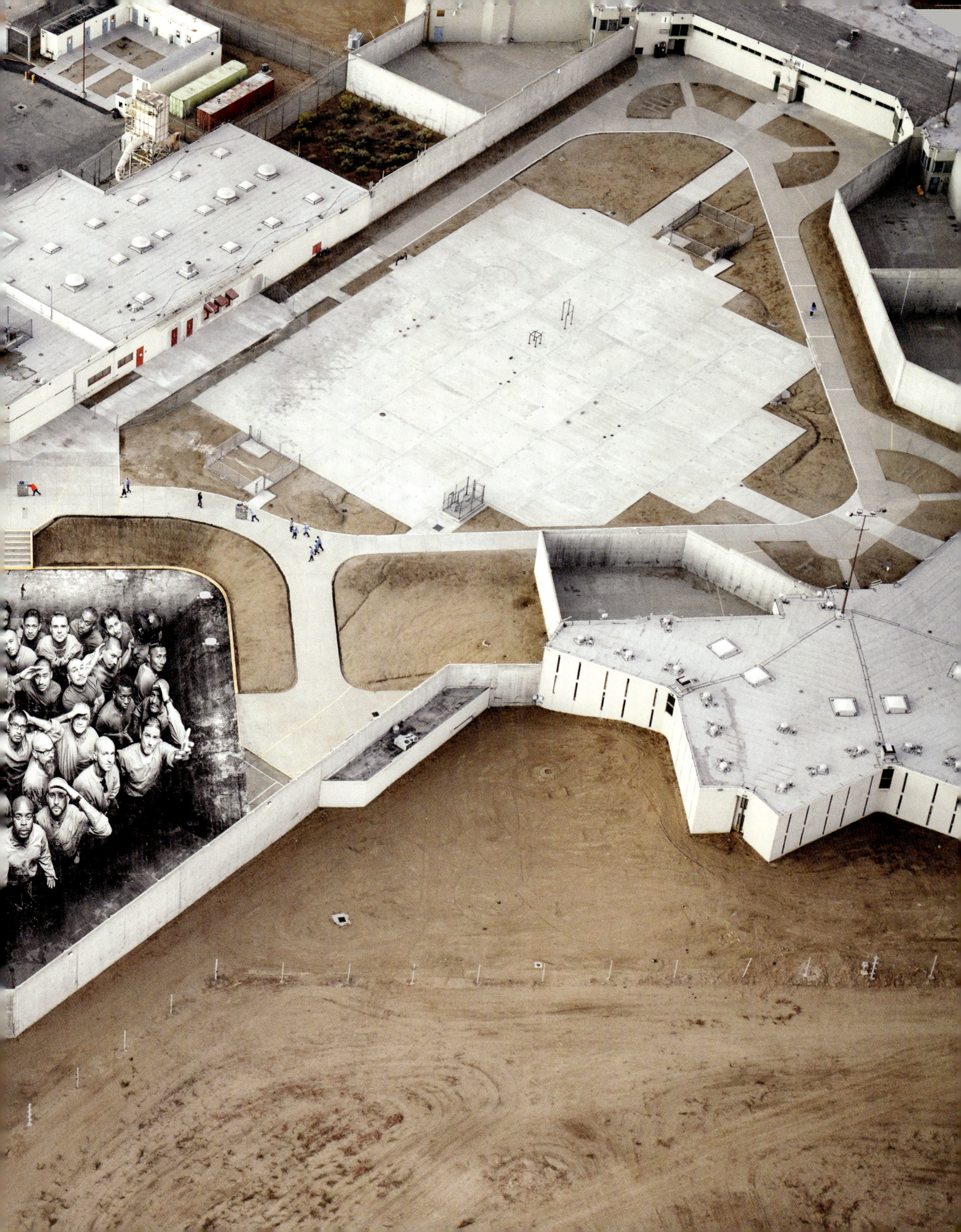

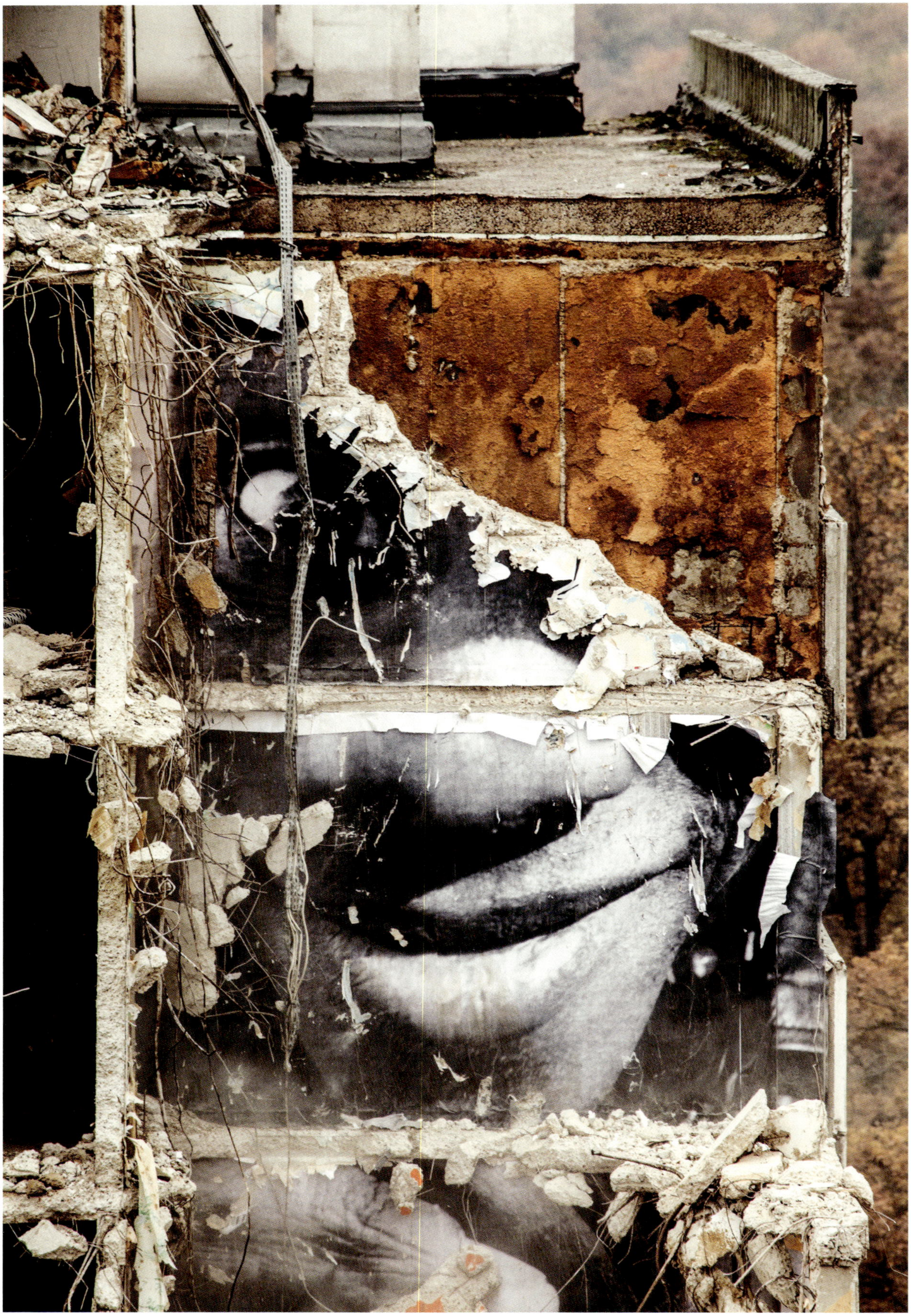

JR and Paris

JR has engaged with architecture in Paris since his tagging days and has an entire body of work that focuses on transforming architecture. Throughout his travels and actions abroad with marginalized communities, he never stopped interpreting the metropolitan area where he was born. He responded even to everyday street furniture with a designer's eye in both his pastings and his photography, as the image of a yellow "pedestal" and a pasted "lookout station" in the Clichy-sous-Bois housing estate La Forestière shows. With its attention to color, balance, and geometry, the photograph could have been taken by a student at the Bauhaus, transposed through time and space to JR's Paris (p. 28).

In 2009, photos from his "Women Are Heroes" actions, featuring women's eyes and one full-body image of a woman, appeared along the riverbanks of the Seine (pp. 94–95) and on the Louis-Philippe Bridge in central Paris—a massive public art project he pasted with his crew and volunteers. With *Portrait of a Generation—Destruction* (two separate actions done in 2013 and 2020, pp. 62, 64–65), JR and his crew responded to the ongoing urban renewal of Clichy-Montfermeil by trespassing at night into buildings slated for demolition. In 2013, they pasted two-story-high reproductions of the *Portrait of a Generation* portraits from 2005 inside the high-rise apartment buildings (p. 62).

JR did not cut open the buildings himself for *Portrait of a Generation—Destruction*, as Gordon Matta-Clark did in the 1970s (p. 63), but he did intentionally embrace the spirit of anarchy found in Matta-Clark's *Anarchitecture*. JR instrumentalized the destruction process as inherent to the "performance" of his images. The documentary photographs of Clichy-Montfermeil faces paired with torn walls became a filmic ode to the people of the neighborhood where JR's artistic development began. By pasting the faces again, even larger this time, JR doubled down on their significance. While it is possible to tear down buildings, it is harder to rid society of institutional racism.

In another project replete with social meaning, titled *The Standing March*, JR collaborated with filmmaker Darren Aronofsky (1969–) to project a "standing

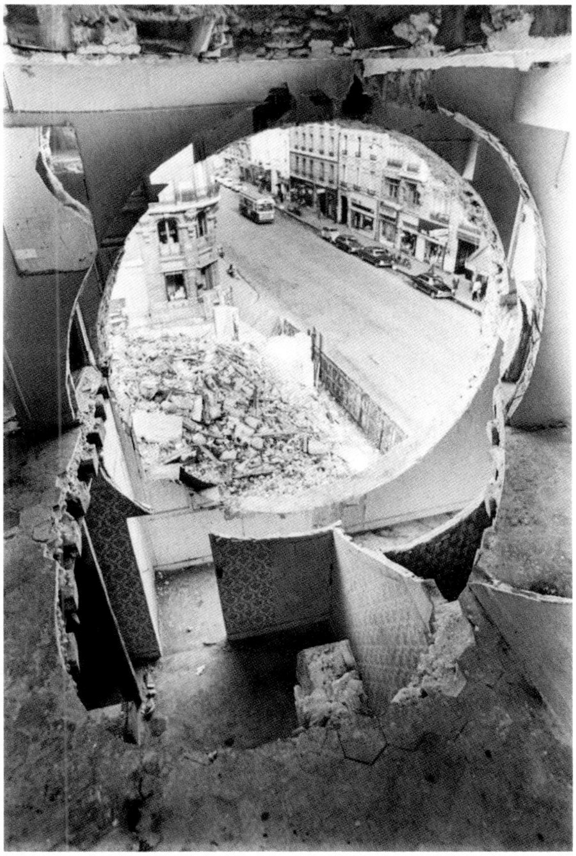

Gordon Matta-Clark
Conical Intersect 3 (Paris, France), 1975 (printed 1977)
Gelatin silver print, 25.4 x 20.3 cm (10 x 8 in.)
New York, Whitney Museum of American Art
Gift of Harold Berg

28 Millimeters, Portrait of a Generation, 2013
B11, Destruction #10, Montfermeil, France

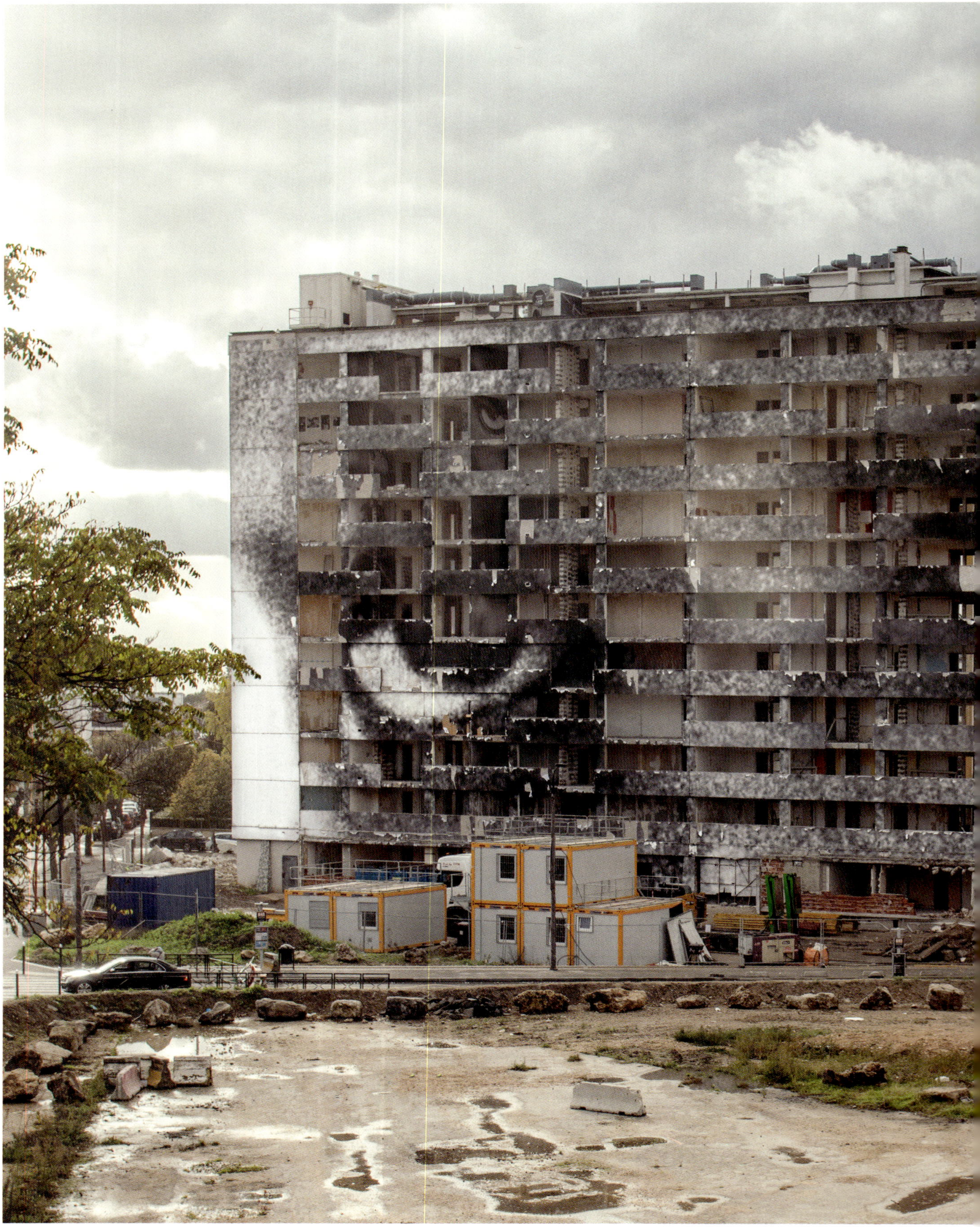

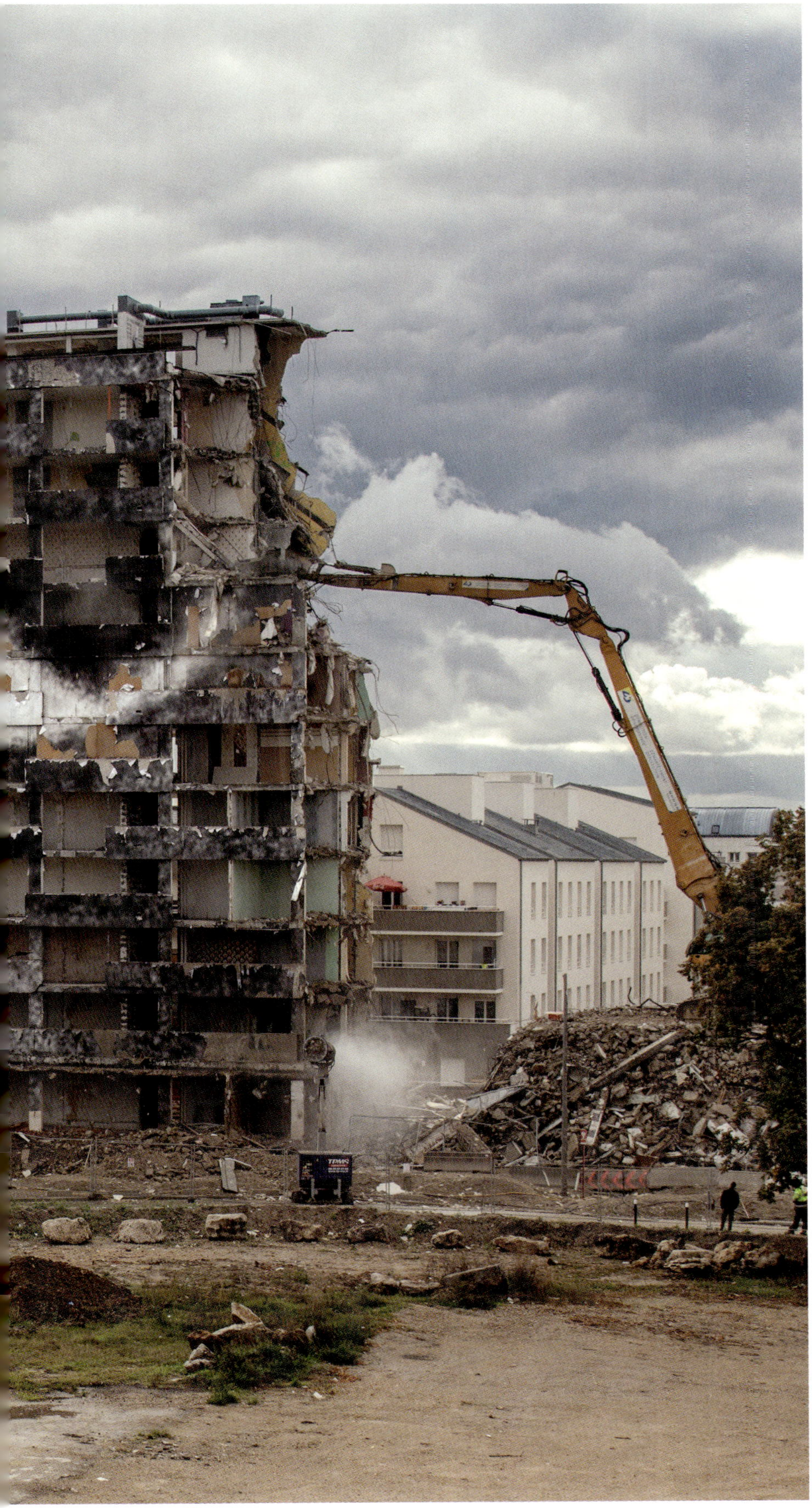

Through careful planning, the upper half of each grimacing face aligned contiguously with its lower half on the story below. As the outer walls came off, the expressive faces of the former residents were revealed—and then toppled (p. 62). These photo actions were witnessed by the demolition crew, who became unwitting accomplices, as well as anyone else who happened by, and by JR's documentary, and carefully composing, camera. Then in 2020, over several nights and in the heroic format of 11 contiguous floors, JR and his crew pasted the 2004 portrait of Ladj Ly with his video camera over the entire height of Building B5, Ly's longtime home.

28 Milimeters, Portrait of a Generation, 2020
Ladj Ly's eyes on B5, side and frontal views
Les Bosquets, Montfermeil, France

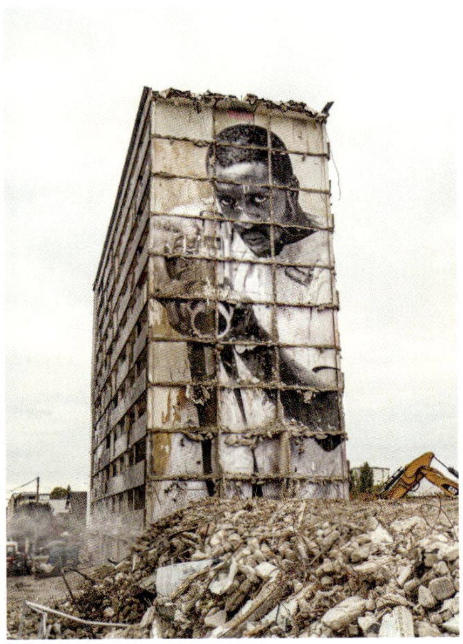

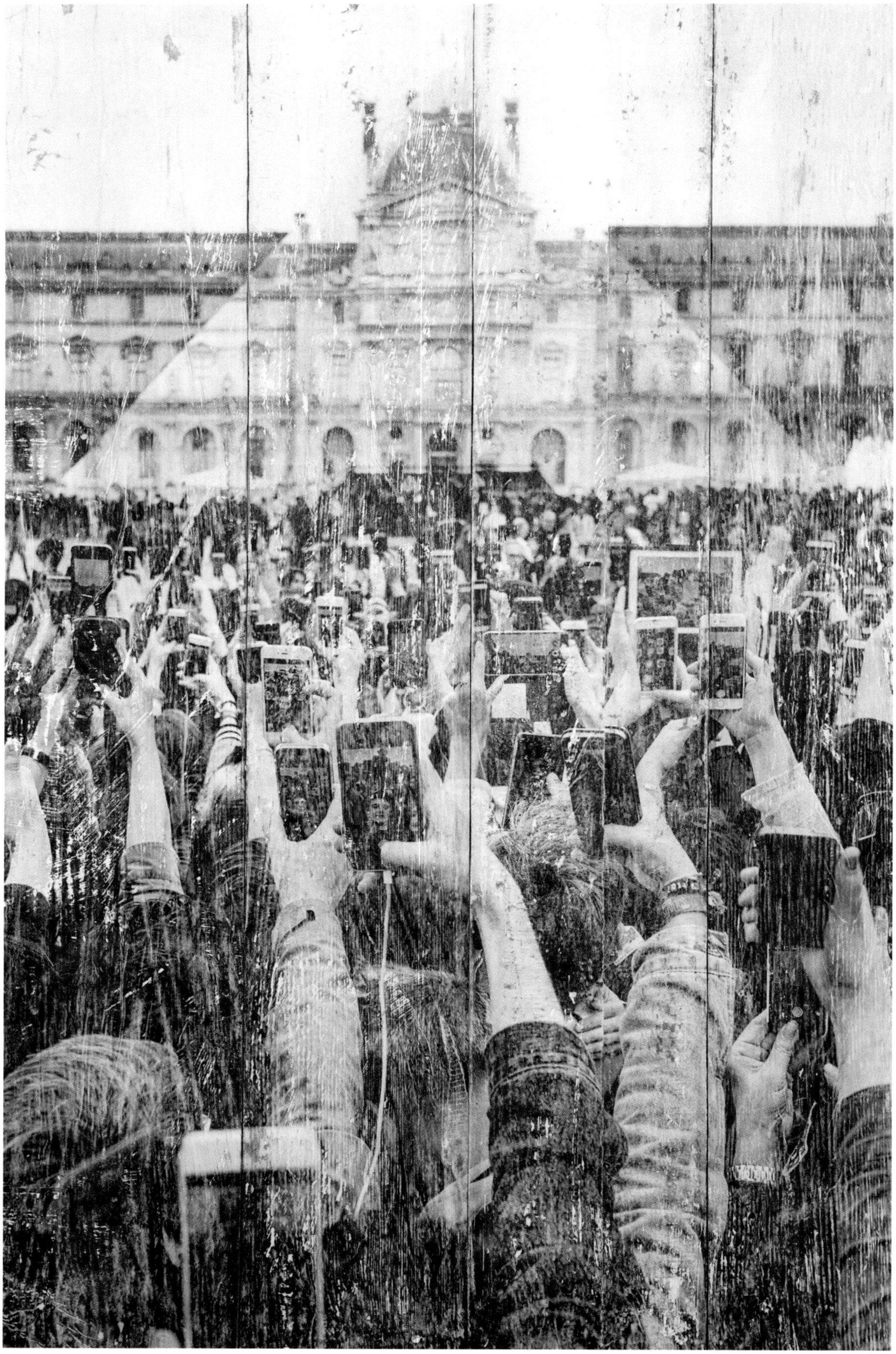

march" onto the National Assembly building in Paris during the 2015 United Nations Climate Change Conference, COP21. The projection circumvented the prohibition of public demonstrations during the conference. As the site hosting the conference, the assembly building held significant meaning: Its Greek temple shape recalled Athenian democracy, it housed a working legislature, and it had been a historic landmark for French democracy since the late 18th century. The media of *Standing March* included light, photography, the facade, sound, and the night. The British band Massive Attack contributed an original soundtrack by the artist 3D.

To assemble the collaged group of demonstrators for the projection, JR had recorded each participant individually rotating against a green screen. Arranged by the artist, 500 somber faces of Earth's inhabitants stood shoulder to shoulder in a "standing march," stretching back and upward toward the temple's pinnacle, covering the north facade of the assembly, impatient for climate action. The video incorporated a brief turn and individually timed movement, so that subtle facial changes and shifts in body position vivified the figures in a time loop that appeared natural and nonrepetitive. The dense arrangement of bodies JR composed recalls historical attempts to visualize the social contract as a body politic, the total of massed individuals beholden to their rulers, like the frontispiece of Thomas Hobbes's 1651 book, *Leviathan* (p. 67). Now, as a 21st-century electorate, they are equipped with the vote to change their government.

Over time, JR has been invited to interact with historic architecture in Paris increasingly often. Within the framework of *Inside Out*, during the restoration of the dome of the Panthéon in Paris, JR's studio gathered black-and-white portraits from all over France to cover the colonnade of the exterior dome, nave, and interior of the cupola (pp. 72–73). JR's vinyl medium, printed with faces, paired well with the dome's construction covering and proved to be a durable surface in the nave. The Panthéon's restoration turned into a people's project.

Two years later, he was invited to intervene artistically at the Louvre Museum in connection with a conference there. JR suggested covering part of the largest glass pyramid designed by I. M. Pei, inaugurated in 1989, in the courtyard of the Louvre, which functions as the main entrance to the museum. By making it opaque from one side, JR would essentially negate the pyramid's transparency. Using a crane, a team of professionals carefully applied the printed vinyl photograph of the old Sully Wing, just east of the pyramid, onto one of the slanted glass facades. The delicate and exact work—JR regretted that no public could be involved here—created an optical illusion (*JR at the Louvre Museum*, pp. 68–71). When viewed from the right spot in the Cour Napoléon, the large 20th-century glass pyramid seemed to "disappear" as the photograph pasted onto its side aligned with the French classical Renaissance facade behind it—even though the colors did not match. This viewpoint turned out to be the most popular spot for tourists to photograph the illusion. A line of picture-takers formed during the month the installation was up, which, as the artist noted, made the architectural intervention participatory after all. The iPhone, with its camera function, has become the medium through which modern audiences consume culture and experience their lives.

The Louvre, originally a royal palace, became the people's museum during the French Revolution and later the largest museum in the world under Napoleon (1769–1821), due to his military campaigns and art theft. JR's now-you-see-it, now-you-don't play with architecture reflected the evolving uses of the Louvre throughout French history. He reminded his audience of the wars and

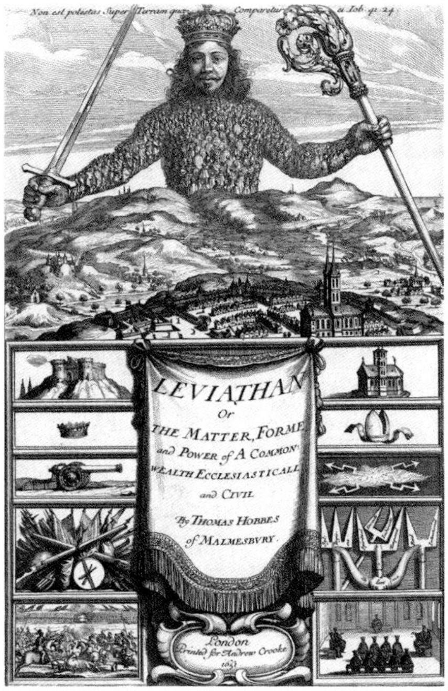

JR's installations are ephemeral. They wear away through wear and tear or weather; some remain pasted for a long time, while others disappear immediately. Sometimes the public or those portrayed remove some of the pasting to keep. His large public pastings, like the one that covered the esplanade at the Louvre in 2019, did not stay intact for the run of the installation, but got stripped little by little as souvenirs.

ABOVE
Frontispiece of Thomas Hobbes, *Leviathan*, 1651

OPPOSITE
JR at the Louvre Museum, 2016
Participatory workshop, May 29, Paris, France
Ink on wood, 155 x 155 cm (61 x 61 in.)

FOLLOWING SPREAD
JR at the Louvre Museum, 2016
June 9, 6:33 A.M., Paris, France

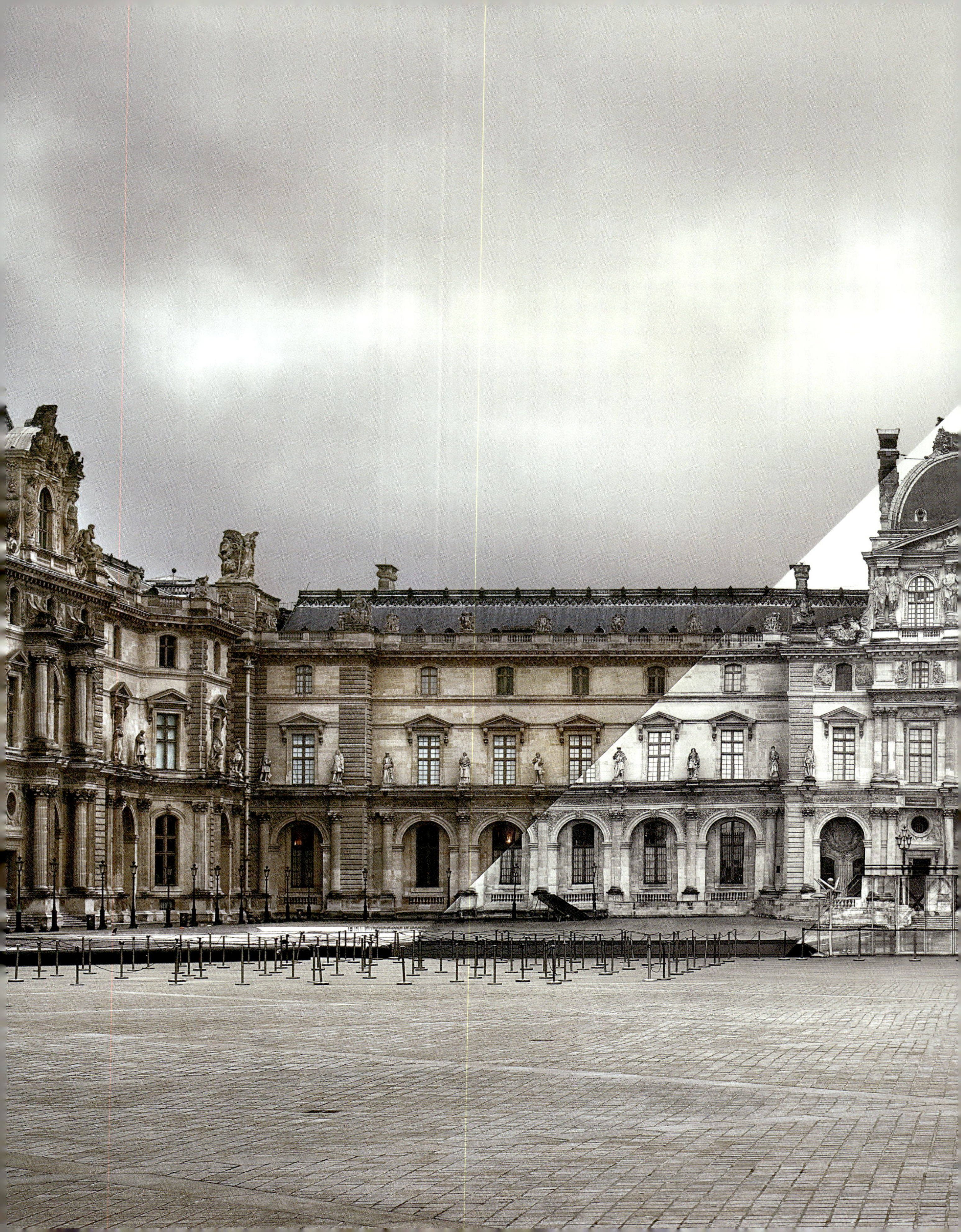

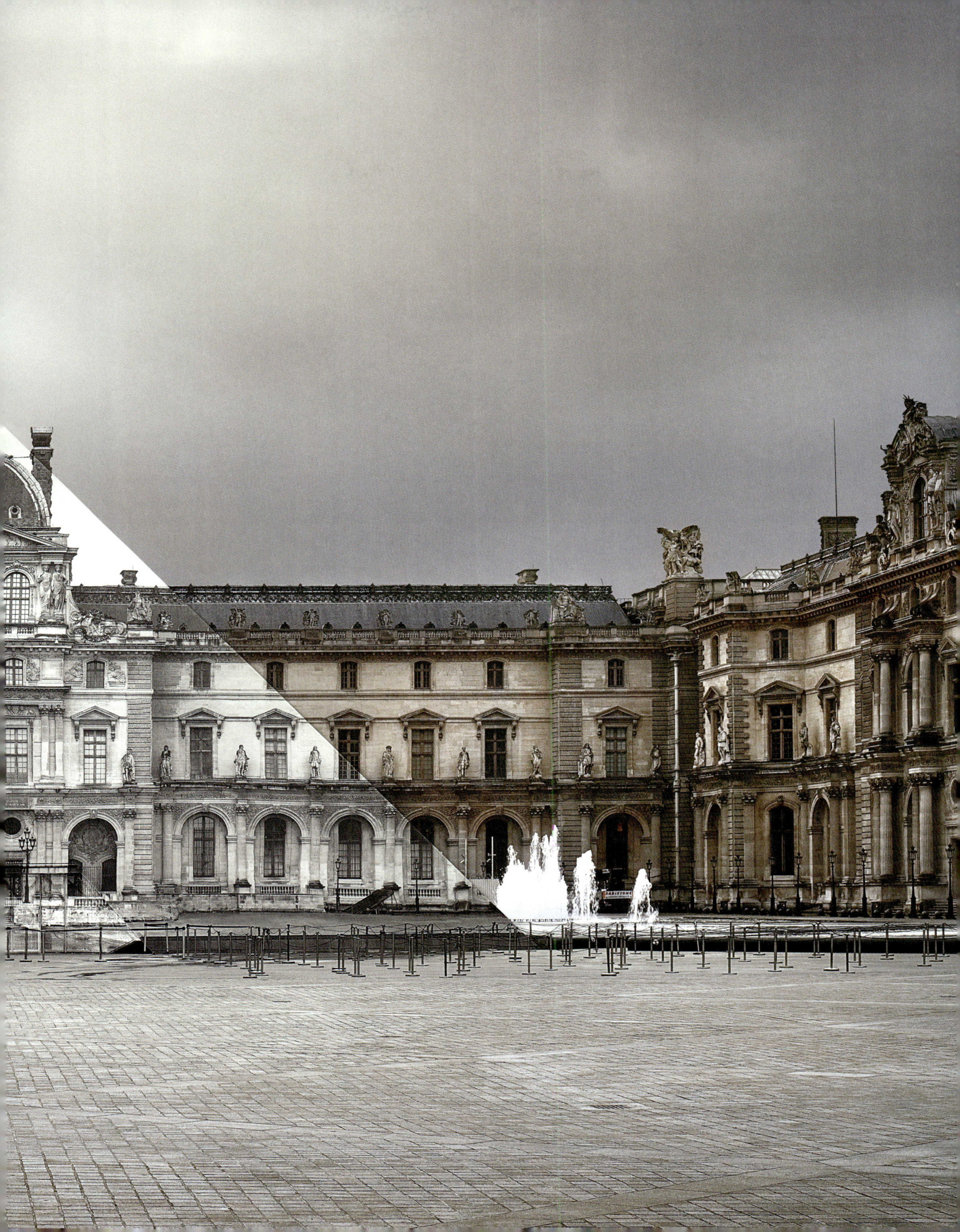

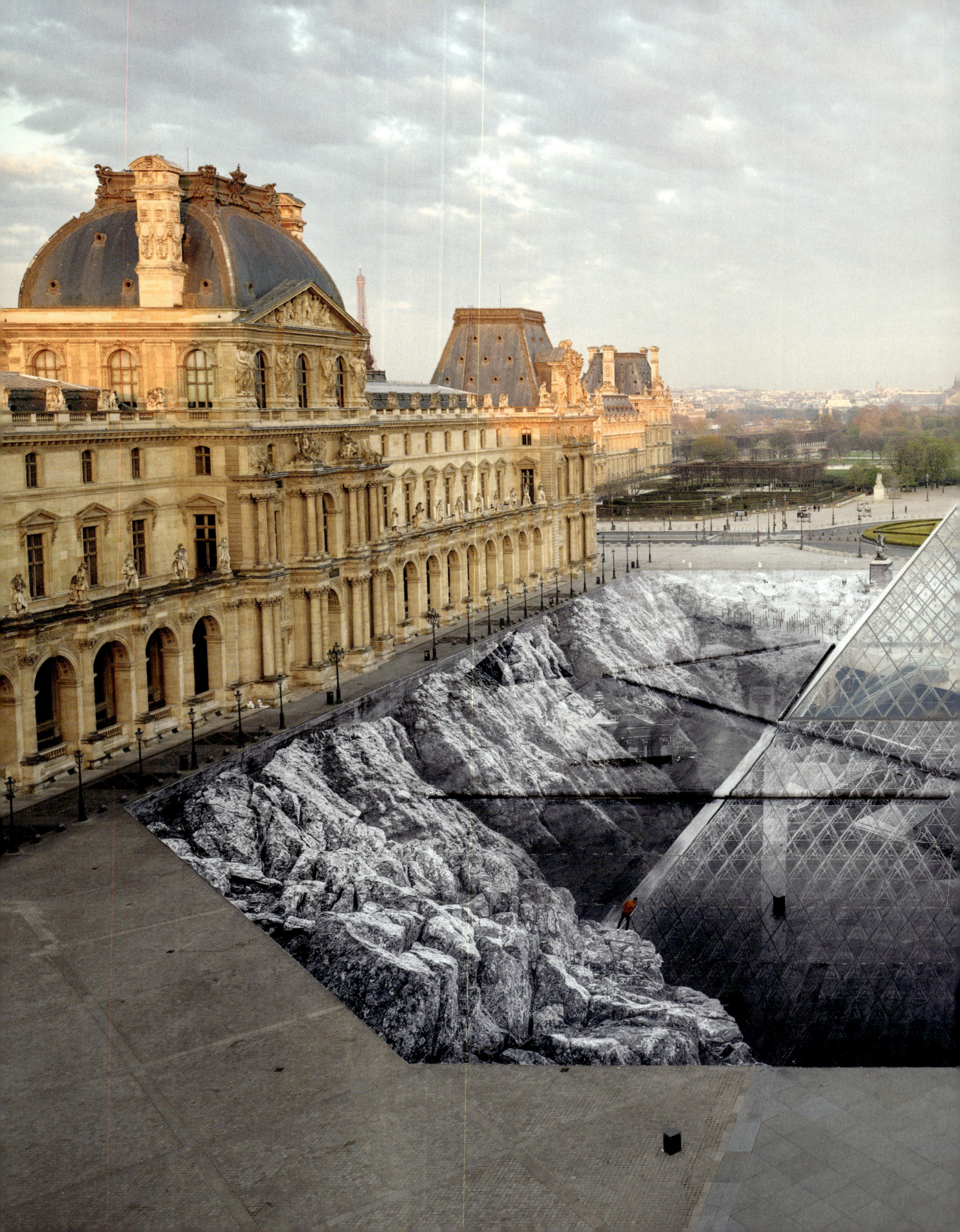

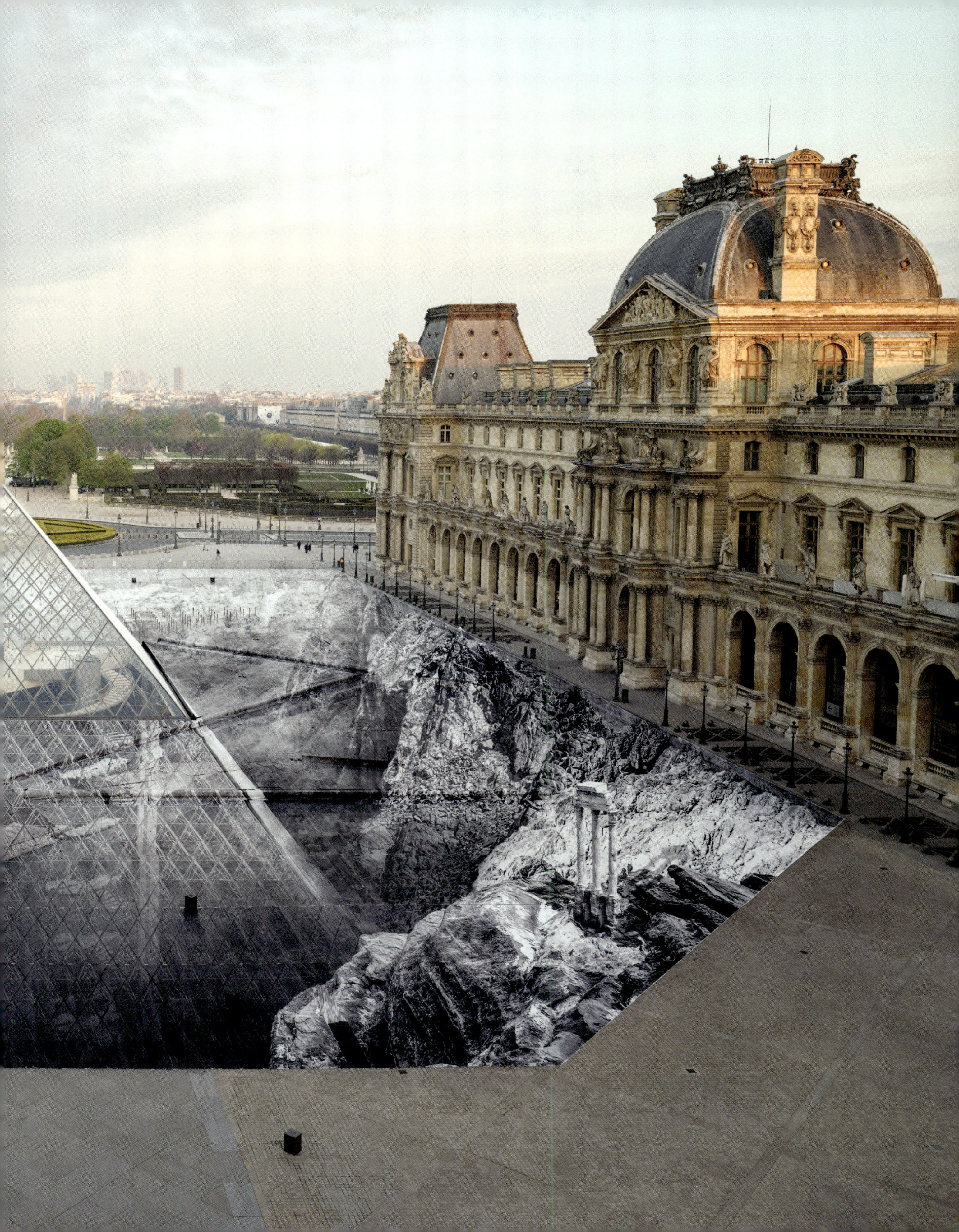

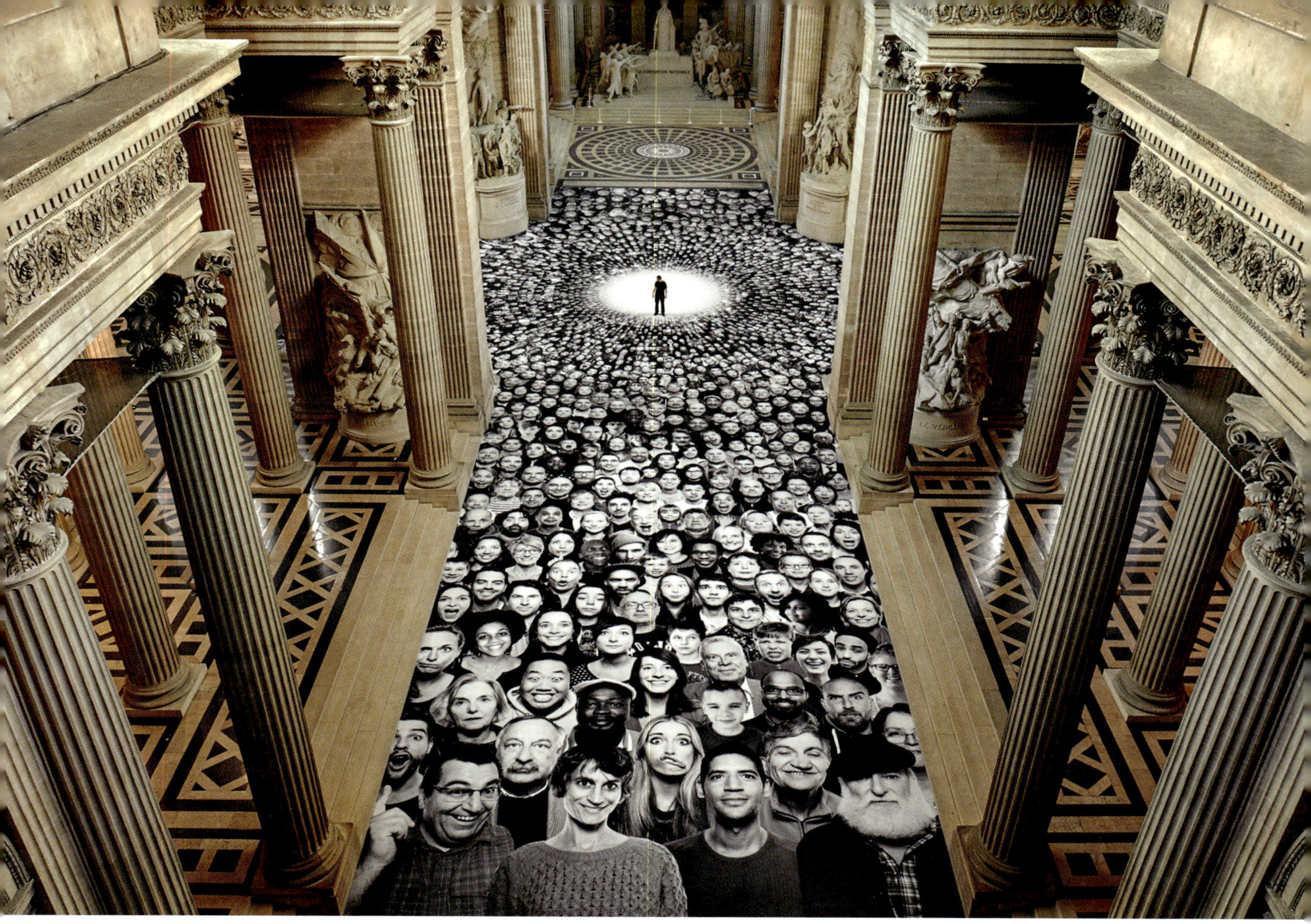

power struggles embodied in the building, as well as the history of the collection—why do works of art end up where they do? The Italian master Leonardo da Vinci kept the *Mona Lisa* (c. 1503–06, or later) throughout his life, bringing it to France himself while employed as a painter, engineer, and architect for the French king. Today, across from the *Mona Lisa* in the Louvre hangs *The Wedding at Cana* (1562–63), a work Napoleon stole from Venice. This feast scene, painted by Paolo Veronese (1528–88), depicts a miracle by Jesus and was originally scaled to fit the back wall of a specific monastery refectory, not a museum (JR is presenting *Il Gesto*, his reinterpretation of *The Wedding at Cana*, at the 2026 Venice Biennale). The Louvre is haunted not just by works of art but by entire stories from the past.

JR's black-and-white pyramid pasting made for a ghostly effect against the stone. A performance by the artist Liu Bolin (1973–) accompanied the project, enhancing its optical illusion and adding an element of fun. Known for his use of camouflage, Bolin, also known as "the invisible man," and JR made themselves disappear in front of the installation with the help of black-and-white paint and makeup. They stood on pedestals, effectively hiding in plain sight.

The Louvre invited JR back to the courtyard three years later to celebrate the 30th anniversary of the pyramid's construction. In a playful gesture, the artist "reversed" the disappearance of his first installation. He pasted the esplanade with paper, enlisting many volunteers from around the world through social

PREVIOUS SPREAD
JR at the Louvre Museum and The Secret of the Great Pyramid, 2019
March 30, 6:50 A.M., Paris, France

ABOVE
Inside Out at the Panthéon, 2014
Nave (left) and cupola (right)
Paris, France

FOLLOWING SPREAD
Retour à la Caverne – Act I, 2023
September 6, 7:11 A.M.
Palais Garnier, Paris, France

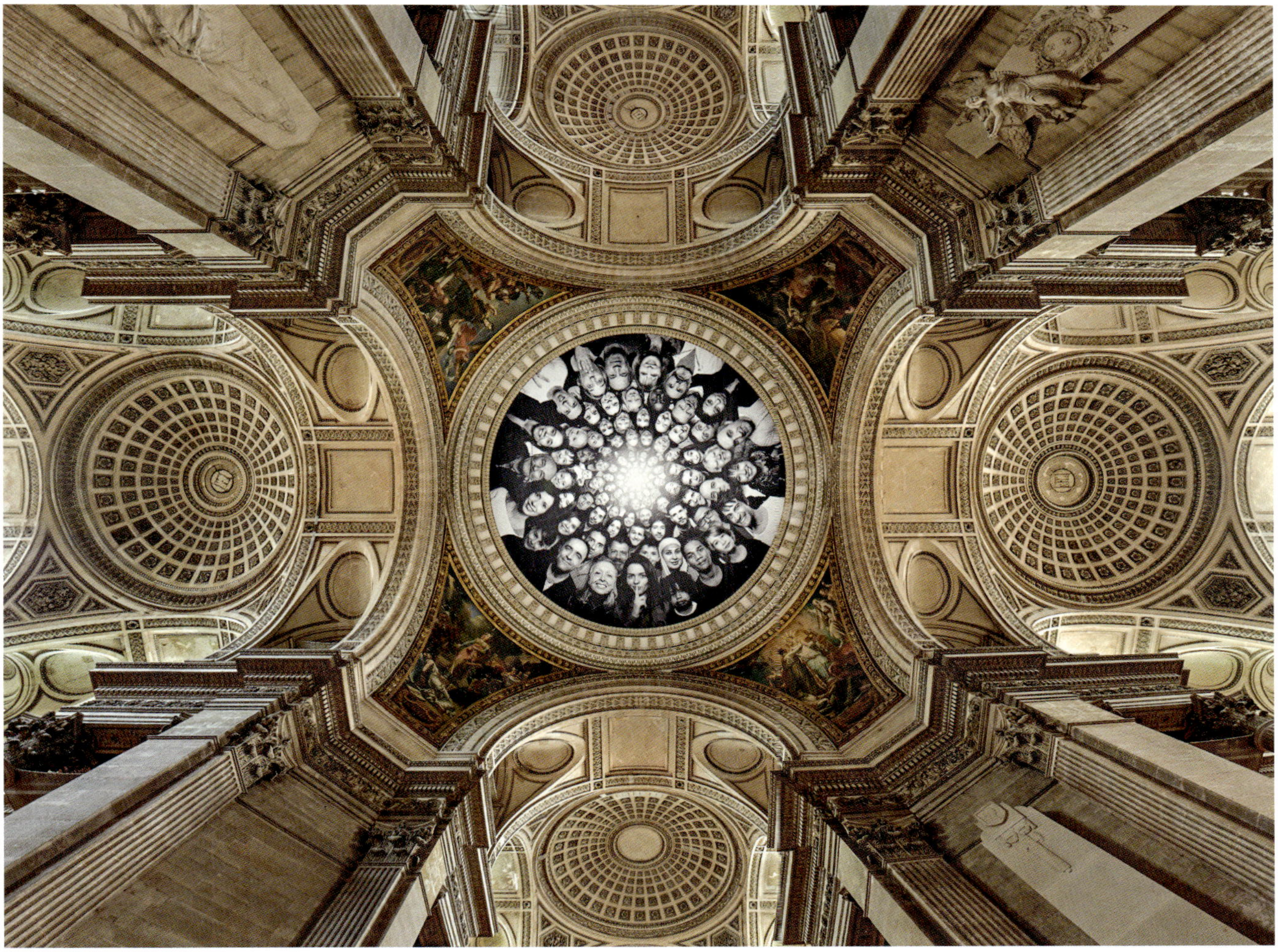

media, and again used printed vinyl to cover all sides of the esplanade's three small decorative pyramids. This time, the large glass pyramid remained its crystalline self. Managing the volunteers and involving them in the process required explaining the numbered structure of each section of the esplanade papering and repeatedly teaching the pasting technique. There were 2,000 pieces of paper to paste, each around 33 feet long. There was paste to mix, cutting to do, and paper to roll and unroll. Not everyone was equally skilled, and some paper strips tore and became bumpy. However, the action was successful, offered filmic moments, allowed JR to climb onto the roof of the Louvre to check for minor visual adjustments, and, like the building of Stonehenge (but with paper, and in less time), brought everyone together in the accomplishment of an extraordinary feat. Viewed from the right angle, *JR at the Louvre and The Secret of the Great Pyramid* (2019, pp. 70–71) revealed that the crystalline pyramid was born from a deep, rough white quarry. The image evoked raw mineral nature, the drama of later civilization's excavation of antiquity, and the haunting call of the void that humans feel when standing on the edge of a precipice. The belly of the earth opening in the middle of Paris introduced a sublime aspect to the classic restraint of the esplanade's architecture. More simply, the secret of *The Secret of the Great Pyramid* might be that the main entrance to the museum lies underground, requiring visitors to descend into its hidden lobby. The title could also poke fun at I. M. Pei's choice of a pyramidal form for such a mundane

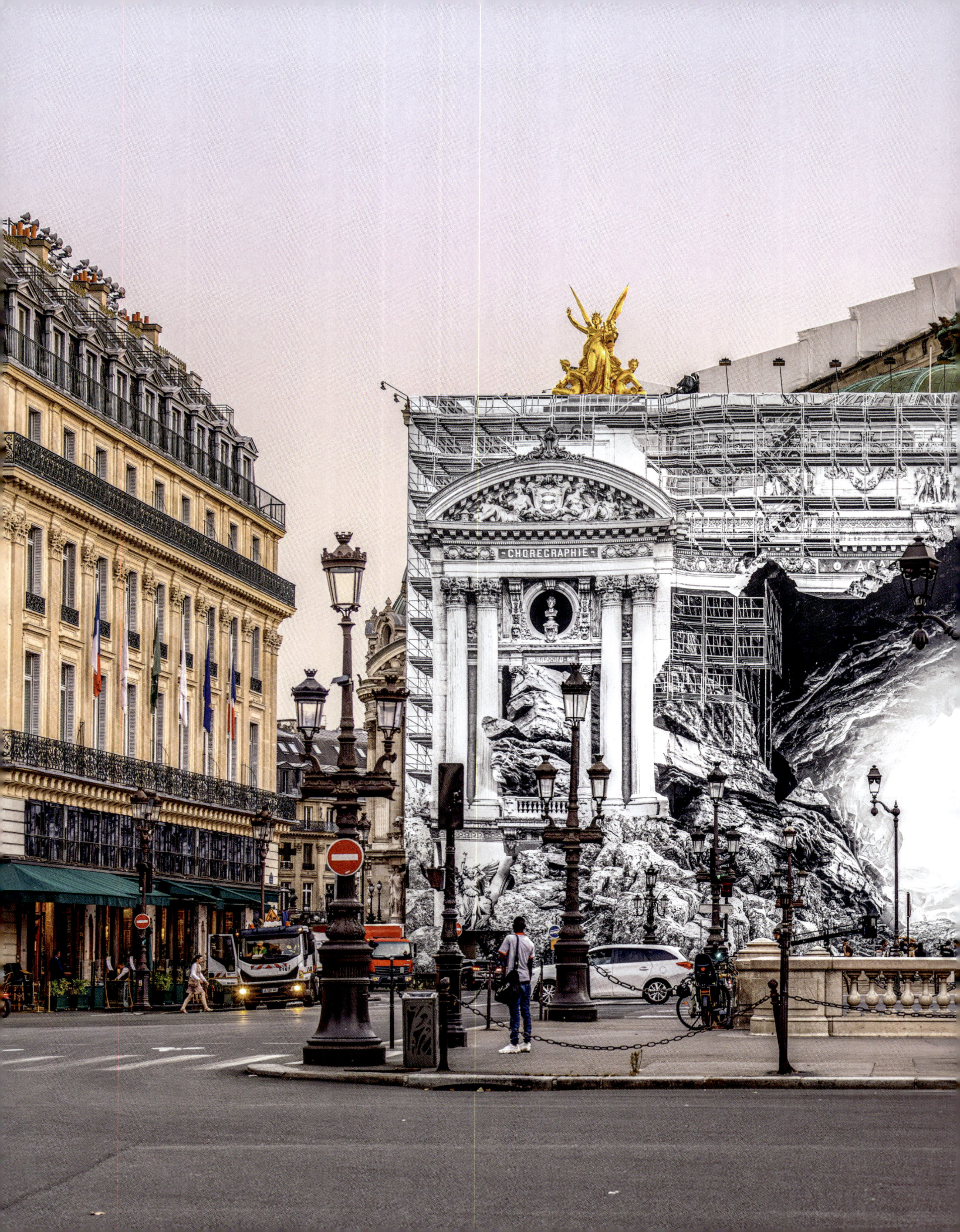
CHOREGRAPHIE

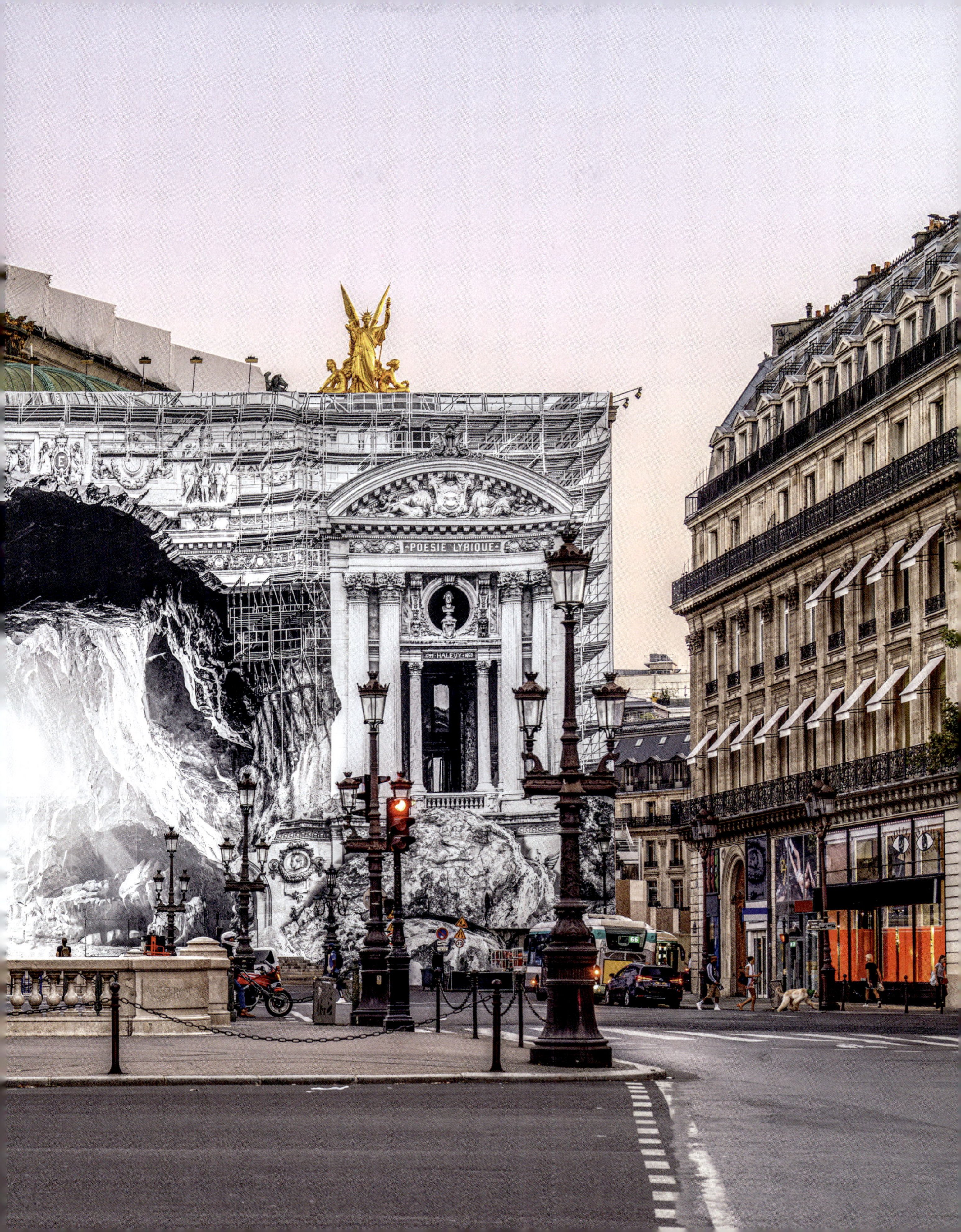
POESIE LYRIQUE
HALEVY

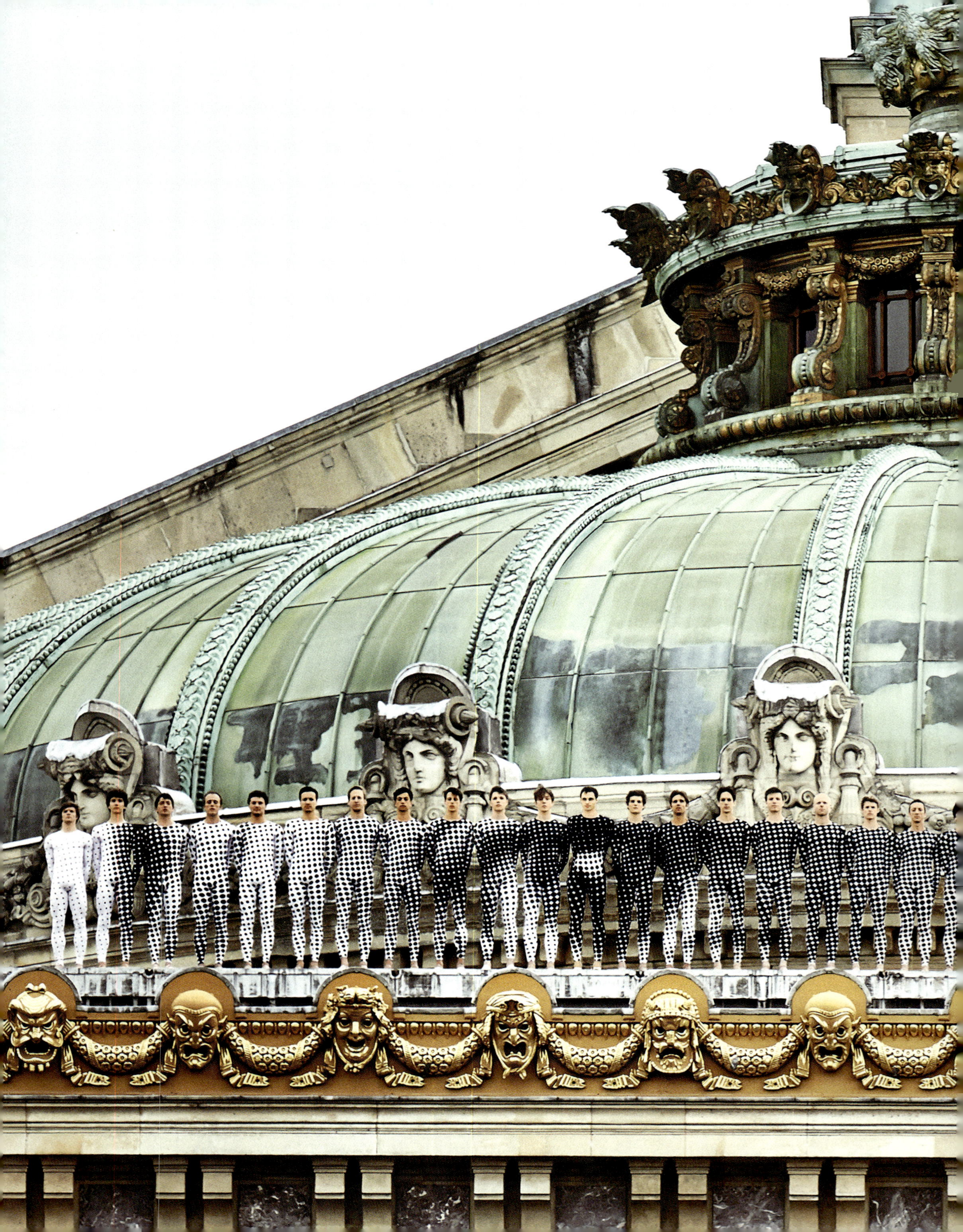

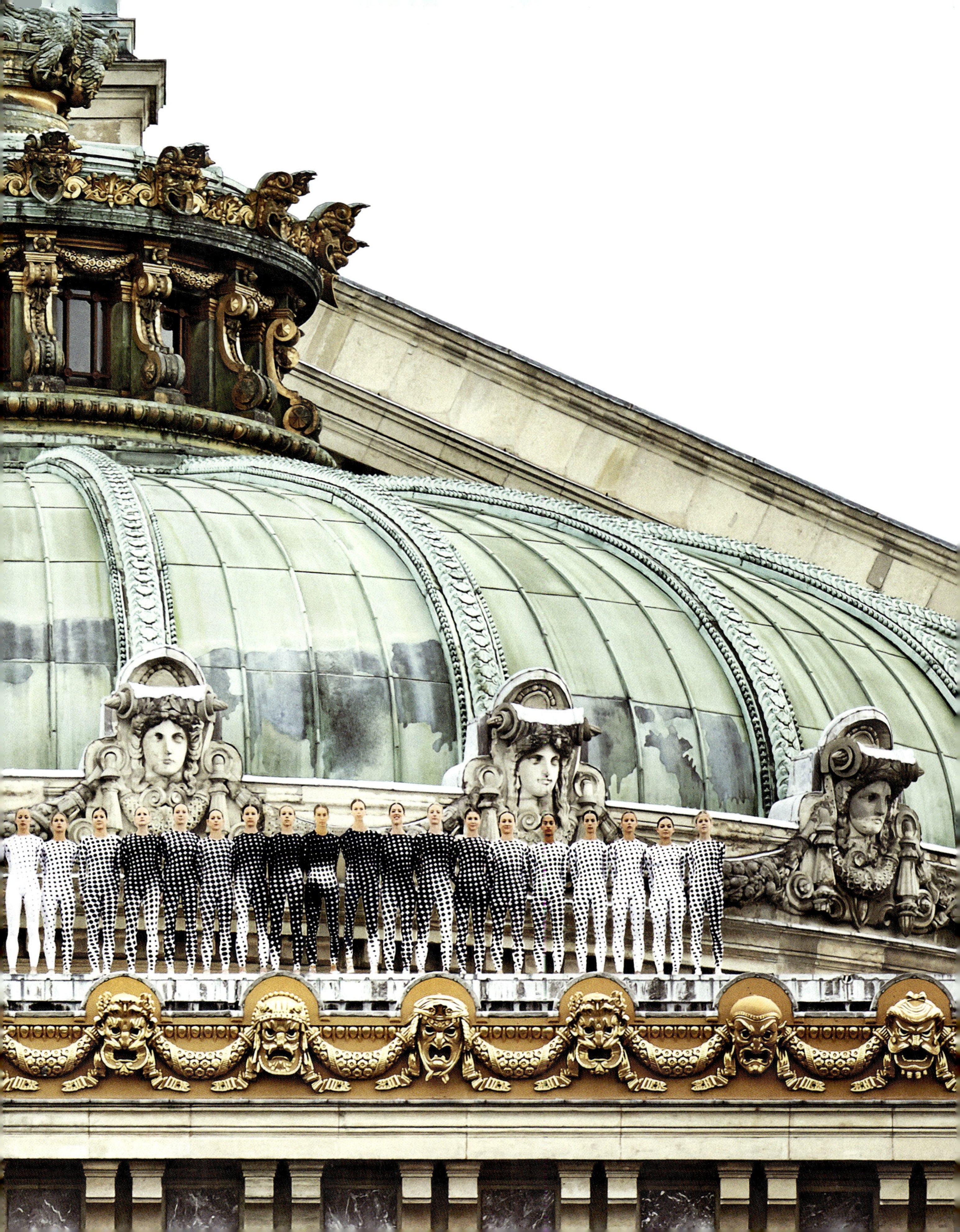

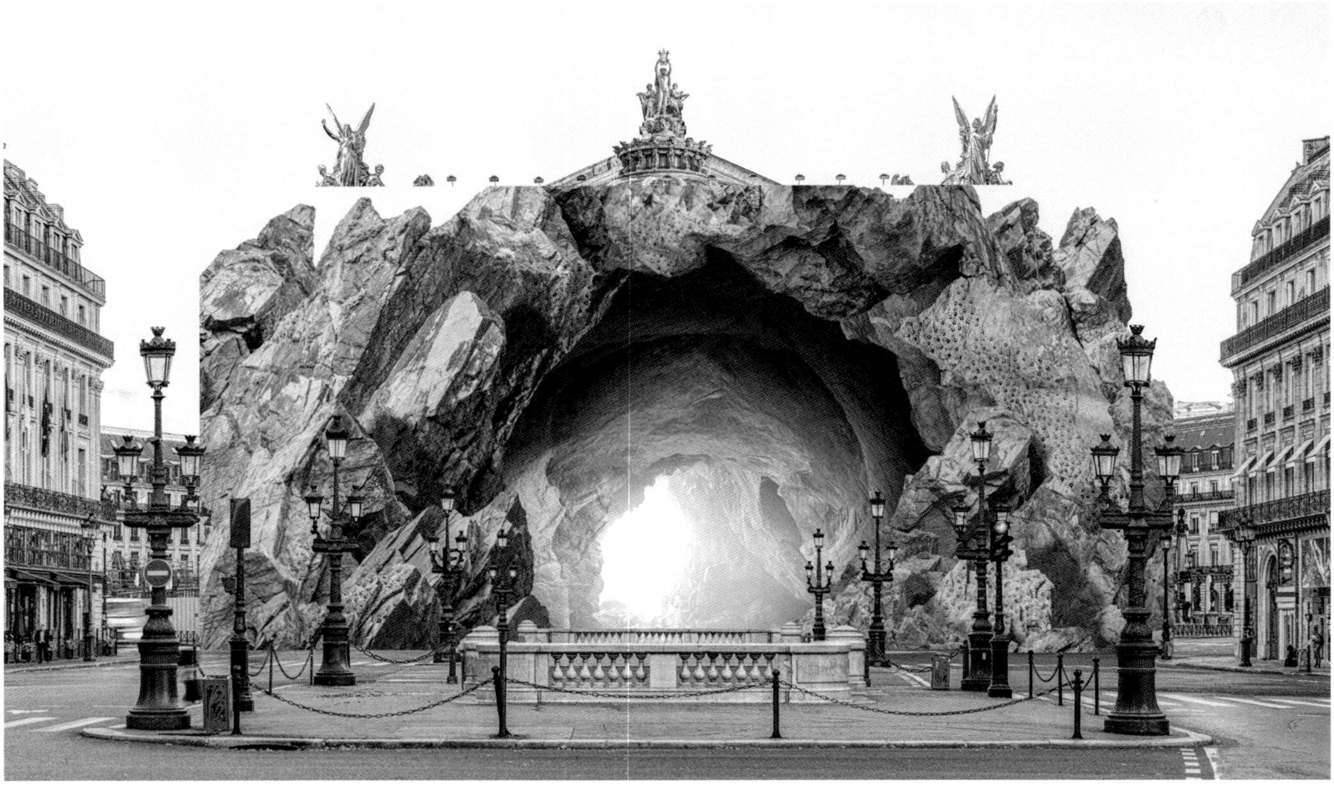

PREVIOUS SPREAD
Ballet, 2014
"Look" above the facade of Palais Garnier
Paris, France, detail

ABOVE
Dans la Caverne, Décomposition #1, 2024

OPPOSITE
Retour à la Caverne – Act II, CHIROPTERA,
Palais Garnier, Opéra national de Paris, France,
November 12, 2023
A project created by JR, Damien Jalet, and Thomas Bangalter with Amandine Albisson, Étoile dancer of the Opéra national de Paris, and 153 dancers from all over the world.

function, as the Egyptian tombs it evokes harbor connotations of deep mystery and secret religious rites. Due to the crowds, entering the Louvre can be as time-consuming as finding the secret door to a pyramid.

Since 2023, JR has been working on the concept of a *Retour à la Caverne*, invoking Plato's allegory of the cave, a story taken from the philosopher's book *Republic* (*c.* 375 BCE). The story describes shackled prisoners who mistake shadows for reality. Troubled by the sense of disconnection in today's world, the artist compares Plato's allegory of the cave to contemporary experiences of reality. While the internet can connect and inform people globally, algorithms can lead to problems. When users only access content and people aligned with their existing views, their outlook narrows, disrupting their reality and leaving them shackled in their own chosen caves.

Plato presents the story of the cave in dialogue form, using the voice of his teacher Socrates. The narrative unfolds in a strange and artificial setting. It describes prisoners who have been shackled by their necks and feet in an underground cave since childhood. They face a wall and are unable to see anything beyond that wall. Behind them, a fire burns. The shackled men see shadows on the wall, created by people behind them who are using the fire to project a show with carved figures of animals and people—the prisoners are being manipulated. The prisoners believe the shadows are reality; they only know the machinations of their manipulators. The rest of the story deals with how painful and difficult it would be to have this belief broken, whether through transformative education or by stumbling out into the light beyond the cave. JR clearly wants his audience to read or reread Plato's story of the cave and engage in a dialogue! The artist's emphasis on the eye in his art—very large eyes photographed all around the world—highlights the importance of how we see. With this story, JR also gives a nod to both photography (literally "writing with light") and the

In *Retour à la Caverne*, one looked at a slight angle into a tall, yawning cave, as if the cave penetrated the classical building. Bright light from an indefinable source simultaneously revealed and blinded. The irregular, protruding rocks, arching cave walls, and craggy ceiling thrilled viewers and challenged them to enter.

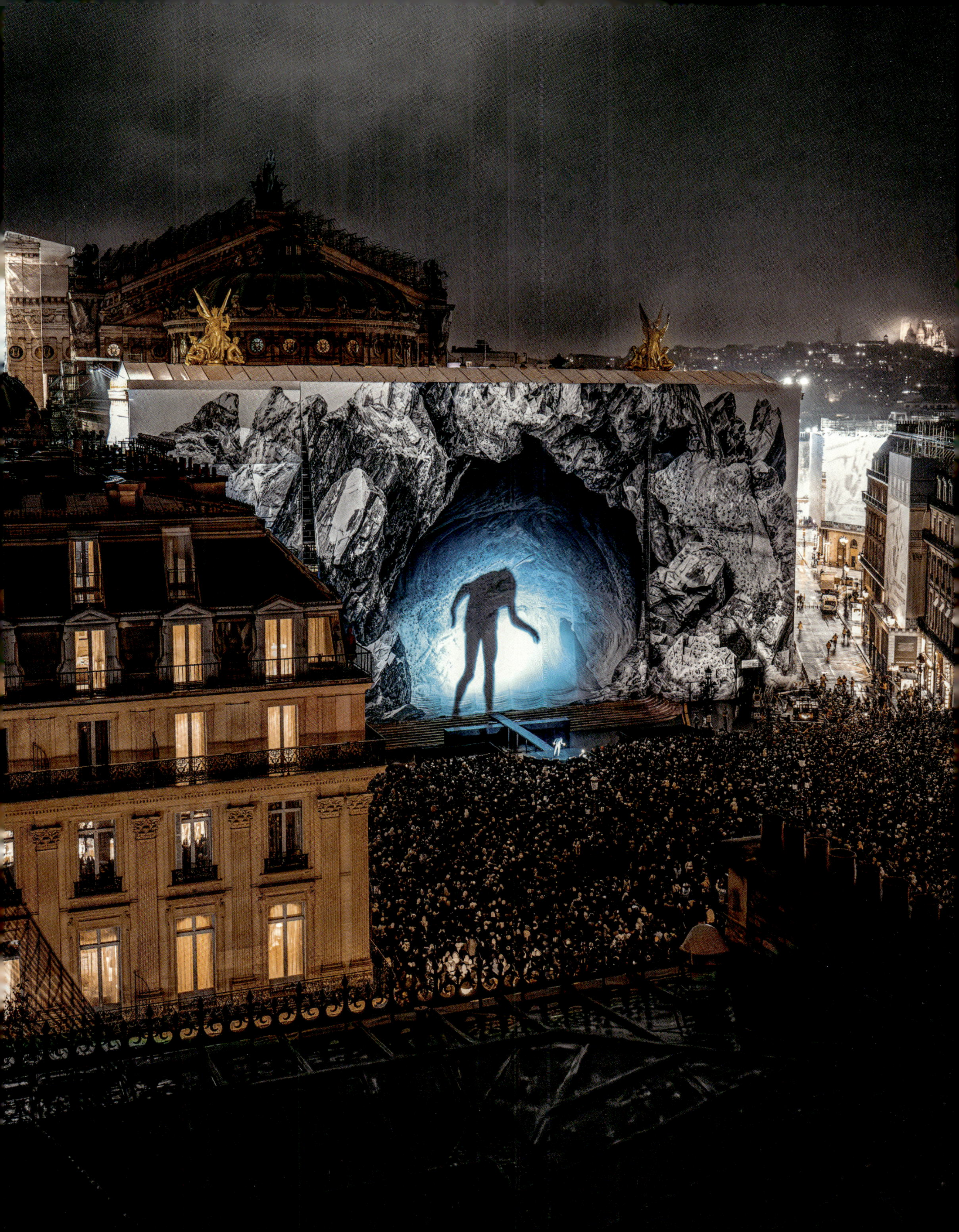

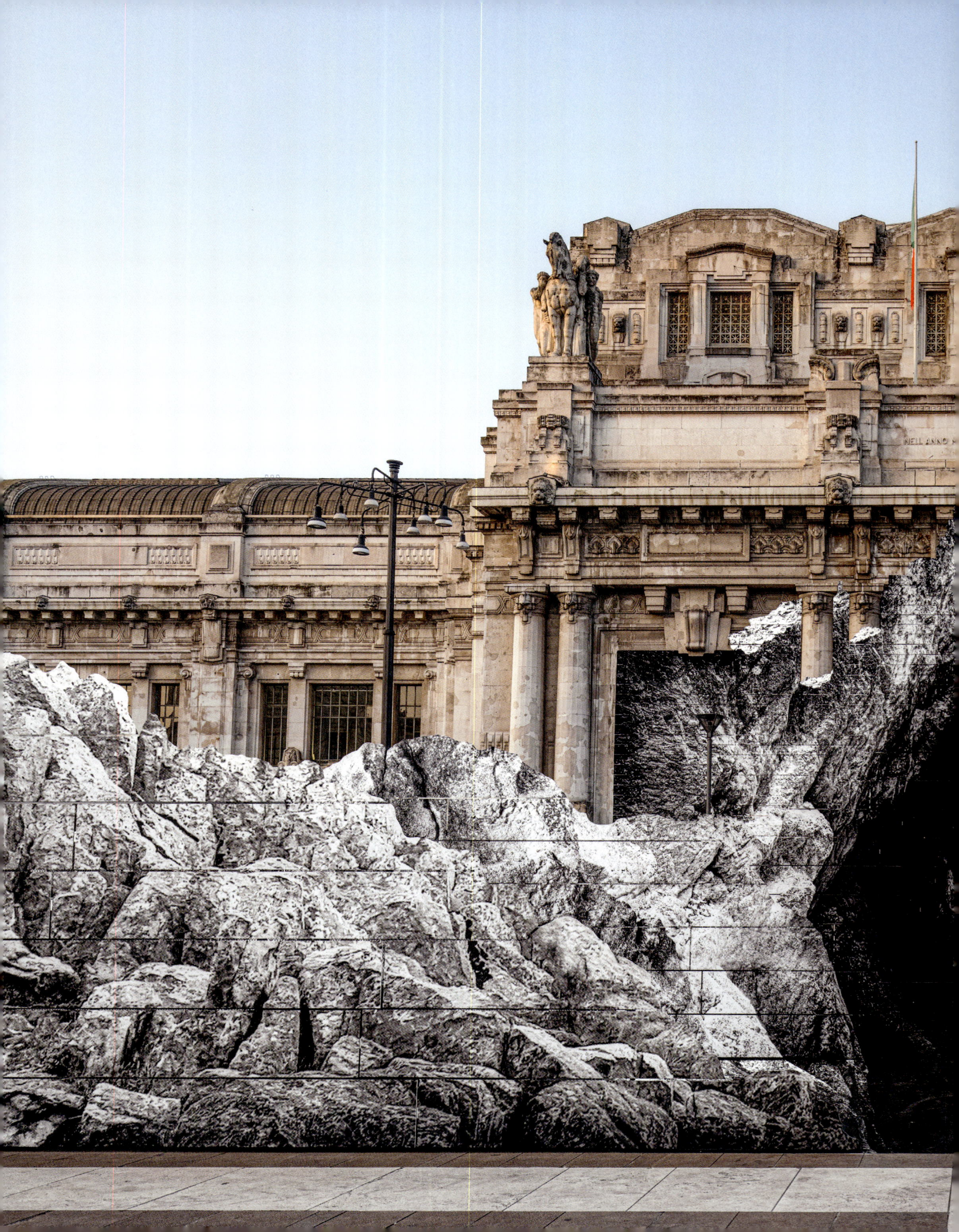
NELL ANNO

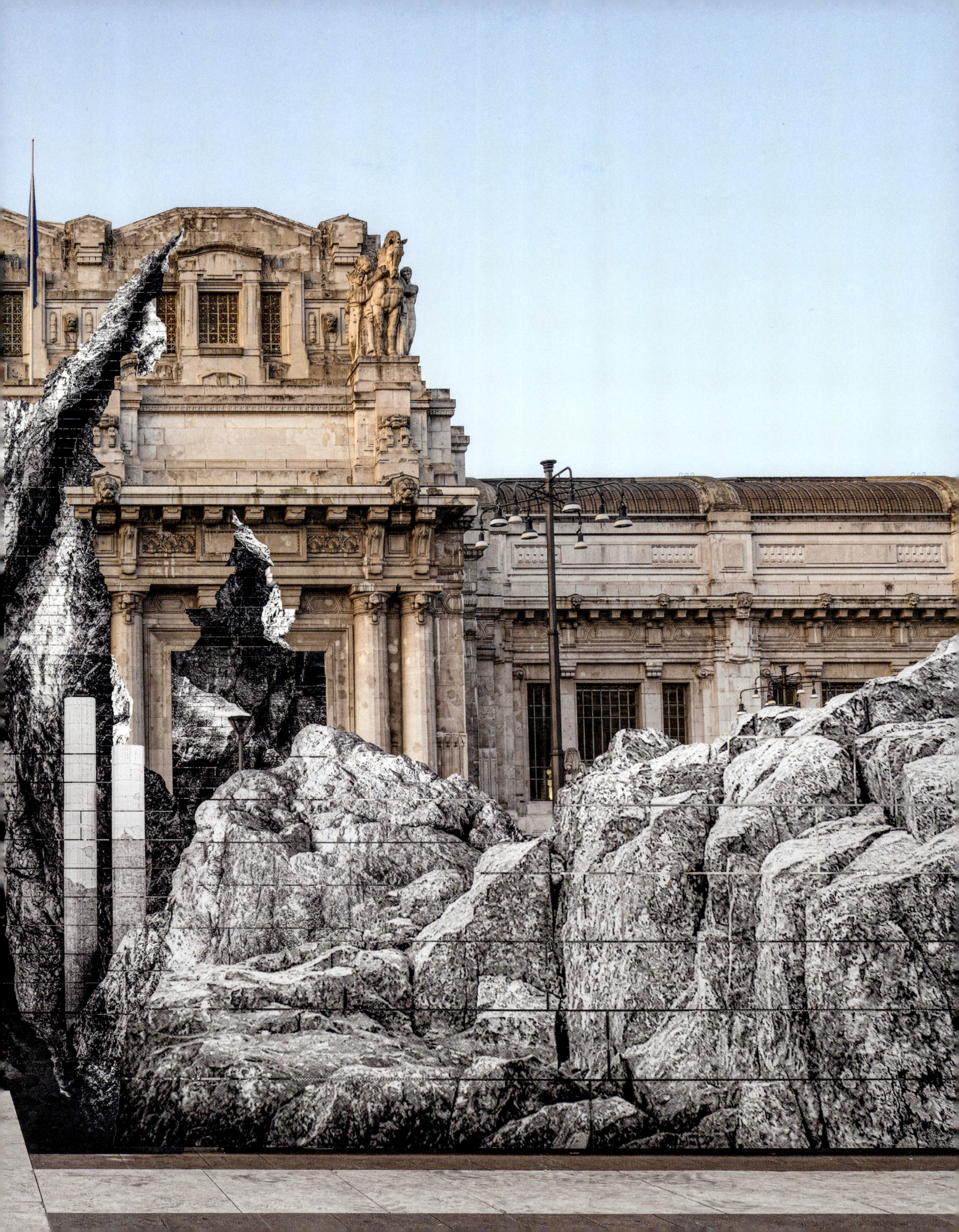

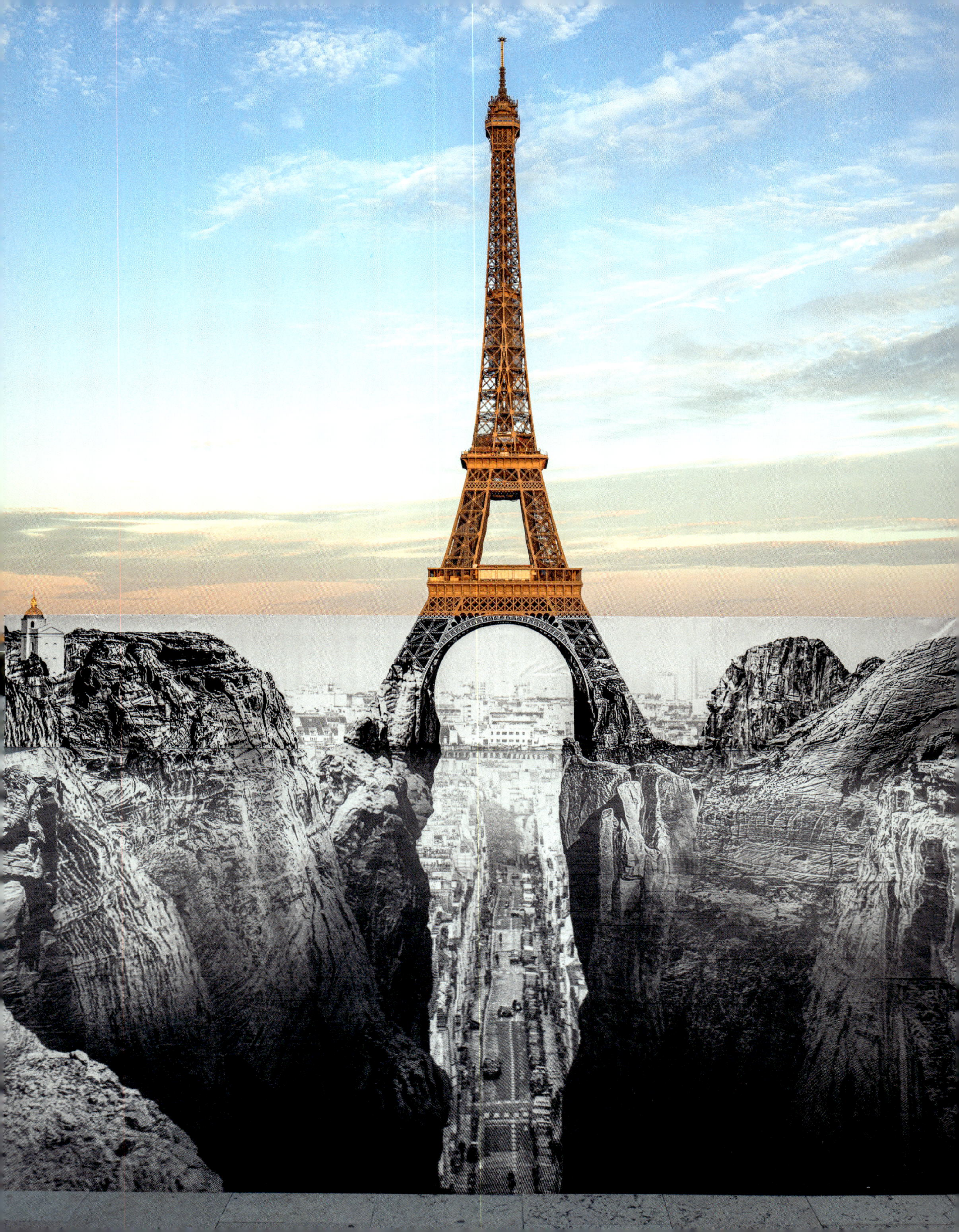

constructed reality of theater, as his first work in the cave series was done for the Paris Opera.

Retour à la Caverne—Acte I began with the renovation of the Palais Garnier, home to the Paris Opera. Scaffolding obscured the historic facade; JR was invited to sheath the building during construction. The image he created for the vinyl sheathing featured a photograph of the old architecture with scaffolding attached, overlaid with an image of a cave opening in its center. As with the sublime ruin images of Giovanni Battista Piranesi (1720–78), and the paintings of Hubert Robert (1733–1808), with their romantic attitude toward landscape, the public was transported to an imaginary world. For four nights in September 2023, projections brought the cave to life.

In November of that year, JR replaced the initial construction sheath image with one that showed only a huge cave spilling light. The public looked straight into it, as if peering into a tunnel to the sun, or down the throat of time, all the way back to the age of the first graffiti artists, who left handprints, devised symbols, and painted hunted mammals, since gone extinct, onto rough walls. Handprints surrounded the opening of the cave, contributed by thousands of people who participated in the creation of this work, titled *Retour à la Caverne—Acte II* by making prints of their hands during public workshops. From September to November, participants learned how decorate their own handprints with embroidery. They were then photographed at an *Inside Out* photo booth. The photographed handprints were collected and placed around the cave's opening, recalling hands stenciled at the *Cave of Hands* (7300 BCE–700 CE) in Argentina, as well as other caves with prehistoric handprints. On Sunday night, November 12, the cave's entrance acted as a stage curtain that opened to reveal the cavern's allegorical purpose. JR, along with dancer and choreographer Damien Jalet and musician and producer Thomas Bangalter, debuted the project *CHIROPTERA*, a performance of 153 dancers and Amandine Albisson, a principal at the Paris Opera. The dancers were tethered by safety harnesses to each of the nine levels of scaffolding. They danced in place, rotating at different speeds and with individually timed movements to reveal the black or reflective side of their costumes, which formed fabric squares when they extended their arms. The costumes resembled sails or wings, and the title *Chiroptera* refers to the only order of mammals capable of true flight: bats, also at home in caves. Lights brought by the large audience—flashlights, cellphones, headlamps—contributed to highlighting the white sides of the costumes, so the dancers became human pixels against a flat dark "screen." Their movements combined into visible moving patterns and waves across the nine-story scaffolding, recalling the chronophotography of Étienne-Jules Marey (1830–1904). The white costumes finally spelled out the message "Darkness holds the grace of light" in what resembled a light-emitting-diode text.

"I always let the architecture dictate the work. That's why [my pieces] fit in the environment like they belong there."
JUXTAPOZ MAGAZINE (2018)

Soon, JR will open the third act of his ruminations on Plato's cave, *La Caverne du Pont Neuf* (The Cave of Pont Neuf, 2026), which will cover the bridge over the Seine. The installation will last three weeks, from June 6 to June 28, 2026. The work will pay tribute to the artists Christo (1935–2020) and Jeanne-Claude (1935–2009). JR befriended Christo in New York and appreciated his work. In 1985, Christo and Jeanne-Claude wrapped the bridge in champagne-colored woven polyamide fabric (*The Pont Neuf Wrapped*, p. 87). It wasn't easy. The entertaining documentary film *Christo in Paris* (1990) could set the stage for appreciating JR's response to that project.

Completed in 1607, the stone Pont Neuf is the oldest and most beloved bridge in Paris. It played a role in many Impressionist works of the 19th century painted

PREVIOUS SPREAD
La Nascita, 2024
Milano Centrale, April 11, 7:20 P.M.
Milan, Italy

OPPOSITE
Trompe l'oeil, The Cliffs of the Trocadero, 2021
May 28, 9:23 P.M., Paris, France, detail

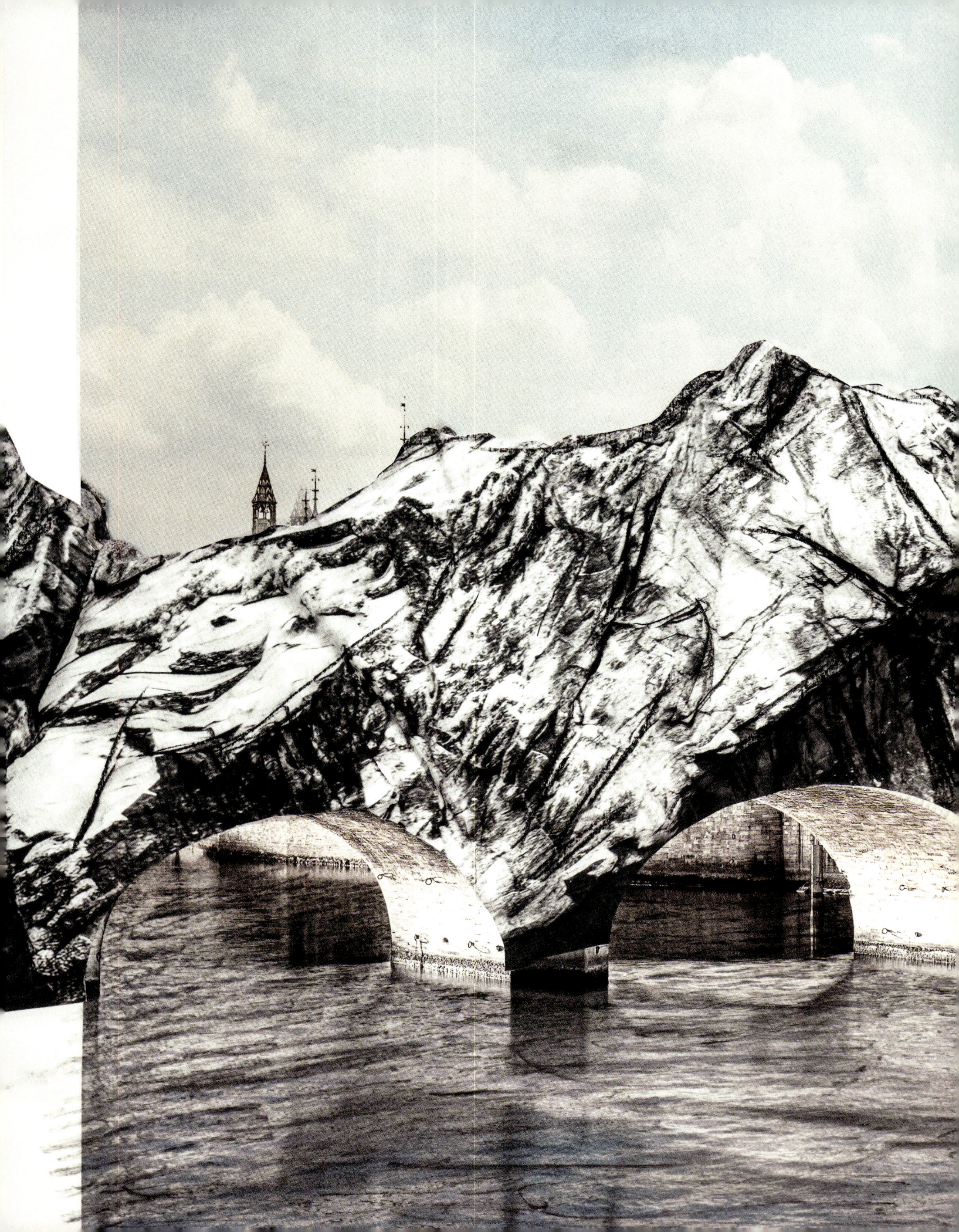

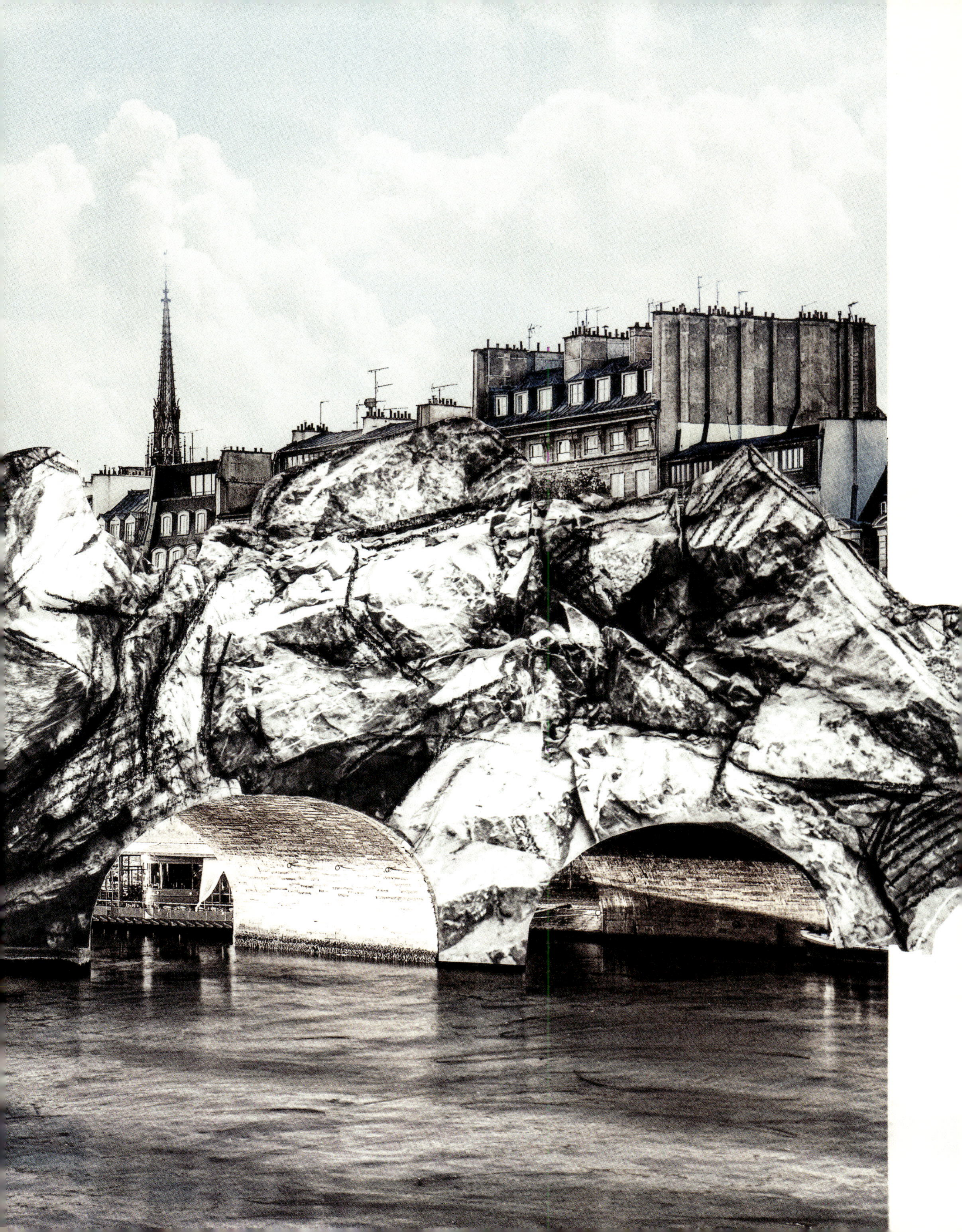

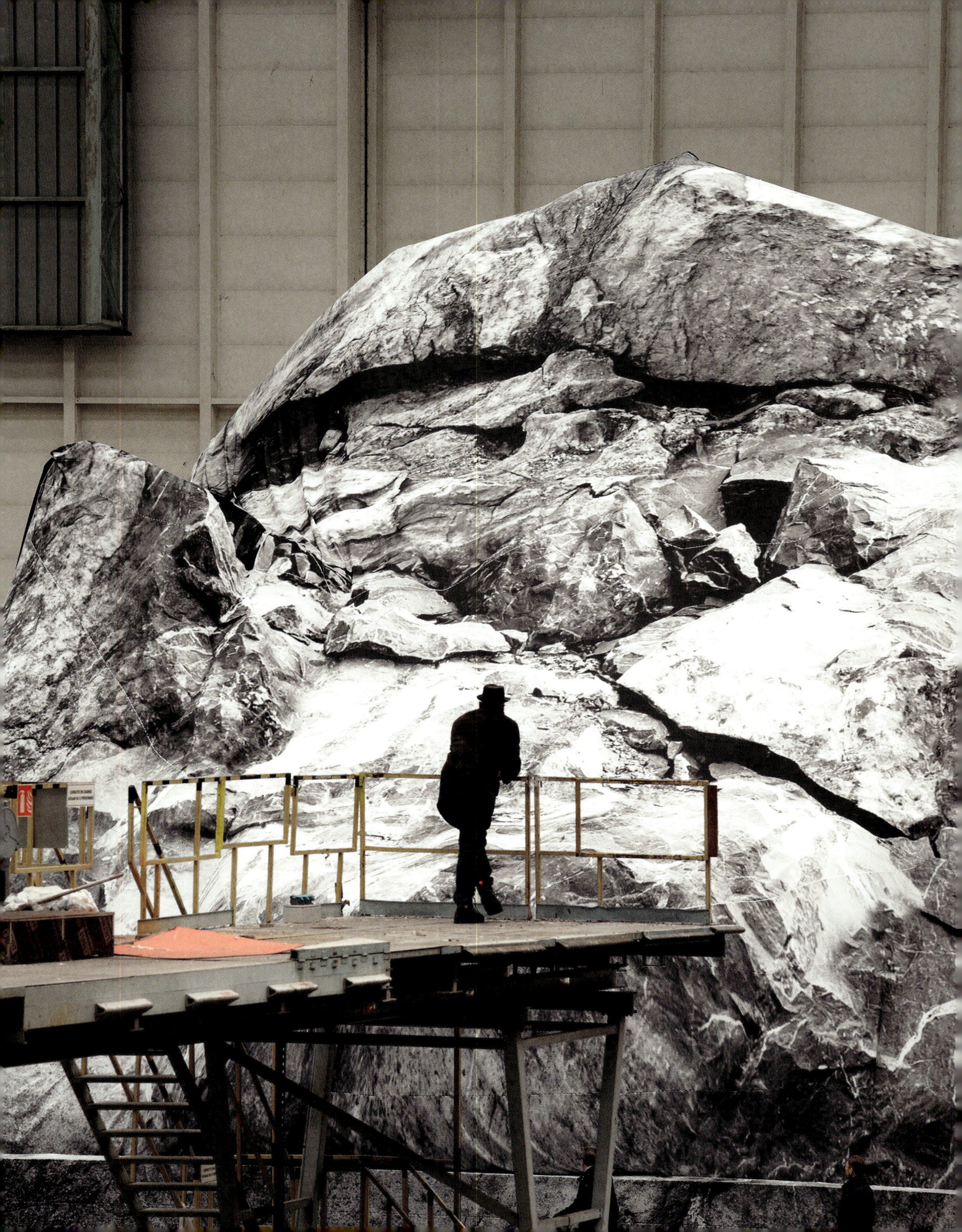

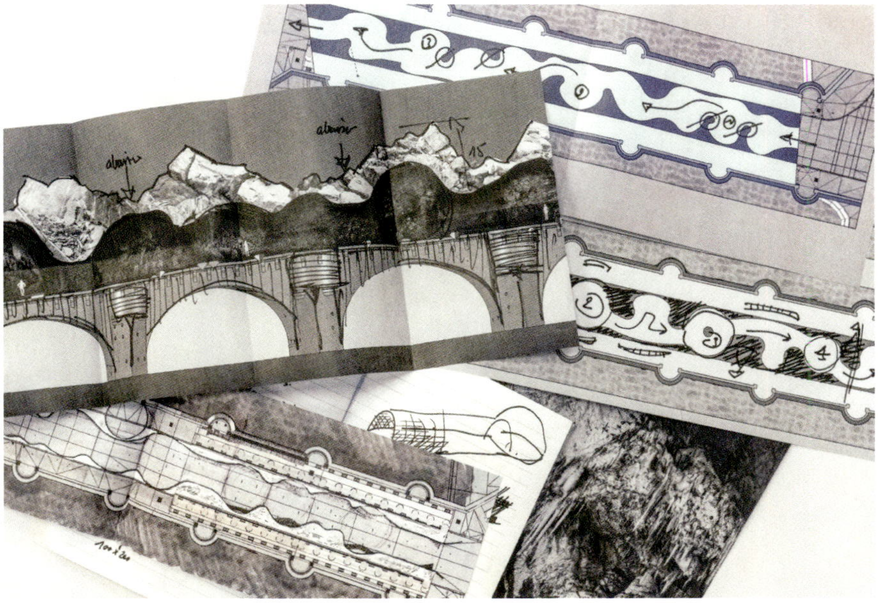

to tempt sightseers of the city, such as *Pont Neuf, Paris* (1871) by Auguste Renoir or *Afternoon, Sunshine, Pont Neuf* (1901) by Camille Pissarro. But what if the bridge disappears? What will contemporary tourists think if the stone quarry comes to the city and decides to embrace the stone it has been missing for centuries? This will happen when JR encases the bridge with his imagery, which will transform it into an inflatable walk-through cave whose walls appear to be made of rock. The installation will use a material printed and sourced from a company based in Brittany, France, that specializes in inflatable structures. The artificial cave will span 393 feet and rise over 55 feet using a built framework. JR intends to break the landscape of the refined architecture of central Paris and send wayfarers back in time. A "Sound Wrapping" by Thomas Bangalter will enrich and color the playful yet philosophical experience. Those daring enough to enter the cave of the Pont Neuf may first lose themselves in darkness, then make discoveries, and ultimately find a new orientation for themselves as they embark on a

PREVIOUS SPREAD
La Caverne du Pont Neuf
Preparatory collage, 2025

OPPOSITE
La Caverne du Pont Neuf
Prototype, Orly, France, 2026

ABOVE
La Caverne du Pont Neuf
Preparatory documents, 2026

BELOW
Christo
The Pont Neuf Wrapped (Project for Paris), 1984
Graphite, wax crayon, enamel paint, photograph by Wolfgang Volz, and masking tape on paper, 35.5 x 56 cm (14 x 22 in.), private collection

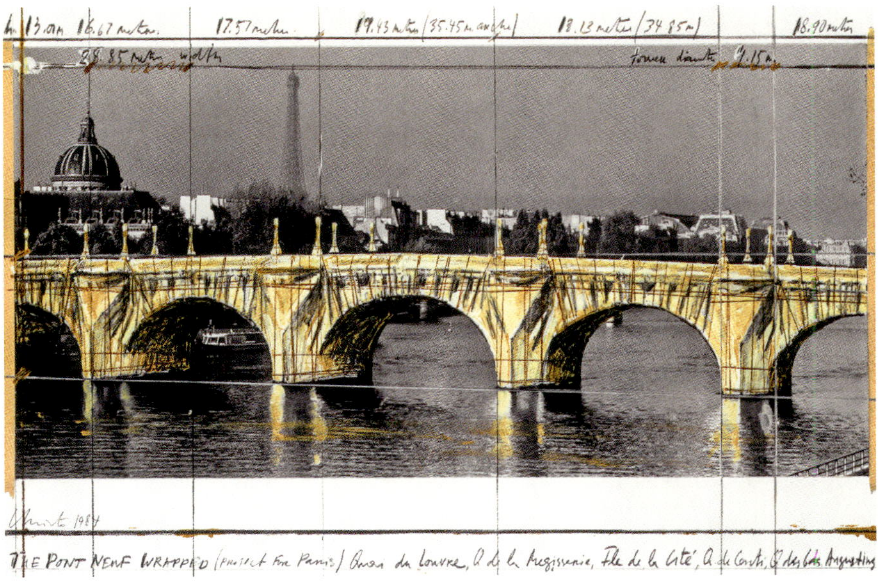

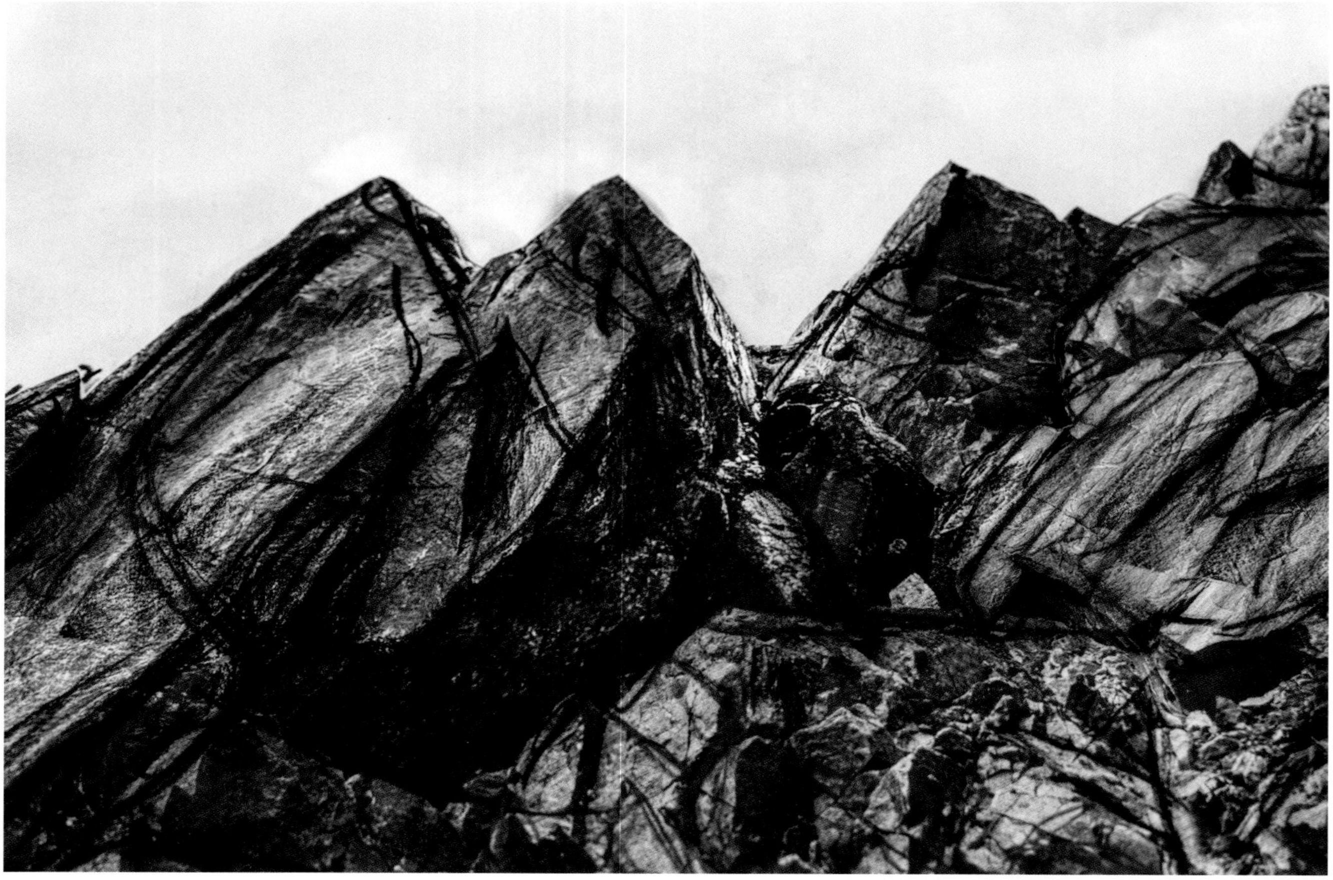

La Caverne du Pont Neuf
charcoal sketch, 2026, detail

OPPOSITE
JR in his studio, New York, United States, 2026

BELOW
A photograph of one of the caves that inspired *La Caverne du Pont Neuf*, texture study

search for light. This could be a heroic quest. Augmented reality options that require the use of a phone will be available throughout the installation, inspiring a sense of play or wonder. In 1942, for the *First Papers of Surrealism* exhibit, Marcel Duchamp complicated viewer experience with webs of string and an environment darkened by a ceiling hung with coal sacks, forcing visitors to use flashlights. At that New York opening, Duchamp instigated children to play with balls and jump ropes. JR's Pont Neuf installation may provoke a related feeling of disorder, energy, connection, and searching.

With his architectural metaphor of the cave bridge, JR hopes to create personal encounters, open minds, and begin conversations about art, time, photography, and more. Public art can facilitate communication and inspire change if the public engages with it beyond their phones.

As JR often says, "Let's see."

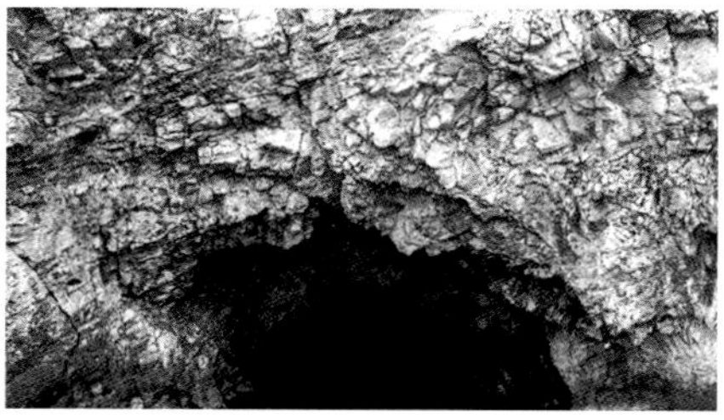

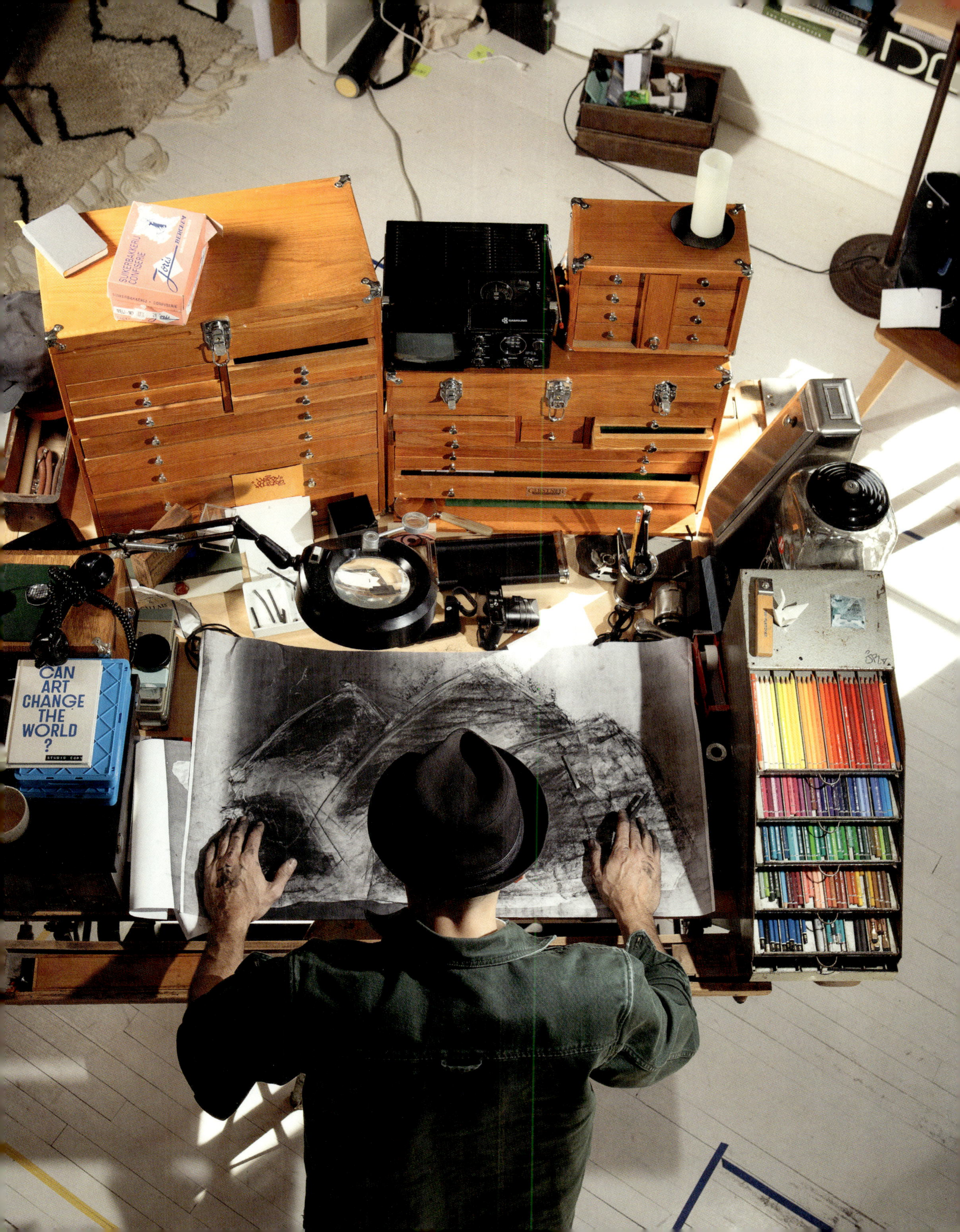
CAN
ART
CHANGE
THE
WORLD
?

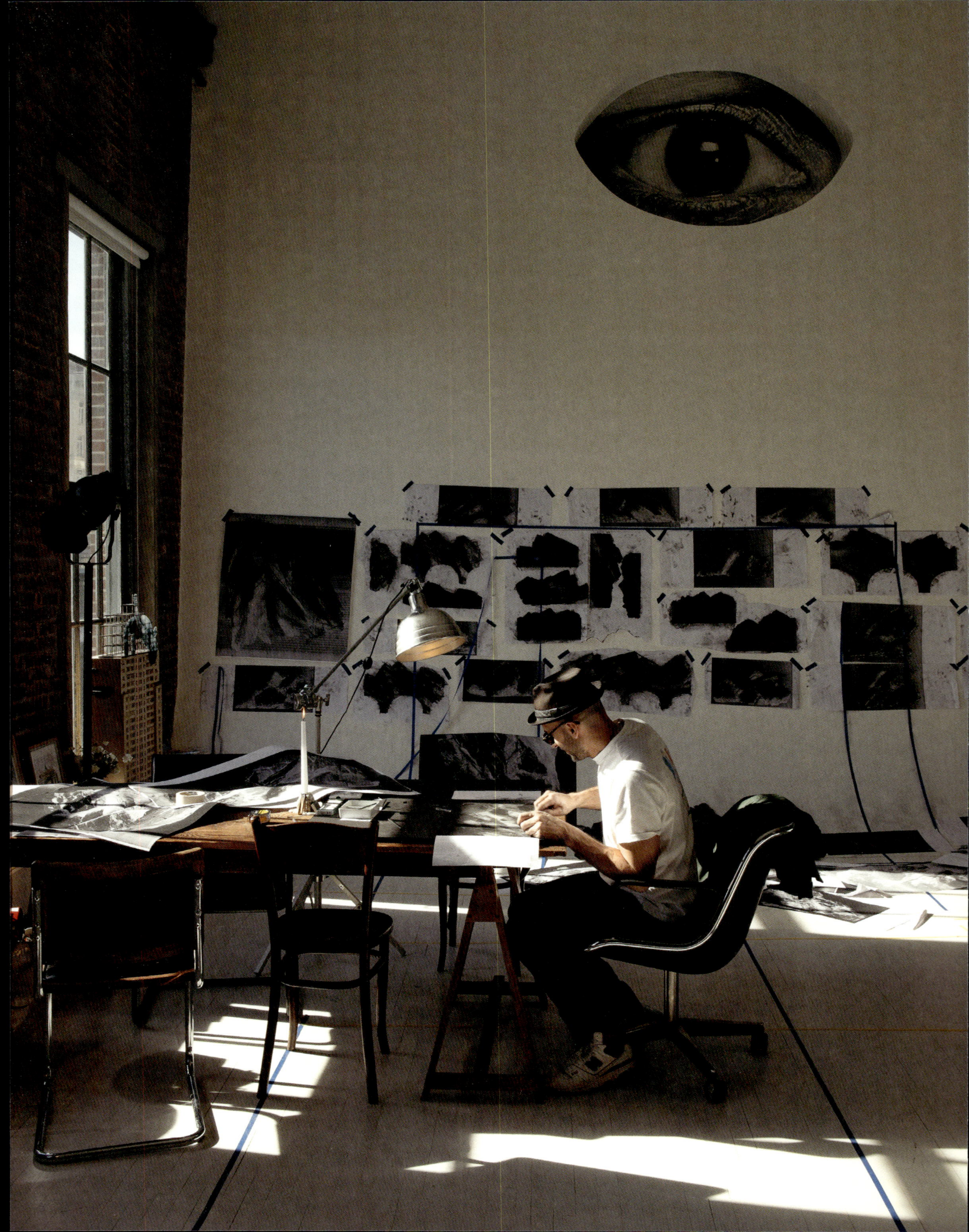

JR
Life and Work

1983 JR is born on the outskirts of Paris.

1996–2000 As a young teenager, he invents the alias “Face 3,” a reference to his DJ work as the “third side” (*face* in French) of a vinyl record. Begins spraying and using markers for graffiti, tagging the initials JR. Follows older graffiti artists. Has access to early internet and email through his father’s computer.

2000 Finds film camera equipped with a strong flash in suburban railway station and transitions to photography. His black-and-white photos document friends tagging graffiti.

2001–4 Begins pasting photocopies of his black-and-white photos on walls in the suburban railroad stations, *métro*, and streets of Paris. The pasted photos function for him as an ongoing public exhibition he calls *Expo 2 Rue*.

2004 Upon invitation of friend Ladj Ly, starts photographing people in Ly’s housing estate Les Bosquets, Clichy-Montfermeil. Makes first large-scale pastings using technique of photocopy strips that assemble into a single image. Together with Ladj Ly, makes video *Clichés du ghetto*. In September, JR leaves Paris to avoid arrest and to research graffiti in other countries.

2005 Publishes *Carnet de rue*, about his own work and graffiti in the United States and Europe. Riots break out in front of pasting of Ladj Ly in Les Bosquets, Clichy-Montfermeil. He sees his pastings from 2004 in background of the news coverage. He returns to Clichy-Montfermeil to photograph grimacing faces for “Portrait of a Generation” and pastes them in bourgeois Parisian neighborhoods.

2006 Receives recognition for “Portrait of a Generation.” Pastes same images now for official cultural spaces in Paris and is invited to paste them around city hall. Travels to Israel and Palestine with friend Marco Berrebi to start *Face 2 Face*.

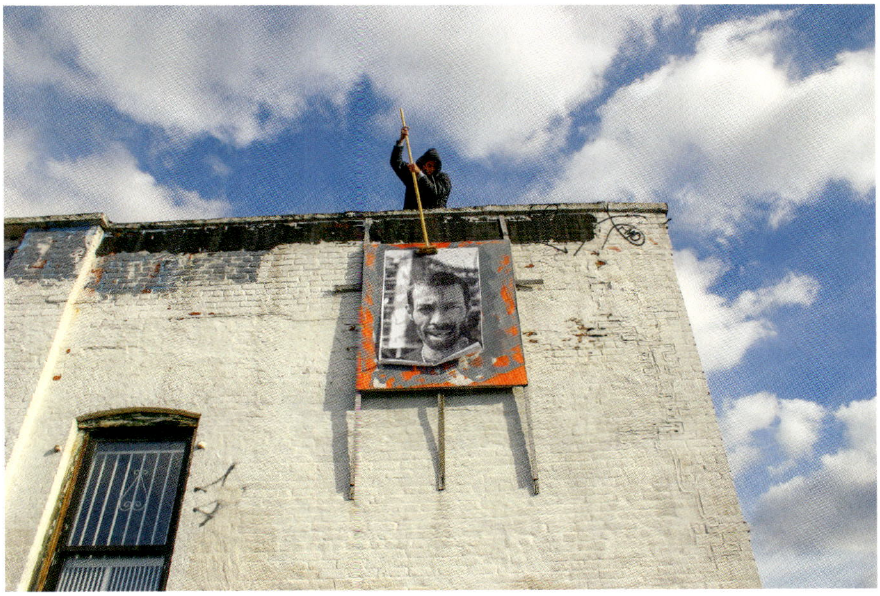

OPPOSITE
JR in his studio, New York, United States, 2026

ABOVE
JR, pasting in New York, United States, 2001

2007 Begins *Face 2 Face* actions in Israel and Palestine. Exhibits pastings in Venice, Paris, Amsterdam, Arles, and Berlin.

2008 “Women Are Heroes” actions with pastings take place in Sierra Leone, Liberia, and Sudan. Begins *Women Are Heroes* actions in favela Morro da Providência, Rio de Janeiro, Brazil. Has solo exhibit *28 Millimeters: Women* in London at the Outsiders Gallery. Begins “The Wrinkles of the City” project, Cartagena, Spain.

2009 *Women Are Heroes* action in Kenya covers rooftops with vinyl tarps printed with eyes and faces of women from the Kibera slum. *Women Are Heroes* action in Jaipur, India, and Phnom Penh, Cambodia. Returns to Rio de Janeiro to paste *Women Are Heroes* onto historic architecture of aqueduct Arcos da Lapa in center of Rio. JR-sponsored cultural and educational center Casa Amarela opens in Morro da Providência favela to serve its population. Begins “Unframed” project using found photographs. Begins production of prints to finance projects.

2010 *Women Are Heroes* film directed by JR premieres at the Cannes Film Festival during Critics’ Week. Participates in the Festival Images in Vevey and the Musée de l’Elysée (now Photo Elysée) in Lausanne, both in Switzerland. *The Wrinkes of the City* in Shanghai. Starts *The Wrinkles of the City* Los Angeles.

2011 Receives TED prize and starts the *Inside Out* project, allowing people worldwide to

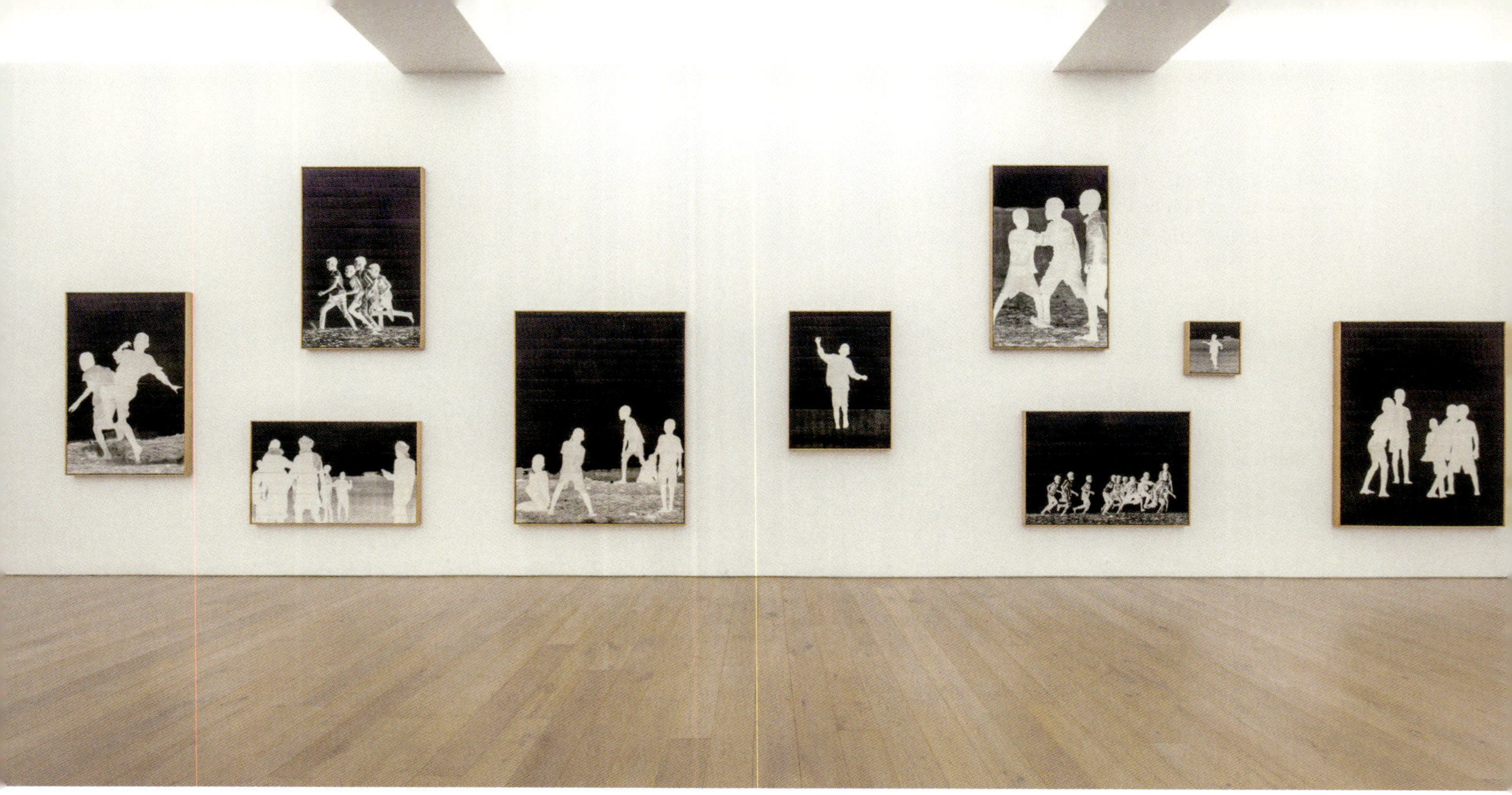

receive large-scale portraits and paste them in their communities in support of their own idea or project. First *Inside Out* happens in Tunisia after Arab Spring. Documentary *Women Are Heroes* released in cinemas. *Encrages* exhibition at Perrotin Gallery, Paris. First *Inside Out* photo booth installation at Centre Pompidou, Paris.

2012 *The Wrinkles of the City* action for Havana Biennial, in collaboration with artist José Parlá. TED talk report on one year of *Inside Out* actions. *Inside Out* actions on High Line in New York and photo booth activations in Vevey and Hong Kong.

2013 First retrospective exhibit, at the Watari Museum of Contemporary Art, in Tokyo, with a pasting on the facade. Returns to Havana with José Parlá to distribute books to participants of *The Wrinkles of the City, Havana*. Screening of the film *The Wrinkles of the City, Havana*. Release of ebook, the first digital art book for iPad. Documentary *Inside Out: The People's Art Project* premieres at Tribeca Film Festival. First solo museum exhibition in the United States, Contemporary Arts Center, Cincinnati. *Inside Out* photo booth truck parked in Times Square in New York.

2014 *JR*, a retrospective exhibition at Museum Frieder Burda in Baden-Baden, Germany, with *Inside Out* photo booth installation, and *Unframed* action in Baden-Baden about German-French history. Installation at Lincoln Center, for New York City Ballet Art Series with pasting on floor and facade. Premier of dance *Les Bosquets*, collaboration with New York City Ballet, music by Woodkid. *Inside Out* installation at the Panthéon, Paris. *Women Are Heroes* action in French harbor city Le Havre: pasting with dock workers on shipping containers loaded on a ship set to travel to Malaysia. *Unframed* action at Ellis Island, New York, in derelict hospital where new arrivals hoping to immigrate underwent health checks from 1892 until 1954. Makes a banner showing Eric Garner's eyes for protest march in New York.

2015 JR's eye strips from faces of killed *Charlie Hebdo* workers carried by the public in the "Je suis Charlie" march in Paris. Short film *Les Bosquets* featuring ballet dancers from Paris Opera premiers in Tribeca Film Festival. Pasting of immigrant for cover of the "Walking New York" issue of the *The New York Times Magazine* on April 25. Releases short film *Ellis* starring Robert de Niro. Creates *The Standing March* in collaboration with film director Darren Aronofsky, projected in Paris onto the National Assembly facade during the 2015 United Nations Climate Change Conference.

2016 Artist in residence of the 2016 Rio Summer Olympic Games, with three giant scaffolding installations, and the first Brazilian *Inside Out* photobooth truck.

2017 *The Chronicles of Clichy-Montfermeil* mural exhibited at Palais de Tokyo, Paris.

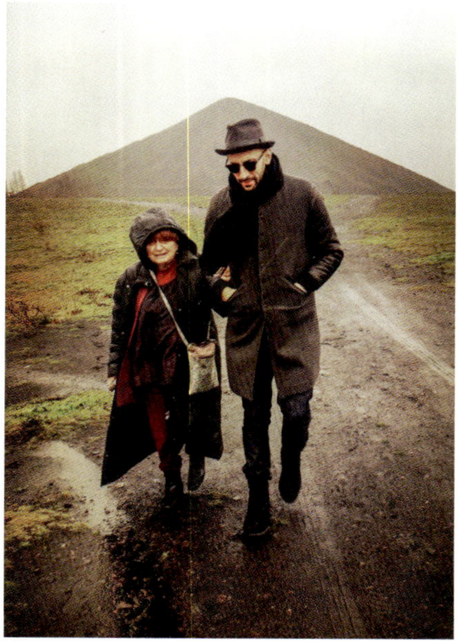

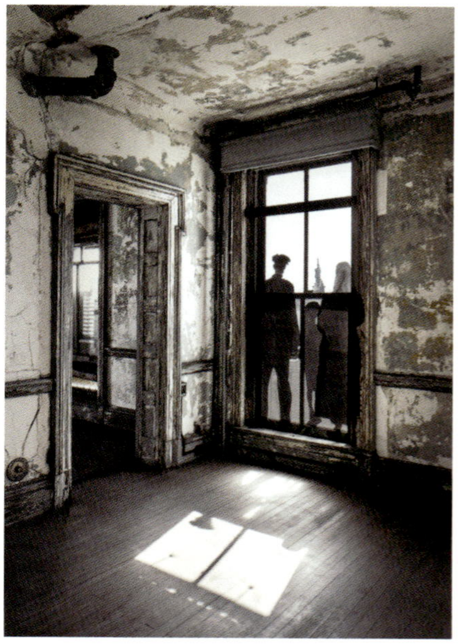

Retrospective exhibition at Qatar Museums Gallery–Katara, in Doha. Codirects feature film *Faces Places* with Agnès Varda that is awarded best documentary at Cannes Film Festival. Installs *Giants,* Kikito, giant mural on scaffolding along Mexican border, and hosts picnic.

2018 Creates community kitchen Refettorio Paris with Massimo Bottura in crypt of La Madeleine church and installs work. Commissioned by *Time* magazine for cover of special issue about gun control, *The Gun Chronicles: A Story of America*, with related video mural shown in 12 US museums. *Giants* action in Berlin, Brandenburg Gate. Beginning of *The Chronicles of San Francisco and New York City*.

2019 Solo gallery shows in Seoul, Palo Alto, New York, Rio de Janeiro. Invited to work in a correctional facility in California and creates *Tehachapi: The Yard*. Installs *JR at the Louvre and the Secret of the Great Pyramid*. Exhibition of finished video mural *The Chronicles of San Francisco* in San Francisco Museum of Modern Art. *JR: Chronicles*, a solo exhibition at the Brooklyn Museum, travels to London, Groningen, Munich, and Seoul.

2020 Creation of *Tehachapi, Mountain*, second installation at the maximum-security prison. Cover for *Time* magazine special COVID-19 issue "Finding Hope." Solo exhibit *Omelia Contadina* at Galleria Continua in San Gimignano, Italy, with eponymous short film by JR and Alice Rohrwacher about plight of farming community.

2021 *Homily to Country* procession with photo-tarps at Lake Cawndilla, near Menindee, Australia, raising awareness about water issues and river health, and exhibition at the National Gallery of Victoria in Melbourne. Award-winning film *Paper & Glue*, directed by and starring JR, premieres at the Tribeca Film Festival. *La Ferita* (The Wound) at Palazzo Strozzi in Florence, *Punto di Fuga* (Vanishing Point) at Palazzo Farnese in Rome, and *Les falaises du Trocadéro* in front of the Eiffel Tower in Paris.

2022 Creates *Déplacé·e·s, Valeriia*, a 148-foot-long tarp with photo of five-year-old Ukrainian child, which volunteers carry through Lviv, Ukraine (also a TIME Magazine cover). *Déplacé·e·s* project in refugee camps in Rwanda, Mauritania, Colombia, and Greece. *The Past Goes Fast*, short film with Robert De Niro about the actor's father.

2023 *Déplacé·e·s* opens at the Gallerie d'Italia in Turin. An exhibition, *Les Enfants d'Ouranos,* opens at Perrotin Gallery in New York. Book release of *Artist Until I Find a Real Job*. Feature film *Tehachapi* premieres at Telluride Film Festival. *Retour à la Caverne—Acte I* installed at the Palais Garnier in Paris. Second installation, *Retour à la Caverne—Acte II,* opens at the Palais Garnier. *Retour à la Caverne—Acte II, CHIROPTERA*, performed on the facade with 154 dancers.

2024 *An Urban Allegory*, short film codirected with Alice Rohrwacher around the *Retour à la Caverne* project. *La Nascita*, a trompe l'oeil installation pasted across the facade of the Milano Centrale Train Station. Creation of *L'Observatoire*, a carriage for the Venice Simplon-Orient-Express train.

2025 *The Chronicles of Kyoto* installed at Kyoto train station; *The Chronicles of Naples* installed on the Duomo, Naples; *Adventice* at Carré Sainte-Anne in Montpellier. Solo exhibitions in London, Beijing, Shanghai.

2026 *Horizons*, first solo exhibition in Los Angeles. *Il Gesto* opens during the Venice Biennale. *La Caverne du Pont Neuf* opens in Paris.

OPPOSITE TOP
Les Enfants d'Ouranos, exhibition at Perrotin Gallery, New York, United States, 2023

OPPOSITE BOTTOM LEFT
Agnès Varda and JR during the filming of ***Faces Places***, 2016

OPPOSITE BOTTOM RIGHT
Unframed, An immigrant family views the Statue of Liberty from the Ellis Island Immigration Station dock seen by JR, courtesy of National Park Service, Statue of Liberty National Monument, United States, 2014

BELOW
Poster for the short film ***Ellis*** starring Robert de Niro, 2015

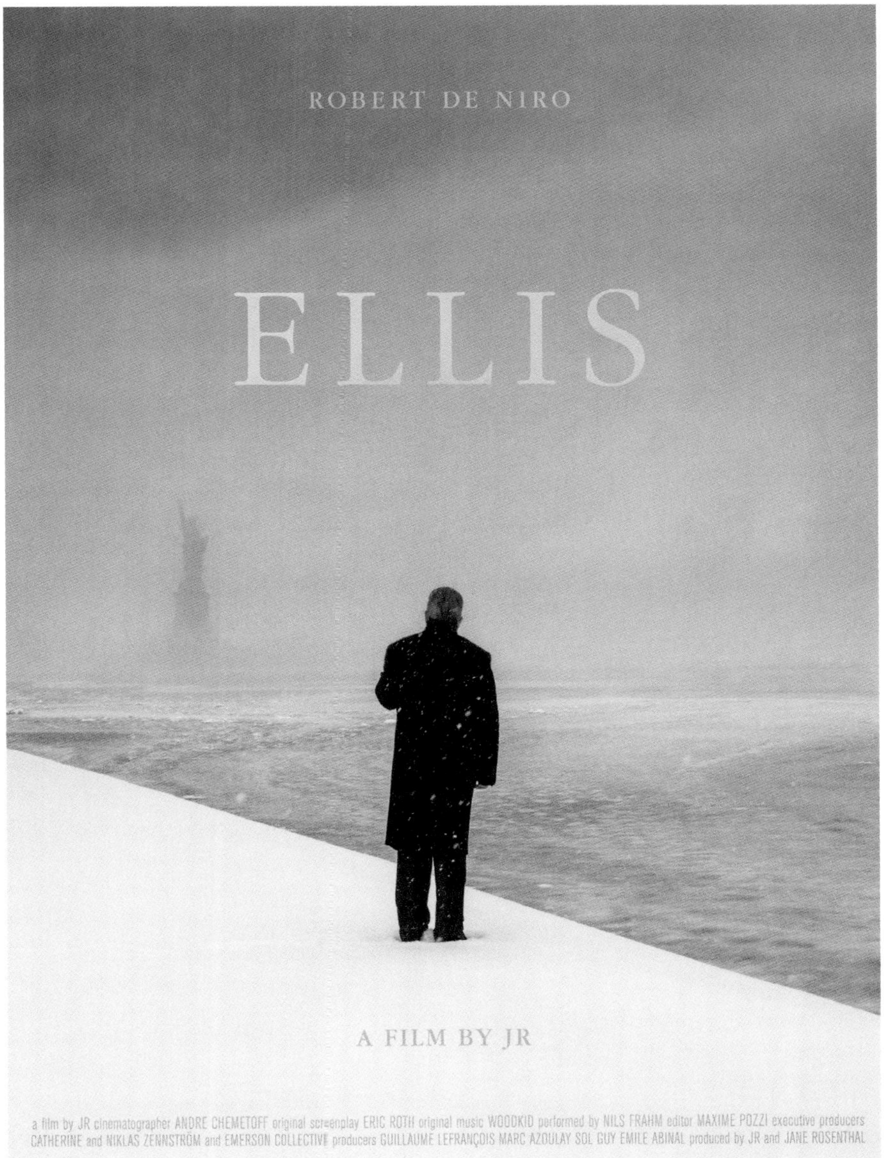

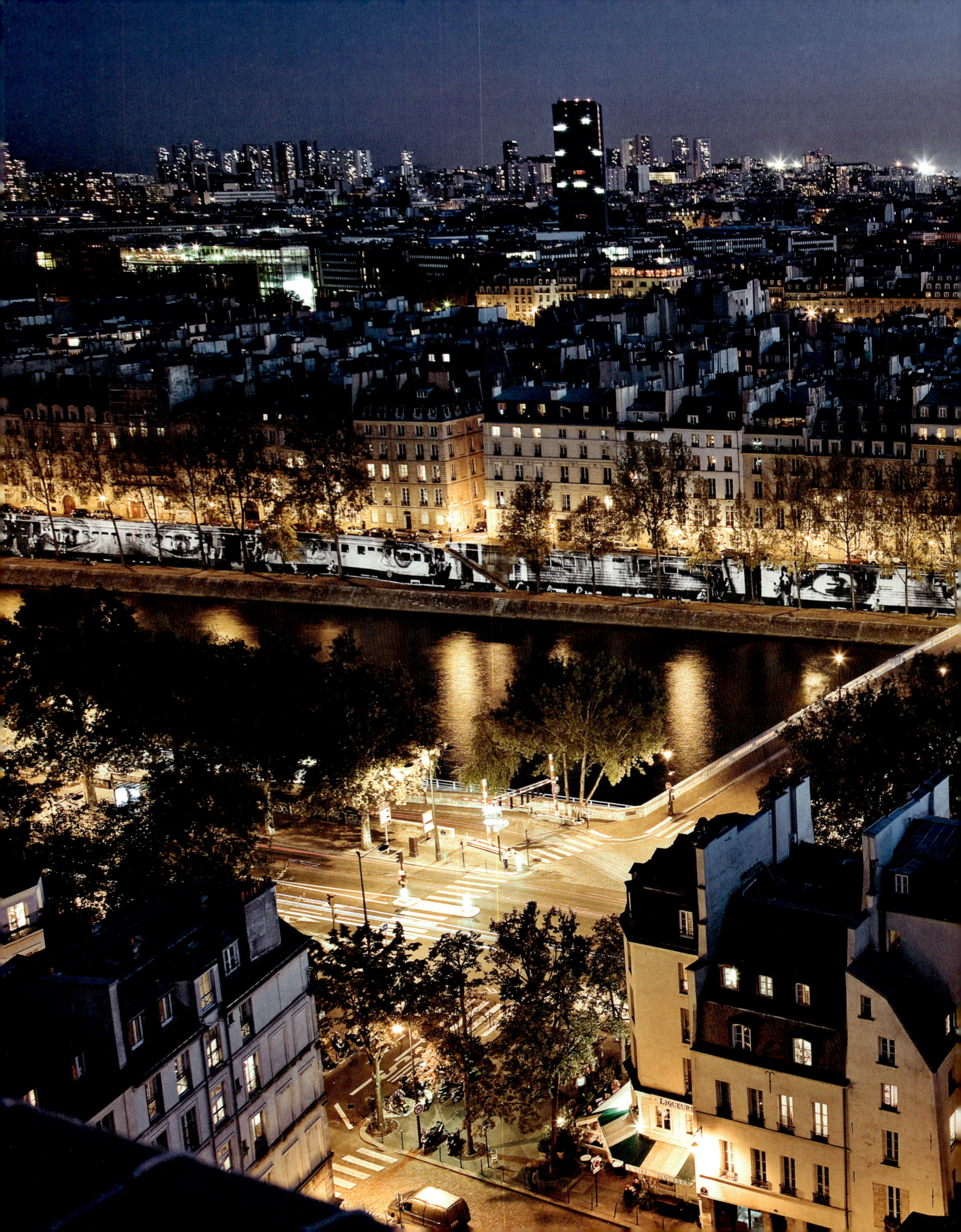
LIQUEURS

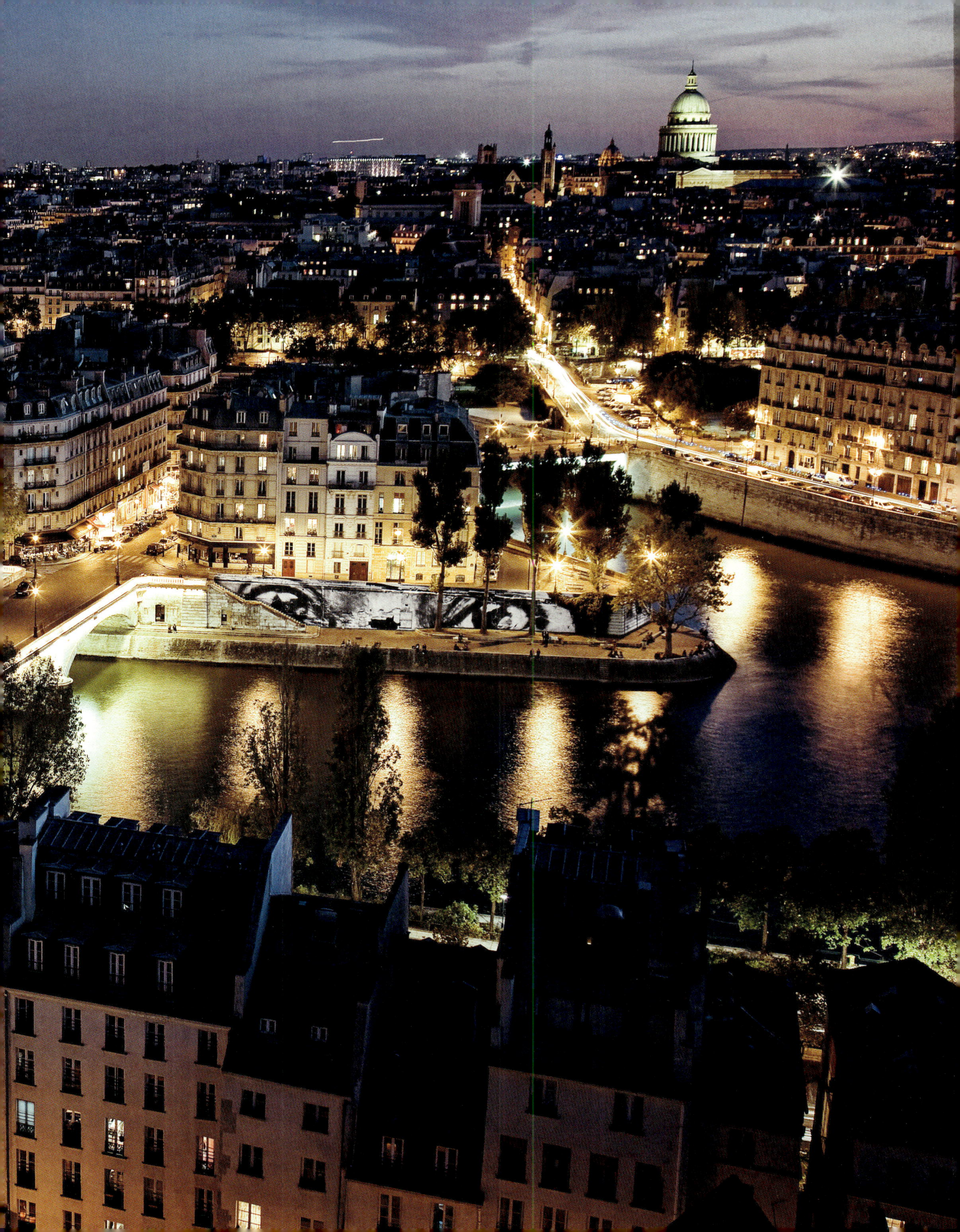

Endnotes

1 JR, interview by Fabrice Bousteau and Hugo Vitrani, “The Retrospective Interview—JR: The Decisive Instinct,” in *Retrospective JR: Chronicles*, exh. cat. (Beaux Arts Éditions, 2021), quoted in *JR-isms*, ed. Larry Warsh (Princeton University Press, 2024).
2 JR, interview with Bousteau and Vitrani, “The Retrospective Interview.”
3 Ibid.
4 Ibid.
5 Anne-Marie Litak and Eyal Levy, “Listening Deeply,” in *The Chronicles of San Francisco*, JR (Chronicle Books, 2019), 13.

Photo credits

All works courtesy of Atelier JR unless otherwise stated. Melvyn Bonnaffé: 4; Paul Salveson, courtesy Perrotin Gallery: 7; Douglas Oliveira: 42; Luana Saltiel: 43; Hesham Alsaifi: 44; Aleš Josifovski: 45; © Ciné-Tamaris: 47, 92; Guillaume Cagniard: 49; Bridgeman Images © Banco de México Diego Rivera and Frida Kahlo Museums Trust, Mexico City: 52–53b; courtesy City College of San Francisco © Cultural Heritage Imaging © Banco de México Diego Rivera and Frida Kahlo Museums Trust, Mexico City: 54–55b; Whitney Museum of American Art, New York/ Scala, Florence: 63; © pyramid architect I. M. Pei, Louvre Museum, Paris: 66, 68–69, 70–71; © Raphael Métivet: 79; Eléa-Jeanne Schmitter: 86; © Christo and Jeanne-Claude Foundation: 87; Cesar Balcazar: 89, 90; © Guillaume Ziccarelli, courtesy Perrotin Gallery: 92t; courtesy National Park Service, Statue of Liberty National Monument: 92br.

The author

Janis Mink studied art history at Smith College and the University of Hamburg. She works as an adjunct professor, writer, and curator.

Acknowledgements

The publisher and the author wish to thank Marc Azoulay and Marie Planel from Atelier JR for their kind support. Atelier JR: Alison Baldo, Julie Bergon, Marc Berrebi, Quentin Besnard, Clémentine Cassard, Mauve Chalandon, Laura Da Cunha, Damariz Damken, Lily Granjon Ashley Hamilton, Soizic Marceau, Camille Pajot, Camille Rousselet, Jaime Scatena, Nina Soutoul, Elodie Terracciano, Juliet Vauconsant, Marie Wlodarczyk.

JR’s projects are made possible thanks to the help of hundreds of volunteers all around the world. Most are self-financed through the sale of artworks. JR is represented by Perrotin, Galleria Continua, PACE, Galeria Nara Roesler.

Imprint

EACH AND EVERY TASCHEN BOOK PLANTS A SEED!
Each year, we offset our annual carbon emissions with carbon credits at the Instituto Terra, a reforestation program in Minas Gerais, Brazil, founded by Lélia and Sebastião Salgado. To find out more about this ecological partnership, please check: www.taschen.com/institutoterra.
Inspiration: unlimited.
Carbon footprint: (almost) zero.

Want to see more? Visit taschen.com to view our current publications, browse our latest magazine, and subscribe to our newsletter.

Hohenzollernring 53, D–50672 Köln
www.taschen.com

Project Editor: Claire Brandon, Madrid
Design: Andy Disl, Los Angeles;
Merrit Schomakers, Cologne
Production: Marion Boschka, Cologne

Printed in Bosnia-Herzegovina
ISBN 978–3–7544–0727–1

FRONT COVER
Giants, Kikito, September 6, 7:02 P.M., 2017
Tecate, Mexico – United States, detail

BACK COVER AND PAGE 2
No Trespassing, 2021
Saint Germain district, Paris, France

PAGE 4
Le Cronache di Napoli, 2025
Duomo, Naples, Italy

PREVIOUS SPREAD
28 Millimeters, Women Are Heroes, 2009
General view, Paris, France